MW00783955

# CLEAVAGE

# CLEAVAGE

## MEN, WOMEN, AND THE SPACE BETWEEN US

Jennifer Finney Boylan

CELADON
BOOKS

NEW YORK

This book was made possible in part by support from the Civitella Ranieri Foundation in Umbertide, Italy, as well as the Radcliffe Institute for Advanced Study at Harvard University in Cambridge, Massachusetts.

www.celadonbooks.com

Designed by Susan Walsh

Library of Congress Cataloging-in-Publication Data

Names: Boylan, Jennifer Finney, 1958– author.
Title: Cleavage : men, women, and the space between us / Jennifer Finney Boylan.
Description: First edition. | New York : Celadon Books, 2025. |
Identifiers: LCCN 2024027354 | ISBN 9781250261885 (hardcover) | ISBN 9781250380067 (ebook)
Subjects: LCSH: Boylan, Jennifer Finney, 1958– | Gender identity. | Transgender people—Identity.
Classification: LCC HQ18.55 .B69 2025 | DDC 305.3—dc23/eng/20240730
LC record available at https://lccn.loc.gov/2024027354

First Edition: 2025

10  9  8  7  6  5  4  3  2  1

For Kenny, Link, John, and Mark

*Bright moments*

# CONTENTS

I was no good at any of it, no good at being a girl;
on the other hand, I am not half bad at being a woman.
—NORA EPHRON

# CLEAVAGE

# BOTH SIDES NOW

## An Introduction

I was born in 1958, on June 22nd, the second day of summer. It was also the birthday of Kris Kristofferson and Meryl Streep, both of whom I later resembled, although not at the same time.

I began the story of my life with these words in *She's Not There,* a memoir published in 2003. At the time it seemed reasonable enough, beginning with the beginning.

Now I wonder whether I chose the right companions. Instead of Streep and Kristofferson, I could just as easily have picked others born that day—Elizabeth Warren, say, or John Dillinger, or Dan Brown. Would my book have landed differently if my chaperones had been the senator, or the gangster, or the author of *The Da Vinci Code*?

Sometimes I think about it, all the other lives I might have led.

At the time of its publication, *She's Not There* was a real brouhaha. I was on *Oprah* five times, Larry King twice. Will Forte imitated me on *Saturday Night Live. Kirkus Reviews* described my writing as "sheer as stockings," which was nice. Though hardly the first trans memoir—not by a million years—it came out at a moment when things were changing, at least a little. I hope *She's Not There*—the book I call SNoT—did push the needle, at a crucial moment. The publisher's promotional copy now calls it "the book that jump-started the transgender rights movement." Big words.

But *She's Not There* was a story told by someone for whom everything was new; the voice is that of a woman who's still in the late stages of an amazing ride, her clothes still smoking after she's been shot out of a cannon. Memoirs of transgender people are almost always about that moment, when a little morning dew is still twinkling on the cobwebs of their transitions.

There's a good reason why so many stories about people like me focus on that passage: it is, by any measure, an astonishing thing. What in the world is it like to go from a man to a woman, or vice versa, or to some identity even more liberating than that?

But a more important, if less scandalous, question is: What's it like for those who finally *have* what they've been impossibly yearning for all their lives? Indeed, what's life like for transgender people as we age, as we inevitably morph from someone covered with sequins into someone whose hair is gray? And what of the people we've been, and our histories from the times before? Surely all of that can't just vanish, like breath on a mirror?

I've spent almost a third of my life over here. I have stories to tell, now that my spangles are no longer aflame, about the difference between the worlds of men and of women, not to mention the fertile territory that lies in between.

But let's also admit there's a huge chunk of the population—the majority, maybe?—that still doesn't understand this trans business at all, people with good hearts who nonetheless could not with any certainty tell you the difference between a transgender person and the Trans-Siberian Railroad. It doesn't help that the best-known trans person in the country is probably Caitlyn Jenner, whom no one could claim has emerged as the transgender Encyclopedia Brown.

The stories in this book examine the differences between manhood and womanhood, as I have experienced them, in everything from food to fashion, from love to loss.

They also address the differences between coming out now, in the current environment of blowback and fear, and coming out twenty-five years ago, when transness—to some people—seemed a thing as obscure as membership in the Royal Antediluvian Order of Buffaloes.

Back then, in an era before people received formal instructions on how to hate us, many individuals encountering a transgender person for the first time were left with nothing to fall back upon, by way of guidance, than their own sense of human decency. When I came out to my evangelical Christian mother, for instance, she didn't respond to her weeping child with a lecture about the dangers of trans women in sports; or concerned theories about "social contagions."

Instead she took me in her arms, and wiped my tears away, and said, *Love will prevail.*

I have been blessed by good fortune in the passage that I have made. But I know plenty of people who were not so lucky, people who even now wait in vain for the people that they love to show them a single crumb of kindness.

Perhaps the central question of this book is not specific to gender at all. Instead, it's the universal dilemma at the heart of so much human trouble: Why is change the thing we all long for, as well as the thing we most fear?

I was born on June 22, 1958, the second day of summer. It was also the birthday of Billy Wilder and Cyndi Lauper, both of whom I later resembled, although not at the same time.

It was Cyndi Lauper who sang, back in 1983, that *girls just want to have fun.* We want other things as well, of course: to be loved; to be respected; to be safe from violence and fear; to be able to make our own decisions about our own bodies. But sure, fun is on the list. Emma Goldman, the anarchist, is credited with saying, "If I can't dance, I don't want to be part of your revolution," although apparently she never actually said that. But she *did* say that everyone had the right to self-expression, and "beautiful, radiant things."

I can tell you that in the Days Before as well as in the Days After I have caught fleeting glimpses of things both beautiful and radiant. I saw them in the sky above me, after the wind in Nova Scotia blew me back from the edge of a cliff I was about to leap off of. I saw them in a dark room, as my future wife unexpectedly stepped toward me from the shadows. And I saw them in my mother's eyes as she folded my weeping self into her arms and quoted First Corinthians: *These three remain: faith, hope and love. But the greatest of these is love.*

Billy Wilder, for his part, directed and co-wrote *Some Like It Hot,* the film that ends with Jack Lemmon (as Daphne) trying to explain to Joe E. Brown (as Osgood, her swain) why they can never be married.

Daphne looks into the distance and says, wistfully, "I can never have children!"

"We'll adopt some," says Osgood, without any reservation.

I have a question about Osgood. Is he generous and open-minded, the kindest man alive? Or is he just, you know: absolutely demented?

After all this time, I'm still not sure, even though I've looked at things from both sides now. Maybe, at this late date, it doesn't matter. It's life's illusions I recall. I really don't know men, or women, at all.

"You don't understand, Osgood!" Daphne cries. She rips off her wig. "I'm a man!"

Osgood looks at her with obliviousness—or what might, just possibly, be love. "Well," he says. "Nobody's perfect."

# I

# FATHERS

I lit the fuse, and we watched the spark race down the long red string: Dad, me, and the Culbertson Rocketeers. Summer was ending. Ahead of us was middle school, and adolescence, and all the forces that would, inevitably, tear us apart. But for now we were gathered together, one last time.

A breeze passed through. The rocket I'd named the Tall Boy—all seven feet of it—swayed precariously on its launch pad, first one way, then the other.

I'd designed the Tall Boy in my father's workshop, gluing together the tubes from a half dozen paper towel rolls, affixing the fins at the bottom, the nose cone up top. I'd decorated it with a can of red spray paint that contained a metal ball. You could hear that ball clacking inside as you shook the little can back and forth.

That rocket was taller than my father. It was the most terribly dangerous thing anyone had ever seen. It was a trip to the hospital in its most basic, unrefined stage. It was fantastic.

And this may be the first piece of transgender apostasy I have to offer you: namely, that while I had known I was meant to be female from my earliest memory, an insight that succeeded in twisting my heart around like an Amish soft pretzel, it would nevertheless be false to describe all my days as a boy as nothing but unending sorrow. Oh, I did spend many hours walking alone in the woods, wondering how in the world I was going to make my way. But there were also plenty of occasions like this one—a rocket launch among a group of twelve-year-old Visigoths. There were many other joyful days ahead of me, too, including my latter ones as a boyfriend, and a husband, and a father.

True, I was not quite myself. But even then I knew full well that *being myself* would come with pretty significant risks of its own. All things considered, I was doing my best, as Mrs. Dilber says in *A Christmas Carol,* "in keepin' with the situation."

My father held his butane lighter to the tip of his L&M King, then shut the top with a metallic snap. It was monogrammed with his initials—JRB. Those were my initials, too, at least they were back then. Sometimes when he wasn't looking I'd toy with his lighter. The butane had a sharp smell—like whiskey, and cumin.

He was a handsome man, Dick Boylan, hair slicked back, and a pair of glasses that made him look not unlike the medieval history professor he'd once wanted to be. There was a little bit of Don Draper about him, a kind of poise. But he also had a quiet, wicked sense of humor. He loved getting everyone around him to debate one another, back in the days when people could pleasantly disagree. Sometimes, at the dinner table, he'd bang his fork against his water glass, and then quietly say, "Okay. Now everybody argue the *opposite.*"

It is worth pausing at this moment to acknowledge the incredible: my parents were named *Dick and Hildegarde.* I still remember lying on my bed during my days as a Rocketeer, staring at the ceiling, thinking, *My parents are named—Dick! And Hildegarde! I'm not going to make it, man! I'm not going to make it!*

The spark sped down the fuse toward the rocket. The breeze blew again, and once more the Tall Boy swung wildly on the launch pad.

It was clear to everyone that the rocket was going to topple onto the blacktop just before its engines ignited. It was even clear to me. But the fuse was lit.

Tub, a blond boy who lived up the road from me near the Du Pont estate, looked fearfully at my father. "Mr. Boylan!" he said. "It's gonna tip!"

My father took a deep drag of his cigarette. He thought this over as he held that smoke in his lungs. Then he blew it all out. "Better be careful," he said.

I still don't know why my father was so sanguine about the catastrophein-progress. Maybe, just like the rest of us, he had never seen anything as dangerous as this up close, and now found it impossible to turn away.

Ted Goodrich shook his head. He was deeply into *Star Trek*, and was given to imitating Mr. Spock, given half a chance. "It is not logical," he observed.

"Shut up," said Howie Finley, who hated everyone. "*Mister Spaz.*"

Ted Goodrich looked at Howie Finley as if he were a grotesque specimen of alien life, which, to be fair, he kind of was, considering that Howie's mouth was replete not only with a set of shining metal braces but a series of complex rubber bands frequently coated with the melancholy residue of peanut butter and marshmallow fluff.

"Fascinating," said Ted Goodrich.

We were on the playground of what had been, up until that summer, our elementary school, William Culbertson, a school named after an Episcopalian minister whose last words were said to be, *God God, Yes!* Our hometown, Newtown Square, Pennsylvania, was still mostly farm country in those days. There were a lot of cows, Angus mostly, black herds on green hills. Some of the farms were for real; others were ornamental. The playground of our grade school was less than a mile from Foxcatcher, the estate belonging to the Du Ponts, although Mrs. Du Pont didn't have cows; she had horses. Many years later, her demented son John murdered a wrestling coach on that estate; a movie was made about that murder, in fact: *Foxcatcher*, with Steve Carell, a film in which he donned a fake nose.

All around the town were mansions, homes to the very last generation of blue bloods, places that in just a few years would be subdivided, or torn down, or shuttered. Just down the street from my house on Sawmill Road was the jewel of the Main Line—the "Big House" of Ardrossan Farms, where Hope Montgomery Scott lived on an estate whose green fields were dotted with Ayrshire dairy cattle. Mrs. Scott had been the model for the Katharine Hepburn figure in *The Philadelphia Story*. Just like in that movie, there really were Quakers in my hometown who would call you "thee" and "thou." It was weird when they did that, but it was also kind of cool. Once, a Friend had looked at me and said, *Thou art a real nut.*

Between these two estates—Foxcatcher and Ardrossan—was a deep green forest owned by the descendants of the former governor, George Earle. His mansion had burned down in the '50s, although the charred wreck of it still stood in the heart of the forest. It was, of course, the coolest and scariest place in the world. Ted Goodrich and I liked to ride our bikes on the old paths in the forest and creep around the mansion sometimes. Once, we got stung by bees there.

The spark was about three feet from the rocket engine now. Smoke from the fuse hung in the air and was then dispersed by the breeze.

"Mr. Scott," said Ted Goodrich. "Beam us up."

This would be the last time we gathered, we Rocketeers. In just a few weeks we'd start junior high school. There was a little bit of *Stand by Me* to this situation, as we prepared to take our leave of Culbertson Elementary, where we'd gone for seven long years, and upon whose deserted playground we were staging this final launch. I wasn't going to Marple Newtown with the others; I was off to Haverford that fall.

I'd begged my father not to send me there, wept and wept as I sat with my parents watching TV in their bedroom—*Hawaii Five-O, The Smothers Brothers, Ed Sullivan.* I told my father that I'd miss my friends, but this wasn't the truth, of course. The only friends I had were these Rocketeers, and most of these friendships were marginal, really based on not much more than parachute wadding and nose cones. We'd been close when we were really little, of course, but by the end of sixth grade, it was clear that I was not turning out like the others. One day, Sammy Walsh asked if I was a *homosexual.* I had no idea what that meant. I told him, I didn't *think* so?

Dad had tried, in his gentle, diffident manner, to steer me into manhood. He'd attempted to teach me how to throw a football, and to get me interested in some of his own hobbies—restoring furniture, building walls from stone. For my birthday one year he gave me H. A. Rey's book, *The Stars,* an introduction to the constellations. On cold winter nights, Dad took me out in the yard with a flashlight, and we gazed up at the night sky. I remember our breath coming out in clouds, the Milky Way shimmering above us. From the little stream that passed along the edge of our property I could hear water trickling beneath the ice. *This is Orion,* said Dad, *the Hunter.*

A lot of boys learn how to be men by taking a good look at their own fathers, and basically deciding to do the opposite. Many of the best memoirs and novels written by men tell the stories of boys who want desperately to grow up, and fathers who refuse to. Richard Russo's *The Risk Pool* is like that. So, in its own way, is *This Boy's Life* by Tobias Wolff. But perhaps all stories of boys trying to grow up in the shadow of a feckless father are descended from Huck Finn, whose Pap is just about the worst person in the world. *Don't you give me none o' your lip. You've put on considerable many frills since I been away. I'll take you down a peg before I get done with you.*

I didn't want to be the opposite of my father. Why would I? He was wise and funny. But in every way it was already clear I was going to become something else. As noted earlier, I'd known I was a girl as early as age four or five, at least on the inside, which—at least back then—struck me as the most important way you *could* be a girl. But this was something I understood, even then, that could only bring me shame.

I knew it would hurt my father's feelings, too, if I ever said the truth out loud. In a way it would be like telling that sweet, wise man, *I'm not going to be like you.* Who would ever want to say such a thing to a father whom she loved?

And so I lived my truth in silence, hoping against hope that some cosmic legerdemain would undo the fundamentals of my soul, so that one day I could wake up and be a boy like other boys, a creature en route to being, someday, a man like other men.

Whenever I write about my parents I am hindered, a little bit, by my profound love for them. They were sweet, dignified, loving people, even if they *were* named Dick and Hildegarde. My father was surely bewildered, at times, by his bookish, goofy, gamine son—not to mention my sister, who had a rebellious streak of her own. But he always treated me with love, and that's the challenge I have in trying to place Dick Boylan at the heart of my life's great conflict. Sure, I think he'd have been happier if I'd exhibited the slightest talent for sports; or if I didn't seem like such an unfathomable, hilarious misfit. But the truth is that he always seemed gently charmed by his weirdo child. I think he thought I was interesting.

Sometimes I wonder what it would have been like to be less interesting. Would I have been happier, if I had been more like him? Would he have been happier, to have been the father of that son?

For his part, Dick Boylan had never known what it was like to have had a father much past childhood. My grandfather, James, had died when Dad was twelve. That was the same age I was now, as the spark rushed into the nozzle.

Once more the wind blew hard against the Tall Boy, and the rocket swayed, tipped, teetered, and then—like a mighty redwood falling in a forest—it crashed down upon the blacktop. Two of its four balsawood fins snapped off as it hit the pavement. The fuse was still burning.

You'd think that we'd all have run and scattered, trying to get as far away as possible from the disaster that was only seconds away. But it was impossible for us to move. We stood there in horror, and in wonder. The rocket engine hissed, and then fell silent. There was a little puff of smoke, followed by nothing.

"Fascinating," said Ted Goodrich.

Howie Finley began to laugh with a cruel kind of joy. "It's a dud!" he shouted, raising his hands. "Of course it's a dud! What a joke!"

Tub looked over at me. We were all still standing there. The ruins of the Tall Boy were pointed directly at Howie Finley. I felt the blood rushing to my face, the tears burning in my eyes. "No wonder you're going to the school for retards!" shouted Howie Finley. "Ha ha ha!"

A small plume of smoke rose from the nozzle of the Tall Boy's engine.

"Wait," said Tub. "I think it's—I think it's still—"

Tub never got to finish that sentence.

The Tall Boy exploded into life, flames shooting out the nozzle, heading straight for Howie Finley. He took off running, but in all honesty, it can be hard to outrun a rocket. As he ran, the Tall Boy in hot pursuit, Howie Finley screamed. How did he scream? *Like a little girl.* Closer and closer to my running, screaming nemesis the Tall Boy drew, scudding along the blacktop, just inches away now from Howie's hateful backside.

Years later, when I saw the video footage of Senator Josh Hawley running from the mob which he himself had encouraged, I thought, *This is a thing I have seen before.*

At last the Tall Boy came to a stop, as the propellent was consumed and the spark burned through the delay charge—material intended to allow an ascending rocket to coast. The delay charge emitted a great deal of so-called tracking smoke, although there was no question as to the location of the Tall Boy: it had run out of propellant not far from the swings, where the Rocketeers and my father and I followed it, as if to the site of a terrible massacre. Howie was trying not to cry, and crying. The Tall Boy lay there, puffing smoke in the late-summer air.

I went over to Howie. I said, "You okay?" and he nodded. He didn't *seem* okay.

We turned our attention to the Tall Boy. The tracking smoke had stopped.

Then, with a sudden *pop*, the nose cone hurtled off the top of the rocket, and the parachute, still attached to the fuselage by a piece of elastic cord, burst out like a champagne cork. For a moment the parachute was filled by the wind. Then, like a plastic shroud, the chute settled gently over the corpse of the Tall Boy. The rocket had traveled. Now it had come to rest.

"It is logical," noted Ted Goodrich.

And at that moment, I heard the sound of my father laughing. He laughed until he started coughing, as heavy smokers sometimes do. The rest of us started laughing, too—me, Tub, all of us, even Howie Finley. It was the most incredible thing any of us had ever witnessed. Tears poured out of our eyes. We raised our hands into the air and cheered.

We would not be little boys much longer. But on that day, we lingered.

Twenty-five years later, I drove home from the hospital through a cold, sharp night. A father.

The windshield wipers slapped back and forth. Snow was falling in heavy wet flakes. The Grateful Dead were on the radio. "*And solemnly, they stated,*" Jerry Garcia sang, "*he has to die.*"

I thought back on the mystery which I had witnessed back at the hospital. I had stood behind my wife Deedie's head as the docs performed the cesarean. They had a sheet raised up so she couldn't witness all the gruesome derring-do that was sustained down below. But I had seen it all, had even seen my precious love's ovaries. They looked just like they were supposed to—the Fallopian tubes grasping onto the ovaries like the tiny hands of a child.

Later, they let me cut the umbilical cord—a mostly symbolic act, really, given that the baby had already been formally detached from Deedie. But they let me have a symbolic snip, like a mayor cutting the ribbon unveiling a new bridge.

How incredible it was to be alive at that moment! *Zach*, Deedie had said. *We'll name him Zach.*

Jerry Garcia was still singing—the song, if I remembered properly, was called "Cryptical Envelopment." It made me smile; in no small measure I too had been enveloped cryptically by the day's events. I'd read somewhere that Garcia had imagined this tune as a kind of update of the Appalachian standard, "Man of Constant Sorrow," a version of which appears in the film *O Brother, Where Art Thou?* It's a story-song about a mysterious man doomed to die. *For in this world, I'm bound to ramble, I have no friends to help me now.* According to tradition, it's a song about Christ, and his lonely journey.

But sometimes when I thought about that tune I thought about Charlie Brown. The boy of constant sorrow.

I had always been something of a Charlie Brown my own self, in my days as a Rocketeer and beyond. As such, I knew the thing the Charlie Browns of the world knew that the Lucy van Pelts did not. Which is this: Each autumn when she holds the football for him, and she pulls it away every time, causing him to crash onto the ground? We Charlies know full well what is going to happen. This is not a story about a person with a feckless sense of hope. This is a story about a person who suffers because he knows something about this exchange is bringing Lucy joy. He pretends to allow himself to be tricked as a favor to Lucy. Because he knows how much she loves pulling off this stunt. Because he pities her. Because his heart is full of love.

I had hoped, when I got married, that I would never have to give in to what I could only assume would be a difficult, doomed life, the life of a transgender woman. It seemed impossible, given the stone foundation of paternity upon which my manhood was now built, that anything could ever erode it. When I fell in love with Deedie, I swore that the whole transgender thing would be sealed away forever, and that I would henceforward focus exclusively on the woman that I loved, and the family we might create. The transgender business, which had haunted my life for my first thirty years on earth, was a secret I was determined no soul would ever know. I would live my life in a spirit of humility and gratitude. I would, in the years to come, be unexpectedly and miraculously *healed*.

But now and again I'd hear songs like this, or I'd see the face of a woman who looked like me, and I'd remember the words a ghost allegedly spoke to the poet Shelley, the day before he drowned. *How long,* the spirit asked, *do you intend to remain content?*

As he had lain upon his deathbed eight years earlier, my father had seen a specter not so unlike that one. It was malignant melanoma that did him in; toward the end it had spread to his liver and his brain.

The spirit he'd seen was dressed up like an orchestra conductor, Dad told me. I'd taken a leave from grad school, down at Johns Hopkins, in order to be with him in his final days. He came to me with his baton, said Dad. And asked me to come away with him, and conduct his orchestra.

I turned up the valve on Dad's oxygen tank. I was afraid, he said. Because I did not know the music.

I was going to have to do something about dinner, I thought now, driving through a snowstorm on the day my son was born. There wasn't a thing to eat in the house, and even if there were, I was in no mood to start cooking at that hour. Before me loomed the lit-up sign for the Oakland House of Pizza. I thought about a hot pepperoni pie, the steam rising from the cardboard box with a picture of a toque-wearing chef upon it. I pulled in, and a moment later was at the counter making my order. There was nobody in the place except the man behind the counter. He threw the dough up in the air, like we were in old Napoli, and he an old-school pizzaiolo. I watched that spinning dough rise into the air; I watched it fall into his hands. Then he threw it again.

I knew it was going to be a while before the pie was ready, so I went back out to the parking lot and watched the snow come down. It was so beautiful, drifting through the cone-shaped light cast by the streetlamps. Everything was so quiet, so still. In a single day the world had become something strange and new.

Maybe I'm not Charlie Brown, I thought. Or, rather: maybe everybody is Charlie Brown, slogging their way through this unfathomable world. Was it possible that I was ordinary, after all? Or that even being ordinary is a profound, indescribable gift? This day I had felt something like the heart of the world throbbing right through me, and it had left me changed.

*Fascinating.*

I remembered sitting in his bedroom right after Dad died. The guy from the funeral home said he was on his way. I had kissed my father's forehead. It was already cool. *Goodbye, old man*, I said. *I promise. I'm going to make you proud.*

There was an old-school pay phone on the wall of the pizza joint. I picked up the receiver, dropped in a quarter, and called my old friend Peter. He'd been especially dear to me during my sophomore year in college, when we were both kind of lost.

"Hey," I said into the receiver. Snow was gathering in my hair. How I wanted to tell my friend everything that was in my heart. How I wanted to let him know that I was going to be all right, that I was finally, ecstatically, amazingly part of something so much bigger than myself!

"Peter," I said. "It's a boy."

# FOOD

How are you doing in there, Miss Jennifer?" asked the helpful saleslady on the other side of the slatted changing-room door. "Let me know if you want to see a different size."

"I'm fine," I lied, looking with sadness at the way I filled out the size 12. I was like one of those Fudge Town cookies, once advertised with the slogan: "So Much Fudge It Pops Out the Top." The saleslady, god bless her, was trying to offer me a way out of hell. *Just ask her for a size 14.* If I swapped what I was wearing for a slightly larger version of the same thing, one that, unlike this dress, would actually fit, well then you'd think our problem would be solved.

But that was not the problem at hand.

The problem, the real problem, was less about fat than soul. Back in the day, by which I mean pre-transition, my boy self had always been slender. I'm six feet tall; on my wedding day (three days after I turned thirty) I weighed about 140 pounds.

Now many years post-transition, as I gazed into the three-way mirror in the changing room, I was probably up to 185.

Even so, the crisis before me was not the fact that I had gained nearly fifty pounds in twenty-five years. The crisis was that it mattered to me now, as a woman.

When I was a man (sic), I can say most definitively that it had not.

I'd had the same sense of myself as a boyo back then whether I was a slender willow tree (as I'd been throughout all my teens and twenties) or whether I was more the size of stately oak (my size in my thirties and forties). To be absolutely honest, when I was male-bodied, I never even thought about my weight. Or compared myself to a tree.

*We did not own a scale.* I could not imagine any circumstances in which knowing how much I weighed would have affected my sense of self one way or another.

Now, in the country in which I had at last attained my green card, it mattered a lot. I had been slender during the early days of my transition, having lost a lot of weight in the process, the result not least because of the profound stress that the presto chango had placed upon me. Before the swap I hadn't known much about the sizing of women's clothing. I think I can be forgiven for this because—let's be honest—the system seems to refer to no known metric. As a gentleman, a pair of size 32 pants—which is what I'd worn, back in the day—meant that a tape measure wrapped around my waistline would come out to, you know, 32 inches. If I gained two inches of belly fat—ta-da!—I'd be a 34. You could see how a person would find some logic in this.

But I'd landed at the bottom of the chute in Girl-land to find myself a size 8, or perhaps a 10, depending on the designer. Eight what? you might ask. Or ten what? No one would tell me.

There was even one blissful day when I'd bought a skirt in a size 6. If you want a perfect example of exactly how fucked-up women are encouraged to be in this culture, may I present to you a snapshot of the idiotic and blissful expression upon my face the day I purchased that size 6 skirt. Because having gone from an eight to a six—whatever those numbers might mean—meant to me something like, *I've made it at last! I'm a success!*

But now those days were gone. I'd long since graduated from an eight to a ten, and from thence to a twelve. Now, here we were, teetering on the edge of the fourteens.

"Miss Jennifer?" said the saleslady. "Can I help you?" It sounded like she was worried about me, like maybe I'd passed out after looking at myself in the mirror.

She was not so far from the truth, and this was the very reason why I could not respond. *No,* I wanted to say. *No one can help me.*

Because now I am a size 14, and I am no longer who I thought I was. *Pour away the Diet Coke and sweep up the SlimFast. For nothing now can ever come to any good.*

When I got home, I checked my dough. I had started it the night before, as is my habit on pizza night. I'd begun after supper, by delightedly doing the very thing to my flour that I now did only with regret to myself—that is, placing it upon a scale. I'd taken 1,000 grams of Italian 00 flour and mixed this by hand with 700 grams of water heated to exactly 94 degrees. I allowed these to autolyze for about a half hour before adding a gram of yeast and about 25 grams of sea salt, then pulled and folded the dough a couple of times over the next couple of hours. Then I sealed it in the special tub I'd purchased just for this purpose and allowed it all to rise overnight. In the morning—before departing for the drama in the fitting room at the mall—I'd opened the tub to find a bubbling, seething goo that gave off an odor vaguely reminiscent of the Adriatic Sea. With my dough scraper, I'd allowed all of this to ooze upon my floured countertop, where I subdivided the sticky mess into five equal portions, rolled them gently in the flour, and then, without deflating them, shaped them into balls and placed these into lightly dusted soup bowls. I'd done all of this wearing a red, white, and blue–striped apron and a white chef's toque, which was less about trying to look like Chef Boyardee than about trying to keep my long blond hair in place.

When I got home I removed the doughs from the refrigerator and spread them on the floured countertop again. Then I went outside, chopped some wood, lit a fire in the pizza oven, and watched as the thermometer slowly rose up to about 800 degrees, which you'd have to agree, is hot. As I waited for the fire to settle into coals, I went back inside, got out my homemade sauces—there was a classic tomato sauce and some pesto and another potion I'd made by letting the shells of cooked lobsters simmer in some red sauce. Then came the cheeses: fresh mozzarella (shredded into small chunks), provolone, shaved parm, some fontina, a little gorgonzola. I had lobster meat marinated in lemon and kosher salt, jalapeño mango sausages, pepperonis and prosciutto and green peppers and red onions and sautéed mushrooms. I had manzanita olives I'd pitted by hand, some sriracha sauce, a tub of mascarpone, some sautéed fennel. From the garden I picked out and then chopped fresh basil, fresh oregano, fresh rosemary, fresh thyme.

We would be seven for dinner, which meant five pies. In the time to come I would assemble them, one by one: the *gabagool* pizza, which was a flat rectangle with fifteen blobs of mascarpone, an olive in each blob, the sautéed fennel scattered overall, the capicola slices layered on top of that, and the final squiggle of sweet Szechuan sauce and sriracha squirted on top. There was the *jalapeño mango sausage pie* with the sautéed mushrooms and pesto sauce. There was the one I called *Downeast*: the lobster meat with the red lobster–infused sauce and the shaved parm and lemon and the kosher salt. There was *Maddy's Meatzapalooza*: with the pepperonis and the prosciutto and the red onion. And, my favorite, the *Classic New York*: red sauce, mozzarella, parm, provolone, and three fresh basil leaves.

We can have a conversation about whether a classic New York slice should have provolone on it, if you want. I say yes, but I didn't grow up there, so, you know: I'm probably the wrong guy to ask.

I didn't make it that night but I have also been known to make *Quackup*. Which is, of course, a pizza with dark duck meat, feta cheese, and a few scattered Maine blueberries. Oh, don't make a face. You'd like it.

I threw the dough in the air. For just a second I looked up at the ceiling, where my pie was spinning around and around. In a moment it would come down, of course, and I'd catch it, and I'd start making the first pie. But let's just pause me there, surrounded by all my ingredients, smoke from the fire oven outside drifting past the kitchen window, my gaze cast heavenward.

I hope that when I am gone, the people I love will remember me just like this, wearing my ridiculous chef's toque, my arms coated up to the elbows with flour, my face made young by an expression of absolute ecstasy, the result of my knowledge that I am deep into the creation of something that will taste so unbelievably fucking good that everyone at my table will fall onto the floor and wet their pants in joy.

I'm a baker. I like baking. I make boules and baguettes, crusty whole wheat free-form loaves. I make classic white loaves made with buttermilk and honey. I make sourdough pancakes. Once, I made ciabatta, as light and airy as a bubble bath. On another occasion I made *schiaccita*— Sicilian pockets filled with hot melted mozzarella, sweet sausages, and spinach that I first had as a college student in Middletown, Connecticut. I've made dark brown bread made with molasses, upon a slice of which unsalted butter had melted into shining yellow pools. I make calzones and focaccia; I make flatbreads, *pain de mie,* and naan.

When I was a man, I ate like a man, I baked like a man, I cleaned up like a man. But when I became a woman, I put the ways of men behind me. For then I baked in a microwave oven, darkly, but now I bake face-to-face. Then I baked in part; but now I feed my loved ones fully, even as I am fed.

And now these three remain: focaccia, baguettes, and pizza. But the greatest of these is pizza.

You want to know how I gained fifty pounds in thirty years? This is how. Do I regret it? You tell me. Does it *sound* like I regret it?

Okay, I regret it. Not during the cooking, which is the closest thing I have to a meditation practice. Nor during the eating, as the ones I love are laughing and talking and clinking wineglasses and filling their plates with pie. But after. When the house is empty, flour dust still scattered all over the kitchen floor, and I step upon the scale. How is it that I have gained weight again? I ask myself, incredulous. It's a total mystery! What possible explanation for this can there be?

When the numbers on that scale get high enough, I declare martial law, and there is no more baking, and there is no more drinking, and there are trips to the pool where I swim a mile every other day. With any luck the numbers go down, and into my clothes I fit once more.

The model Kate Moss once said, "Nothing tastes as good as being skinny feels." She's since retracted that statement, but every woman I know understands what she meant.

But then I will find myself at a table with my family and my friends, and we are drinking Negronis, or a hearty Valpolicella, and upon the table before us are slices of my homemade pizza pies, kosher salt clinging to the outer rim to produce my famous *pretzely finish,* deep green basil leaves scattered on top, bubbles in the crust dark with the char produced in my fire oven, mozzarella and prosciutto and pepperoni and provolone in a glorious shining wheel, and one of my children will raise their glass and say, *To all of us!* and I will think, O Kate Moss. *This* is the thing that tastes better than being skinny could ever feel.

I mentioned the drinking. It is this, in fact, rather than my pizza kitchen, that I think is most responsible for my size. Maybe it's just my metabolism. Maybe it's something else. But what I know is that if I have zero drinks over the course of a week, I am likely to shed pounds. If I have one drink a night, I will maintain the weight I have. And if I have two, or more? Then you will find me in the dressing room trying to avoid looking at myself from the side.

Since I became the writer in residence at Barnard College, I have split my year between the four and a half months of spring semester in New York City—January through May—and the rest of the year in Maine: summer, fall, and early winter. This means that Deedie and I are often apart for the first third of the year. It is the only fly in the ointment of the spectacular life that Barnard has made possible for me.

And it's this, more than anything else, that is responsible for my size.

It works like this: when Deedie and I are apart, we are sad, so we drink. Then, when we are together again once more, we are happy. So we drink.

It is not that hard for me to lose weight, especially when I am in New York, because at least in the pre-pandemic days, I could get myself over to the Columbia University swimming pool and do some laps. I love being in the pool, even though I am a sight to behold. When I am fully decked out in latex bathing cap and surrealistic tinted swim goggles, I look a little bit like a giant walking Q-tip from Mars.

But swimming provides a time of the day when no one can get at me. I can't check my email, or get angry on Twitter, or even answer the phone. As the saying goes, I just keep swimming.

If I'm in a lose-weight phase, the day will begin with fifty laps— seventy-five, if I'm up for it—then a salad for lunch, then a humble dinner. No cocktails, no Valpolicella. If I start the semester at 185 pounds—my usual default after a summer making pizzas in the fire oven—I can work my way down to 165 by May, if I'm dedicated, and carefully avoid spending time with any other human beings.

But all it takes to throw me off the wagon is the prospect of actually enjoying my life. I'll think, Well, why not join the gang down at Burp Castle for some Belgian ales? How much damage can that do, in a single night?

Answer: a lot.

And so this is what I have learned: it is perfectly easy to lose weight if that is the only thing you are doing, if you have a system for counting calories and getting exercise and never try to enjoy anything. Weight comes off slowly, and goes back on fast. I can lose a pound a week over the course of a month, swimming four days out of seven, staying on the wagon, not overdosing on the carbs. Then, after single night at Burp Castle? Once again, I am beautiful from the front. From the side: a one-way trip to Fudge Town.

It was not like this when I was a boyo. Of course, part of the difference is also the difference between being old and being young, of being a person driven by speed and fear, and being a person of some contentment and solace. When I was a young man my metabolism was that of a jackrabbit; once, in high school, when we all took our pulses, my heartbeat averaged out at 120 beats a minute. I was so fast in those days that even

at a state of rest I shook, very gently, very softly. I made big pots of coffee
in one of those old-time percolators with a clear bubble in the top, and
it was against this bubble that I would watch the brewing coffee pulse
with the intensity of my soul. I would listen to Stravinsky's *Rite of Spring*
at top volume while socking back pot after pot of coffee, then write my
stories out in bleeding peacock-blue fountain-pen ink upon long sheets
of yellow legal paper. In addition to the differences between male and female, and young and old, I should surely add this one: when I was young,
I was fast. Now, I am slow.

Is it any wonder that in the days Before I could pretty much eat whatever I liked, drink whatever I pleased, without any effect whatsoever? I
could have eaten a whole side of beef without gaining a pound—and
indeed, when I was a child, twice a year my mother bought a side of beef
subdivided into portions wrapped up in butcher paper, each one with
an identifying stamp: T-Bone, Porterhouse, Filet Mignon, Rump Roast.

But it's not just that my speed kept me skinny. It was also that neither
my mother nor my father had much interest in dining, per se, as a way
of spending the time. It may be that they had each lived through the Depression, and thought of mealtimes as traumatic—especially my mother,
who, growing up on what she called a *dirt farm*, in shocking poverty, spent
most of her childhood hungry.

It might also be that my mother and father, being German and Irish, re-
spectively, come from cultures not especially known for their fine dining—at
least not back then, anyway. My father loved sitting around a big table with
his family, smoking a cigarette and arguing philosophy—but I don't know
that he especially cared about anything that was actually on his plate. He did
reach a certain point in his life, though, when he decided that no one could
ever force him to eat vegetables again, and that was that. So Dick Boylan's
tastes in food were primarily about the things he hated.

Given my grandmother's choices in cooking—Chicken a la King,
brisket slathered in heavy sauce, creamed onions, frozen peas—it is not
hard to figure out how he wound up that way.

I didn't have a lot of meals with my parents when I was in high school. My father, traveling the world and working late in those days, usually had his dinner with my mother after nine o'clock at night. For my part, I'd come through the doors around five to find a pan of Shake 'N Bake chicken on the stove, where it had already been warming for an hour or two. I would eat this by myself while reading the comics in the *Philadelphia Inquirer,* which maybe sounds lonely, but I can tell you I think of those suppers with happiness. Dondi! Terry and the Pirates! Mark Trail! Rick O'Shay! Dick Tracy! I loved the comics, and to enter that world with a big plate of Shake 'N Bake after a long day of wearing a coat and tie at my all-male prep school (sic), well, that was a sweet escape indeed.

It may explain why to this day, if I am alone in a strange city, my favorite way of having dinner is to sit alone at a bar with a book.

It simply never occurred to me, before I went to college, that food could taste good, or that there was anything especially pleasant about sharing a meal with someone else.

Also, there were fairly strict rules around meals on those rare occasions when we all ate together. I remember at college wrinkling my nose when I learned that the dining hall was serving spaghetti one night. My friend Peter Frumkin asked me why, and I sighed that it was just so exhausting using the soup spoon to twirl the pasta around your fork. Peter just looked at me like I was from Mars—which was not so far off—and then he said, Watch. He put his fork directly in his plate, spun the spaghetti around it, and then popped his fork directly into his mouth. I had never seen anything like this. Seriously? I said. You can do that?

I tried it myself. I started eating spaghetti that day. I have never stopped.

Still, the biggest change in my relationship with food happened after Deedie and I got married and moved to Maine. In the late '80s, there were no Thai restaurants north of Portland, so one of our friends sent us a huge box of Thai ingredients and a cookbook as a housewarming gift.

In no time at all, my sweetheart was making me drunken noodles and shrimp with coconut milk and pad Thai chicken, meals which we ate in our little farmhouse at a dining room table with candles. Would you like more? she'd ask me as I cleaned my plate.

*Why yes,* I said to my beloved. *I will have more.*

It was not just that Deedie's meals—containing lemongrass and fish sauce and galangal—were delicious. It was also that eating a meal changed from a kind of stop-in at a gas station into something else. I guess they call it *dining.*

For most of my life, I had snarfed down my supper while reading the comics, in hopes of moving on to the next item on my agenda. This was not universally true—there were certainly happy nights out eating pizza with my friends or stopping in at a diner to have a cup of coffee and some pie. But having dinner with Deedie was about something more.

When I was in college, the campus priest had given a sermon one Sunday morning about the meaning of the Eucharist. He wasn't that enthused by the whole *let's eat Jesus's body* business. What was important about breaking bread was sharing it with other people. That's what was meant by communion, he said. If you wanted to know the love of god, he suggested, order a pizza for your hall.

And it was not only this aspect of breaking bread that meant the world to me now. It was also the fact that someone I loved was cooking for me. In those early days, Deedie's ability to trash the kitchen was magnificent; a simple supper of noodles and meatballs could lay the kitchen to waste. It fell to me to clean up the mess after dinner, which I did, mostly, without complaint, because in its own humble way, washing and drying the dishes was part of the Eucharist, too. *These are my soapy bubbles, broken for you.*

Over the years, Deedie and I developed an understanding. When she cooked, I cleaned up. And when I cooked, *I* cleaned up. You see what I did there? The system works.

We lived in Ireland the year I turned forty, and I spent that year enjoying the carvery lunches at the pub, a kind of Irish smorgasbord that turned every day into Thanksgiving. There'd be a guy carving a roast beef for you, and stacks of chicken and little meatballs, and an unstoppable battery of root vegetables: turnips and carrots and onions and parsnips. And then there were the potatoes: boiled and baked and French-fried chips. All of this was piled on top of a plate and then drowned in brown gravy, and you'd take it back to your table along with a nice pint of Guinness or Murphy's or Beamish and life was good.

For most of my male life I'd paid no attention to my weight because, quite simply, there'd been nothing to pay attention to. Until I was thirty, I'd stayed rail thin because my metabolism was so fast, and because there was no one to linger over a meal with. That last decade pre-transition I'd begun to morph. I went from 140 to 150. Then sixty. Then seventy. I looked down sometimes and saw a belly, like Santa. Deedie and I made little jokes about it. Go on, she'd say. Shake it when you laugh.

The gain in size didn't really bother me, in part because I'd grown up without food or weight issues being on my radar. I'd been able to eat whatever I wanted, in whatever quantities I'd desired, for so long that it never occurred to me that this was something I should even remotely be concerned about.

When we returned to America in late 1999, though, I began to understand that transition was in my future. Shortly after that, the fact that I'd been living in a dream world, and never even known it, was made clear to me.

To be a woman in this culture meant being thin, or so I was led to believe. And so, on top of everything else I had to worry about, as I began hormones and electrolysis and therapy and grew out my hair and saved my blood for autologous blood transfer (don't ask), I now had to think about food.

I was six months into transition when someone offered me some cake at a party. *Oh I don't know,* I heard myself say. *Maybe just a little sliver.*

And so the attempt to be thin was now on the radar, and not only because I was committed to a repressive, anorexic version of womanhood. It was also that the belly I'd acquired had a particularly male shape to it, and that it was this, more than any other aspect of my embodiment, that could out me against my will. I could take voice lessons to change from baritone to mezzo-soprano; a trip to an electrologist's trailer in Livermore Falls left my cheeks and neck as smooth as a harbor seal. But if I shook when I laughed, like a bowl full of Jell-O, I sometimes got that look, the one that said, You are not who you are pretending to be. Or so I convinced myself.

Weight loss thus became not only the traditional locus of female neurosis for me; it also became a handicap unique to transgender women, the thing that might ruin my hopes of passing, and thus—in the worst-case scenario—put me at risk for cruelty, or violence, or murder.

It seemed like a heavy price to pay for moo goo gai pan.

My first attempt to lose weight was with something called SlimFast powder, which, from what I can see, is the same as Nestlé's Quik with some vitamins thrown in. Every day I'd enjoy a big gloopy milkshake, instead of actual food, and it was surprising how swiftly this appeared to work. I counted calories, and fat grams, on a small plastic wheel I'd bought somewhere, the anorexic equivalent of an abacus. Every day I weighed myself, and I also checked my measurements with a tape measure: thighs, bust, stomach, neck. The change was so rapid that first year on hormones that every day was sort of like opening an Advent calendar of the flesh: you never knew what each morning's weigh-in might reveal.

I lost a lot of weight that year, but I think that an even stronger motivator of my diminishment was the worry I carried around before coming out in public. I was so uncertain what the future held: Would I lose my family? Would I lose my job? Would I ever be able to write another book? What was going to happen to me?

Most of the trans people whom I knew then lived desperate, marginal lives. I was friends with a woman who'd been thrown out of her house; I knew another who'd been fired; I knew a third whose child was relentlessly teased and tortured on the school bus. Was this what my life, and the lives of my loved ones, was going to be like? I read a news report in which a transgender woman had been taunted by a crowd of thugs, a woman who ran from these villains, was caught by them, and beaten within an inch of her life. This incident took place on a street which I myself had walked down *en femme*. Night after night I lay awake in my bed, listening to the clock chiming: 3:00 A.M., 3:15, 3:30. It was hard to imagine that the future before me contained something other than violence and loss.

It didn't leave me hungry for chipotle mac and cheese, I can tell you that. Or drunken noodles. Or pasta primavera.

Mostly I pushed my food around on my plate, hoping that no one else would notice that I wasn't actually eating anything. It is probably worth saying out loud that no one ever falls for the *pushing your food around* strategy. If no one says anything, it's not that they haven't noticed. It's that they're embarrassed for you, or too full of pity to puncture your balloon.

One friend, taking a good look at me during this period, shook her head and said, Ah. I see you're on the Stress Diet.

I'd read somewhere that the lowest safe weight for me, based on my body mass index, was 135 pounds. Dish by dish, I began to approach this: 160, 150, 145. I notched my belt tighter. Then I notched it again.

*Oh Jim,* Deedie said to me one night toward the end of transition. *It's like you're disappearing in front of my eyes.*

I found talk like this annoying, of course, because for one thing, didn't she see how much more beautiful I was becoming, as the Irish belly slowly receded? Was it possible that she was really all that nostalgic for the times when I could jiggle when I laughed?

More important, I wasn't disappearing. I was, if anything, at last becoming visible. Couldn't she understand that?

145, 140, 135 . . .

One time, I looked down at my chest. I could see my heart pounding through my ribs. Excellent, I thought. That is just great.

Of all the untrue things I convinced myself of in early transition, I think the most harmful one was the idea that womanhood meant *being little*. In its way this idea does more damage even than the idea that womanhood means *being pretty*. Little sends a different message from pretty, of course. Pretty says, *Judge me by my looks*. Little says, *I'm not even here*. Little says, *You don't need to worry about me, because there's not enough of me to challenge you*. Little is an invitation to being ignored.

I need to swiftly add that there are some little women who are the largest people I know, including at least one friend of mine who is an actual Little Person. No one would ever mistake my friend Barbara for a person of no consequence; as a teacher and an activist she has fought for justice and for change, and her work has helped improve the lives of Little People—and some big ones, too, including me.

I'm also aware that beauty is no small thing, and that looking good can make people feel happy about themselves. I'm not here to make anybody feel bad about the things that make them feel good.

But willingly diminishing yourself in order to fit some feminine ideal is a different matter, especially when that ideal has at its core the erasure of women and the foregrounding of men. That's something I want to fight.

Women—and men—in the grips of anorexia aren't necessarily experiencing a political dilemma; many of us are trying, against all odds, to have control over something in our lives. This is especially true of women who feel that they have lost—or never had—agency over their fates. I know the euphoria of stepping onto a scale and realizing that I've reached a goal. In a world in which so much of our agency is constantly being stripped from us, that kind of high can provide a rare sense of ownership—especially since the thing that we get to own at those moments is *our own bodies*.

It is, of course, exactly that control which is most frequently under attack, by everything from infectious disease to Republican congressmen.

Of all the things I struggled with in transition, one of the hardest was the need to *fit in*. I've written before about the ways in which transgender people often go through a kind of second adolescence in transition, and if that adolescence happens—as it did for me—in one's forties, the results can be, ahem, a little awkward. But it's not just getting used to being in a differently shaped body that's hard; even weirder is trying to negotiate the truly adolescent urge to be like the cool kids, the pretty ones, the thin.

I remember thinking about all this back when I was in the throes of all the changes, remember looking upon the behavior of so many pre- or non-feminist women, living their lives as if determined to succeed only when they had *oppressed themselves*. And all I could think, as I looked with contempt and disdain upon all of this behavior, was, I want to be just like that! If being a woman means making myself invisible, well by all means let's get on with the business of erasing ourselves! Because only then, when people look upon me and see a woman as fucked up and sad as all the other women I know, only then will people see that at last I have succeeded.

I managed to shake off this insanity in time, but it took a lot longer than you'd think. Maybe, at six feet tall, I came to realize that I was never going to be little, no matter how thin I got. Maybe, as the hands of the clock whirled around and around, and I turned forty, then fifty, then sixty, it became clearer to me that the graveyard doesn't care how purty you were.

Or maybe it's just that my wife, Deedie, is a really incredible cook.

I don't think that food is a good substitute for love, but if someone gives you a gift to show you how loved you are—and what is a plate of food if not a gift of love?—that's not the time to start counting calories.

When I finally flew home from Neenah, Wisconsin, after my surgery, I was driven in a limo from the Portland airport back to our home in Belgrade Lakes. Deedie and our friend Richard Russo had come to Neenah to be by my side during the actual surgery, but after I was safely out of the woods—and waking up in a room with balloons that said, IT's A GIRL!—Deedie and Rick headed back to Maine, and my friend Timothy Kreider joined me for the follow-through. The car that met Tim and me was a hilariously over-the-top stretch limo that had been used just the night before to take kids to a prom. There was glitter on the seats. A tiara had fallen onto the floor. Incredibly, there was a single cassette tape in the deck, and that cassette tape featured the music of Yanni, the New Age keyboard player. Tim and I climbed into the limo, high on the painkillers I had been prescribed in the wake of the switcheroo, and we laughed ourselves silly listening to Yanni and taking turns wearing the tiara.

At last the driver pulled up to our house, and Tim and I came through the front door.

And there were my children—eight and six years old at the time—holding signs that said, WELCOME HOME MADDY WE LOVE YOU. Yes, they called me Maddy—Zach's mash-up of "Mommy" and "Daddy." (Sean had briefly advocated for "Dommy," but that one didn't take.) At the stove was Deedie. Water from a lobster pot steamed behind her.

She embraced me and sat me down at the kitchen table, and we had a cocktail. A little later, she put a plate before me. On it was a two-pound lobster, and some melted butter with lemon in a small ramekin, and two ears of fresh sweet corn. She opened a bottle of sauvignon blanc, and we raised our glasses (the kids raised their tumblers of milk).

"Welcome home," said Deedie. "We love you."

I looked down at the feast before me. "Hey," I asked my wife. "Can I roll my corn right in the butter?"

Deedie smiled. "Of course you can roll your corn in the butter," she said. Which I did. The melted butter glistened on the kernels. I shook some kosher salt and ground some black pepper on it. Steam rose from the hot lobster.

"I'm going to roll my corn, too, if that's okay," said Tim.

"Of course it's okay," said Deedie. "Hey, listen. Did you know you're wearing a tiara?"

"I am wearing the tiara," explained my friend, "because it makes me beautiful."

My children laughed. Sean turned to me. "Maddy," he said. "That's a silly man."

# FRIENDS

It was my second car wreck in six months. Back in September, on the very first day of my senior year, my friend Mickey had mixed up the clutch and the brake, sailing the Volkswagen off a cliff. Next thing you knew, *blammo*.

There was an explosion and a bright light. Something in my skull rang like an iron bell. Then this beautiful blue was everywhere and a dark blob spoke to me with forgiveness and love. *Son? Son?*

This turned out to be the head of a cop, bending over me. I was looking up at the blue sky, all banged up. But not dead.

So a few months later, when Ben Simmons lost control of the Vega, I was like, *Don't worry, it takes a lot to kill a person.*

In this, of course, I was wrong. It hardly takes anything at all.

We whirled down the hill, the road before us black ice. A stone wall loomed ahead. "We're gonna hit!" Ben shouted.

People who didn't know us sometimes thought we were brothers, two hippie boys with identical John Lennon glasses, identical mops of straight blond hair. We wore corduroy pants, we had bandanas. We wore Wallabees.

It was pretty easy to get us confused.

Ben jammed on the brakes, and we went around and around. A Beatles cassette was playing on the eight-track. *Somebody spoke and I went into a dream.* I closed my eyes, waiting for the impact.

We smashed into the wall, bounced back, spun around some more. He yelled, and I yelled, and we both kept yelling. The front end of the car pitched into a ditch, and then everything went silent except for snow crystals ticking on the windshield. We were okay.

"Oh, man," Ben said. The front fender was crumpled up like a love letter. "My dad's gonna kill me."

"Listen," I said. "Just tell him it was me."

He thought about it. "You know," he said. "I *could*."

Ben was the sweet one. He had a giant fluffball of a dog, a Newfoundland named Lucy. He was the head of our school's stage crew. He spoke French. He had a girlfriend named Pam. They hadn't had sex yet, though you never know. Ben had hopes.

I wasn't the sweet one. I had a terrible dalmatian, Penny, whose eyes oozed an inexplicable brown goo. I spoke German. I was in love with Pam's best friend, Poppy, but to her I was just an irritation, like a leech or a tsetse fly. She wanted Ben instead. Of course she did.

We both lived in haunted houses in a town called Devon, on the Main Line in the Philly suburbs. On the walls of my house I often saw shadows. One night, looking into a mirror in my bathroom, I saw the reflection of somebody who was not me. Even worse than this was the vibe of the place. There was a feeling you'd get when you climbed the creaking stairs up to the third floor. Whatever was up there, it was always watching. A string hanging down from the ceiling released a Jacob's ladder that led into the attic. Nobody went up there, ever.

Ben's house was haunted, too. His grandfather passed right through him one night like a cold mist—scary, but also kind of dear. Ben had loved his grandfather.

There were a lot of specters back then.

After the accident, we drove away with the front fender all smashed up. When Ben stopped in front of my haunted house, I grabbed my schoolbooks off the back seat and jumped out, then Ben headed on to his. The snow was still coming down.

I climbed those long stairs up to the third floor and felt the presence of that watching thing. I pulled the dead bolt on my bedroom door, and it snapped closed with a *snick*. I took off my clothes and laid them on the bed—the corduroy pants, the Oxford cloth shirt, the schoolboy tie.

On one wall there was a secret panel. I opened it up.

Once, at school, Tim Ling and I had a conversation in which it became clear almost immediately that he'd mistaken me for my sweeter-tempered friend. A normal person would've told him instantly about his mix-up, but I felt sorry for him, and thought the kindest thing I could do would be to imitate Ben until we finished talking.

So I told Tim Ling about Pam's refusal to take things up to the next level. I told him that the stage crew was preparing the fall performance of *Our Town* in the gym. I even told him that I worried about my parents, about whether they'd stay together. It felt good, in a way, to be him instead of me.

But at some point I gave myself away. I can't remember what tipped him off. "What's wrong with you, Boylan?" Tim said, pissed off. "You think it's funny, lying to people?"

I thought he was going to punch me out, and I hung my head in shame. "No," I said. "I don't think it's funny."

It was a sunny day in California, with the waves rolling on the blue Pacific. Ben lay there in the sand watching his friends playing in the water. He was almost thirty now. After college he'd moved back to Philly and got a gig at a video production house, now and again working on films of his own. He made a silent movie called *The Fan*, in which an electric fan blows people away. All the dead wind up on a green hill, feasting. Then they disappear, one by one.

As for me, I was in Baltimore and finishing up grad school at Johns Hopkins. I lived in an ornate first-floor apartment with a fireplace and mirrors on the wall. I was trying to write a novel about a wizard who owns an enchanted waffle iron.

That place had a secret compartment, too.

Ben dove into the waves. For a moment he was underwater, in a dark, cool world. Then he came up for air.

When a big wave rose behind him, Ben decided to ride it in.

It curled above him. Then he was tangled up in the churning surf. He came down *hard* as the wave crashed. The foam slid past him, the wave withdrew.

Ben lay there in the sand. He could hear the voices of his friends, the calling of the seagulls.

But he could not move.

Twenty-five years later, we went to our fortieth high school reunion together. Ben was in a wheelchair, and I was a woman. Lots of guys showed up for the occasion, though not Tim Ling. He'd died of a heart attack at a Phillies game.

The Haverford School was supposedly an all-boys school, but in our class of sixty-nine, two of us had emerged as trans women. There were jokes about something being in the drinking water. In response, I laughed. "Ha ha," I said, "yeah I guess."

The other trans woman, Chelsea, lived on an island off the West Coast now, selling tie-dyed clothing.

Chelsea didn't make it to the reunion, but lots of us did. Curiously, among the returning alums were lots of former boys who'd gotten expelled. The headmaster had loved throwing people out whenever he got the chance. Back in the day, Moats climbed onto the roof of the cafeteria with a bucket of water and waited for the librarian, Mr. Kupersmith, to pass below. They expelled him for that, and you couldn't really blame them. You can't pour a bucket of water on somebody's head and expect the world to remain unchanged. Now Moats was fifty-eight years old, with a long beard he'd tied into a braid.

They'd come from New Jersey, from Florida and Los Angeles, from Chicago and Ohio and Maine, even some from Pennsylvania. There wasn't a lot of love among my classmates for our alma mater. The headmaster, a Frankenstein named Davis Parker, had lurched around the hallways, yelling at us for not having enough *gumption*. Now he was dead, confined to an oil painting hanging in the hallway of the Upper School.

Earlier in the evening I'd stood there, studying him, mesmerized. The smells of this place—the pencil shavings and floor wax and cold sweat—still made me shudder. It hadn't been much fun, being a trans girl at an all-boys school. On the other hand, several teachers had changed my life: Mr. Hallowell, who wore three-piece suits and carried a pocket watch on a chain. Mr. Pearson, the German teacher, so young: *Alle Menschen werden Brüder!* And terrifying Mr. Jameson, whom we called "Chopper." There were times when being there was all right. I felt like a clever spy, a mole behind enemy lines.

Ben and I loved this song by Rahsaan Roland Kirk, "Bright Moments." I recalled listening to Rahsaan playing his heart out in Ben's barn one hot summer night, the lyrics just that one wonderful phrase chanted over and over: *Bright moments! Bright moments! Bright moments!*

So I stood in the hallway, my hair down to my breasts, and I stared at Davis Parker's painting. *Who's got gumption* now, *motherfucker?*

Why had so many of us flocked to this terrible old place? Was it just morbid curiosity—the simple desire to see what had become of us? There were social workers and venture capitalists, hand surgeons and insurance salesmen. Keith Jones, who'd played the part of Katisha, in drag, during the high school production of *The Mikado*, became the guy who announced the horse races at the Liberty Bell raceway. "And they're off—" he'd shout, and the race would begin.

It was Ben who'd made the calls, tracked down the e-addresses, sent out the invitations, won everybody over. Sure, that school had been the source of beatings and mortifications. But Ben—beautiful, generous, damaged Ben—sent out the summons. And we answered it.

Once upon a time, in the same hallway over which Davis Parker presided, there had been a corkboard listing the names of everyone in the class. If you were failing anything, they *popped your cork*, and a light shone through the empty hole so your classmates could be amused by your struggles. There was a cork for Late Session, which was detention, and another—with a red light—for Saturday Session, the most humiliating cork of all.

Now, ten thousand years later, I was an alumna among alumni, with gumption out the wazoo.

Ben and I paused before an assortment of cheeses, cocktails in our hands. This was in the old study hall, a huge space known simply as the Big Room. A slideshow of our younger selves was playing on a screen behind the cheese. There we were, putting together the set for *The Mikado*. Look: there was Keith Jones in his bra. Look, there was my friend John, wearing a tuxedo, raising an invisible glass of champagne. And then there was a shot of Ben and me in a field of green grass, holding beer steins on Senior Cut Day.

"You know, Jenny," he said. "When I look at these pictures, it's like I'm looking at some whole other person."

This, of course, was the fundamental question. *Was* it some whole other person? Were the boys we'd been gone forever, or did we carry them in our hearts? How do you build a bridge between your present and your past, especially if you've been sundered from your former self by trauma?

What does it mean to be a woman who never had a girlhood?

Ben had shattered a vertebra in his neck when he smashed down on the sand that day. He couldn't move his legs. He could raise his arms, but could lower only one of them.

Ben looked at me, all willowy in my black dress. "You're looking kind of saucy tonight," he said, grinning sweetly.

It was weird to be back in the Big Room after all these years with a martini and a vagina. "You know, if Mr. Parker found out I was a woman," I said, "he definitely would've popped my cork. Given me a Late Session."

Ben nodded. "A *Saturday*."

We looked out across the room, once full of wooden desks that were nailed to the floor. There had been little holes on top of each one, in the corner. That's where boys long dead had once emplaced their inkwells.

Now, all the desks were gone and the room was filled instead with middle-aged men. Even among this rarefied demographic—upper middle class, East Coast, conspicuously white—it seemed as if there'd been a lot of different answers to the question of what it meant to be a man. One of us had played football for the New York Giants. Another dropped out of Kenyon to follow the Grateful Dead. A third had run for mayor of Pittsburgh.

A photo of Young Me flashed across the screen, another one from Senior Cut Day. I was sitting next to Peter Hunter, who held his arms spread wide, as if to fly. The camera had caught me in an unguarded moment, wearing a look of hope and hurt. It broke my heart, a little bit, to see that face. How I loved the boy I'd been! If it wasn't for him, and everything he'd silently suffered, I wouldn't even be here.

"You and me, Jenny," Ben said. "We each had a before, and then an after."

I have been blessed, over the course of a long life, with good friends, both men and women. The friends of my childhood were almost exclusively boys. There was Ben of course, but there was also the man I call Zero, with whom I listened to the music of Frank Zappa. One time we drove around in his car throwing pancakes out the window.

Then there was John, whose father was a beloved television weatherman. For his part, John wasn't all that interested in talking about the weather. You could kind of see why. Another thing about John was that in a few short years, he would come to own a tarantula. What did he name the tarantula? He named it Fido.

And there was Link, who in another era would've been a shepherd. His great gift was the ability to look out for other people. He made sure we buckled our seat belts, conversed with our parents, used condoms. We called him the Safety Officer.

In our senior year, John and Link had a car accident, too, a smashup en route to a summer house in Maine that left Link with a shattered skull and a bruised brain. For a week or two it wasn't clear if he was staying or leaving. In the end, he made it through all that, although nobody can come so close to dying without being forever shaken. It wasn't lost on me that Link, the most careful and solicitous among us, turned out to be the one who most needed the rest of us to look out for *him*.

But I wasn't a very good shepherd, not when we were young. I hope I'm better at it now. Still, there probably are better people to choose if what you need is someone to guard your flock.

I'd carried a spectacular burden back then, as a trans girl in an all-boys school. But now, looking back on it all from the vantage point of old age, it was clear to me that I was not the only encumbered soul. Each of the men I loved had struggled with *something* during those years. Who's to say that my own troubles were any more profound than theirs? Link had been fundamentally changed by his car accident; John sometimes struggled with his weatherman father. Plus, his tarantula wasn't doing him any favors. Zero, meanwhile, was so fidgety in high school that he'd found it very hard to read a single page from a book without getting distracted. And Ben's parents would soon divorce.

A couple weeks into our junior year my friend Ginger just vanished. He'd sat right next to me in Mr. Houston's American History class, in one of those desks nailed to the floor, with the hole for the inkwells in the desktop. But then that desk was empty, day after day.

Mr. Houston, a round man known as "Thumper," was a member of a particular religious order that believed that the first-person pronoun was sinful, an indication of pride. He'd say things like, *He wants you to get out a sheet of paper and number it one to ten.*

We'd say, who?

*He does*, said Thumper.

Who's he?

He'd point to himself. *Him.*

And so on.

Eventually we got word that Ginger was in the hospital, his fists all bandaged up. He'd destroyed his bedroom. There were holes in the wall where he'd punched it.

Ginger never did come back to school that year, although eventually we got back to hanging out at his house. We listened to *Tubular Bells* in his room with the holes in the wall. We drank 16-ounce Pabst Blue Ribbons. We played Rock 'Em Sock 'Em Robots.

Nobody ever asked about what had happened to him. The thought was inconceivable. That wasn't the way it was done, among boys.

Instead, we made jokes, spoke of it all obliquely, or through irony, or through spectacular acts of public stupidity, like throwing pancakes out the back of the station wagon as we listened to "Dark Star." In our own way we were working it out, I guess, trying to let our friend know that we loved him, and that we were sorry.

But we could not say this in any words that you could hear.

Then, at college, I had lots of female friends for the first time. Annie was a writer from New York; Judith was a dancer from East Hartford. With these women, and others as well, I developed friendships based, at least in part, on a kind of sympathy. We'd often reassure one another— *We're going to survive this, we're going to be okay*—as if we'd all arrived in our early twenties after surviving some gruesome chagrin.

It's not impossible that this sensibility was hardwired into the experience of growing up female. Of course, I hadn't suffered in the ways they had, or for that matter, known the unique joys they'd found, either. But I still felt that I was their sister. It was a shame that they did not know it.

How I longed to tell them that we were, you know, the *same*! I came so close sometimes. One time, Betsy Manlove and I wound up in an old graveyard, singing two-part harmony into the dark abyss of a crypt built into the side of a hill. *Betsy*, I imagined myself saying. *Betsy, I'm actually* . . .

But it was impossible to say such things. All I could hope was that the song we were singing might stand in for the truth, that Betsy might hear in that melody the aching secret that clenched my heart like an octopus.

She didn't hear it, though.

It had never occurred to me to spill the beans to my boy friends, not ever. Was I afraid of letting them down? Or was it because male friendships weren't about sharing secrets—at least not in words? With the boys I had a sense of adventure, of conquest, even if what we were exploring was nothing more than a song, a book, a plate of spicy food. We'd head off to dives in the middle of the night like we were the bar-crawling equivalents of Thor Heyerdahl. There were so many scuzzy new worlds to discover!

During those missions we almost never provided one another with a sense of consolation for the various burdens we privately hauled around. That just wasn't how it worked. Instead, the truths of our souls could only be revealed through irony or dumb jokes. There was a secret language among boys, a silent code that gently revealed some—but never all—of the things we'd left unspoken.

It might be that we were repressed, or that we lacked a language for describing our inner lives. But maybe we also feared that describing them in words would violate those secret selves. Our inner lives were like those creatures that live at the bottom of the sea, like tube worms or the flapjack octopus. Hauled into the light of day, these things could only shrivel.

Many years later, long after transition, I drove my friend Lefty home after a jam in the barn of my friends Nick and Shell Laroux; back in the day I used to be in a band with them, along with our friend Cindy the Drummer and Big-Head Chester on rhythm guitar. It was always a good time, the Laroux's Halloween party, and their barn that night had been full of vampires and Frankensteins, Jasons and Slutty Nurses. You know: the usual.

I'd worn a tight black dress for the occasion, fishnet stockings. All the way home, Lefty looked out the window at the shining harvest moon, humming softly to himself. Earlier, he'd had a knife sticking out of the side of his head. But he was okay now.

We'd always been friends, Lefty and me, even though I was a college professor and he ran his own karaoke company. He'd come to your bar, or your party, and put on a whole show. The company was called Championship Karaoke. Nick, one time, had explained to me the difference between Championship Karaoke and the regular kind. "Your ordinary karaoke comes in about here," he said, carefully holding his palm parallel to the floor, as if measuring the level of water in a pool. "But Championship Karaoke?" he said. He raised his other hand about a foot above the first one. "That comes in up here."

I'd see Lefty around the jams, even in local bars now and again when

Championship Karaoke and I accidentally crossed paths. I'd always liked Lefty. He had merry eyes, a small braid down his back.

I pulled up at Lefty's apartment, put the car in park, and I leaned over to give him a hug.

Lefty's arms wrapped around me, and without warning his tongue shot down my throat. I tried to pull back. But Lefty wasn't having it. "No," I tried to say, but it came out *nggghhh*. At last I got loose.

He looked at me, hurt. "Lefty," I said. "It's not like that."

Lefty just shrugged. "You know I've always thought you were hot," he said.

I didn't know what to tell him.

"Nevertheless," I said.

"Come on, Jenny," he said.

"Come on what," I said. "You know I'm married."

"Yeah, well," he said, crestfallen. "That didn't seem to make much difference when you were flirting with Baloney Dog."

Baloney Dog was a guy I'd met at another one of the other barn jams. I'd been playing the Hammond organ that night through an old Leslie, a kind of amp in which the speakers whirl around inside the cabinet to create a classic B-3 Vibrato sound. He had a beautiful old National steel guitar, its body full of the many dents it had received over a lifetime of musicians playing their hearts out on the thing.

I don't know if I'd been flirting with Baloney Dog per se, but I'd definitely been coming on to his guitar.

"Nothing ever *happened* with Baloney Dog," I told Lefty. "I just loved the way he played."

"Jenny," said Lefty. I could smell the beer on his breath. *"I can play."*

He leaned in and grabbed the back of my head, and kissed me hard once more. "No," I tried to say, but it was hard to talk. *"Nnnggg!"* I pushed him away. I looked at the dashboard. My keys were still in the ignition. They were the only weapon that I had.

But Lefty just sighed, smiled, and then opened the door. I didn't watch him walk toward his apartment. I just drove off as fast as I could.

The next day, when I woke up and remembered the whole scene, I was angry: angry at Lefty for putting me in that situation; angry at myself for having been so blind as to what was coming.

And angry at the cleavage between the worlds of men and women, worlds that in some ways I understood even less well now than in the Days Before.

It's like I've crossed the briny ocean, I thought, to take up residence in this new land, only to wind up deaf and blind to its rules. Years had passed, but even now I did not know how to protect myself, how I could still, in spite of everything I knew about *both* of these worlds, wind up in this dangerous situation. Was that my fault, as a newcomer to this world? Or is that what it meant to be female, to constantly be suspicious, even of the friends that I held dear?

After the reunion, as Ben drove me home in his wheelchair-accessible van, I thought about the boys we'd been when we were young, and the men—and women—we'd all become. Chelsea, who'd been deeply into war games and military strategy as a teenager, and who'd rowed crew at Princeton, was now a musician, a weaver, a poet. Looking at her, you wouldn't know anything at all about the person she'd been. But that boy was still in there somewhere. I hoped that he was a source of joy for her, just as the person I'd been was, mostly, still a source of joy for me.

Music was playing softly in the van as we drove toward home. Was it the Beatles again? *Somebody spoke and I went into a dream.*

I looked out the window. Over there was the diner we used to go to, Minella's, just down the street from the Wawa. Over here was the Ludington Library, where I'd spent rainy Saturdays looking at James Thurber cartoons. There was Old Gulph Road, the street that once had led to Poppy's house. She gave amazing parties back then. Once she gave a luncheon where she served peach melba.

A dark blob spoke to me out of a blue sky. *Son? Son?*

I almost never get back to Pennsylvania anymore, though I always thought I'd wind up back there someday. But we sold Mom's haunted house in 2011. She had died there in her bed, aged ninety-four. My sister and I were at her side, holding her hand. *It's okay, Mom. You can let us go.*

At the reunion I'd wanted to tell the boys that I was sorry for every mean thing I'd ever said, that I wished I'd been more forgiving when I was young, less concerned with conquest, a little more concerned with forgiveness.

I looked over at the man who'd once been my twin, as he drove us down the streets of our old hometown. A wave had picked him up and left him changed.

But then a wave had lifted us all.

I think of all the differences between manhood and womanhood I've experienced, there is nothing more profound than the way men keep their emotions bottled up, and women let them loose. There are advantages to both approaches, I guess. I mean, sure: it's sad that men so often seem bereft of the language to describe the things they feel. There are times, in thinking of my younger self, when I just want to shout at him: *Tell somebody you're a girl! Tell Zero! Or Ben! Or Link!* I could have spared myself decades of trouble if I'd only been able to share the thing that was in my heart.

But I was afraid of speaking the truth back then, as so many men are, because saying the thing I felt out loud would have made it real. And the fact that I was trans struck me as the worst possible curse; I would have done anything not to constantly, endlessly feel the thing I felt. So I kept it silent, and hidden. There was a secret panel in my room, to be sure. But even more tightly sealed was the one I kept in my heart.

I think sometimes of the lines in the Gospel of St. Thomas. *If you bring forth what is within you, what you bring forth will save you. If you do not bring forth what is within you, what you do not bring forth will destroy you.*

Without diminishing the truth of St. Thomas's words, though, I do want to acknowledge that the opposite condition has its pitfalls as well. I had a girlfriend in college, Nora, who used to knock on my door, sweep into the room, and burst into tears. "What?" I said, looking up from my Smith Corona. "What?"

Nora rushed in, her eyes already red, and collapsed into my arms. She was a world-class crier.

It made me mad sometimes, that she was so loose with her tears. Come on, I'd think. Show a little gumption. You think I don't want to cry like this sometimes? Well, you don't see me keening about it.

But man. I longed to. It was bad enough not being female. It was worse to be surrounded by women for whom being themselves was a source of zero consolation. Oh Nora, I'd think, as I watched the second hand sweep around the dial. If I were myself, I'd never shed another tear again.

Which is, of course, completely untrue. That was the very first thing that estrogen changed. A few weeks on Premarin and I was crying at anything—television commercials, songs by James Taylor, the songs of birds.

I understood something about Nora now that I had not comprehended when I held her in my arms. Her tears had brought her joy.

I had cried many tears the summer that Ben died, in 2022. It didn't take much. For a while I wondered if I'd ever be able to listen to the Beatles again. It was just too hard. I'd hear "Sgt. Pepper" while I was in the supermarket, and I'd stop for a moment, traveling in time, mourning the man that I had loved, my former twin.

Tim Ling was yelling at me. *You think it's funny, Boylan, lying to people?*

We went to his funeral, Deedie and me, back in Pennsylvania, at the old St. David's Church. There were all the boyos, now transformed into old men. Some of them still couldn't get my pronouns right. One of them said right to my face, "You know, I don't think of you as a woman." It occurred to me to reply, *You know, I don't think of you as a gentleman.*

But instead I said, "Maybe one day that will change."

Afterward, Deedie and I got back in the car and drove home to Maine. She was behind the wheel, as usual, while I sat at her side, looking out the window. The Bruce Springsteen channel was on the satellite radio. "Glory Days."

I thought about Ben and me, about Link and John and Zero. I thought about the empty halls of the Haverford School, the portraits of the former headmasters hanging on the walls. How creepy they all were, their eyes following you as you walked to get your books, late in the evening, after you'd served your time in Late Session! There was one dude with a pair of pince-nez, headmaster in the 1930s. Mr. Boocock. He was always on my case. *You're going to go home and open up one of those secret panels again, aren't you, son?*

Yeah, I told him. Probably.

"Are you okay, Jenny?" asked Deedie. She turned down the Springsteen.

"I'm okay," I said.

"You're awfully quiet."

"Yeah," I said. We were heading toward the Tappan Zee Bridge now, preparing to cross the Hudson. "I was just thinking about all of those boys I grew up with."

She nodded. "They're good guys," she said.

We started to drive across the bridge. It was a beautiful summer day. I looked over at my wife. We had crossed a lot of rivers together. I have many friends, male and female. But there is only one Deedie. She can whistle with two fingers in her mouth. She loves roasted potatoes, hot fudge, and Jameson Irish Whiskey. At the end of the day she stands by the lake and watches the sun turn the trees on the opposite bank to gold. So deeply does she love that glow that our friends, observing the rays of a setting sun touch the pines, call that "the Deedie light."

I've written about the two of us before. I admit I'm reluctant to do it again. Deedie would much rather be a reader of my books than a character in them.

But, as this book makes clear, there is more of our story to tell.

The Hudson stretched before us. To the south, way off in the distance, was the skyline of New York City. I remembered the first time I'd crossed this bridge. I'd never been to New York before. The far-off city had sung out to me, with its danger and its promise.

Deedie changed the station, landed on the Beatles channel. We crossed over the water. Ringo was singing. *In the town where I was born.*

"Oh, Dee," I said, tears rolling down. I raised my hands to cover my face. "I can't believe he's gone."

She reached over and held my hand.

"Ben . . . he was always my Beatles friend," I said. "I was the Stones, and he was the Beatles. We used to bicker about it, you know, Beatles versus Stones."

"Is that how people told you apart?"

"He was the nice one, the one girls wanted to be in love with. Me, I was the weirdo," I sobbed. "Nobody wanted to be in love with me. I was just some giant spaz."

"Jenny," she said, and squeezed my hand. "*I* want to be in love with you."

Deedie never seemed to have a problem, sharing the things inside her heart. But who knows? It was possible that there were some things, even now, she had not yet revealed to me, or, for that matter, to herself.

We were still on the bridge, she and I, suspended above the deep river. But we had not yet reached the opposite shore.

# VOICE

*Let me outta here,* said the figure in the trunk. This was at the bar, after hours at the National Ventriloquists' Convention. *Please, somebody, you gotta help me.* The guy next to me had been trying to pick me up all night. He hadn't gotten anywhere, not yet anyhow. He looked down at the trunk on the floor. "C'man," he said, irritated. "Just go back to sleep."

*I can't sleep, it's too noisy in this place. C'man, lemme out.*

On the dance floor, more than a few of the conference-goers were slow dancing with their puppets—or *figures,* as I'd learned they were more properly called. The ventriloquists had their arms wrapped around their figures: floppy dogs, sloe-eyed cowboys, even a bright green alien, as they swayed back and forth to Elvis Presley. *Wise men say, only fools rush in.*

*Who are you talking to?* said the voice from the trunk. Interestingly, it sounded slightly muffled. *Is she cute?*

"Yeah, she's cute," said the vent, casting a sidelong glance my way. He had slicked-back black hair, a southern accent. "But she's not interested in me. She thinks I'm *stupid.*"

*Laaady,* said the voice in the trunk, like Jerry Lewis. *Laaaaaady!*

"That's not true," I said. He looked at me. "Tell him that's not true."

*Is that her?* asked the voice in the box. *She sounds weird.*

"Hey," said the vent. "That's not nice."

*Laaady!* said the voice in the box.

"What do you mean, weird?" I said, feeling the blood rush to my face. Even now, these many years after transition, I still felt funny about my voice. I'd taken lessons from a therapist at Bates College, had done tutorials online from all sorts of people who claimed that they could teach you how to change your voice from a male-sounding one to a female. And for a while, I'd succeeded: my speaking voice had morphed into a more lilting and resonant instrument. I'd pick up the phone and a telemarketer would say, *Hello, ma'am, can I speak to the man of the house?* and I'd have to explain, *There is no man of the house, not unless you want to talk to my nine-year-old.*

But over time my voice had morphed from the feminine one I'd perfected with my therapist to something more androgynous. In part this was because I was just too lazy to continue making the constant effort to sustain that voice. That was the very problem: it was a voice I had to *sustain*, rather than being the thing that just came out of my mouth au naturel. I didn't want to have to keep thinking about how I was sounding. I just wanted to talk.

Another issue was that the *Jennifer voice,* as my wife began to call it, didn't project very well. It was fine if I was sitting in a quiet room with a friend, drinking cocoa and talking about pound cake. But if I was in a classroom and trying to reach the back of a lecture hall? Students sometimes had a hard time hearing me.

And it wasn't just a matter of volume. Everything about what I'd been taught in creating the Jennifer voice seemed to suggest that I should sound more uncertain of myself, to be asking, with my tone of supplication, for my audience's permission to be saying the things I was saying. It rubbed me the wrong way.

As time went by, my voice slipped out of its first flash of femininity and into something a little more androgynous. It was not, to be certain, the voice I had used back when I was a boyo. But it was a less overtly girlish voice now, too. It felt natural to me, and if there were any proof needed that it was the one coming from my heart, it was the fact that I didn't have to think about it anymore. I opened my mouth, and there it was.

This was swell when I was in front of a classroom, or trying to hail a cab, or drinking wine with my friends.

But it was awkward when I picked up the phone. *Hello, sir*, said the telemarketer. That was when I'd feel the blood rushing to my face, a sense of fury building up in my heart. There were also situations when my androgynous voice could, potentially, put me at risk. It was one thing to be on a college campus, where most people knew my history, and were fine with it (or pretended to be).

It was another thing to be at a ventriloquists' convention in Fort Mitchell, Kentucky, sitting at a bar where a dummy in a box thought I sounded weird. It made me think, and not for the first time, about the question of our true voices, and what these might actually be. And how do we find them? How do we know when the voices we speak in are our own?

Even before transition I had spoken in different voices over time. Once, in high school, I had wound up so stoned that I *forgot what I sounded like*. For a few terrifying minutes I spoke in the voice of my friend Link, who was the person I looked up to, and in so many ways wanted to be. But this only hurt Link's feelings. What are you talking like that for? he asked. Are you making fun of me?

Later, in college, I was roundly mocked during my freshman year because of my Philadelphia accent. There was an occasion when I had announced that I wanted to get a glass of *wudduh*, and a whole room full of hippies laughed hysterically. *James,* said my friend Tad, *say that again! You want to get a glass of what?* By the end of that year, I'd lost my Philly accent completely.

In the late '90s, after our year in Cork, our whole family came back from overseas with gentle Irish accents, and with the residue of a few curious Hibernian expressions. In particular, I loved the use of the Corkonian negative interrogative. Like: *Will you not turn down that music?*

Now, at a convention of ventriloquists, I was in a potentially more dangerous situation. What would happen if the man at my side—already a few drinks in—was able, by the tenor of my voice, to detect my history? All at once I had gone from a pleasantly absurd situation—the slow dancers cradling their figures were now on to "Dust in the Wind"—to one in which I was, quite possibly, at risk. Quite possibly, about to be unveiled. Quite possibly, to be on the receiving end of violence.

"He says you sound weird," said the ventriloquist.

"Oh no," I said, shifting subtly into Jennifer voice, just in case. "That hurts my feelings."

"Ah, don't mind him," said the ventriloquist. "He's just never heard a Yankee before."

Trying to figure out what I should sound like, post-transition, was not the only instance in which I would have to confront the gnarly question of *passing*, a subject so highly charged and complex that we should just agree at the outset that I'm not up to the task of exploring it in full. In its most basic form, though, *passing* refers to the degree to which any member of a marginalized group resembles, either by accident or design, the majority group, and as a result of that resemblance receives a kind of immunity from the prejudice and hatred that the majority group dishes out to outsiders. Historically, darker-skinned African Americans have been more likely to be on the receiving end of violence and bigotry from racists than lighter-skinned people of color. Jews around the world know that there's a difference in the way anti-Semites treat you if you "look Jewish." Gay men and lesbians learn early on that there are some places where you can be happily out, and other places where, if you want to be safe, you have to shift the code (if you can stand it, and if you are willing) to avoid violence and cruelty.

It's that very question of code-shifting—changing the way you look, changing the way you sound—that makes the issue of *passing* so volatile. Because there are some things you can change—your clothes, say—and some things you cannot—like the color of your skin. Michael Jackson was widely mocked for supposedly bleaching his skin in order to look white, but his autopsy confirmed that he had vitiligo, a condition that causes the skin to lose its pigment, and which he attempted to correct through the use of makeup.

It's fair to say, though, that some things are easier to change than others. What is it people are detecting when they say they have gaydar, or t-dar? Is it something physical, or is it something about the way you sound, or act? And why is it that some people have it, and others do not?

(I still remember the boredom with which I experienced the movie *The Crying Game*, since the heroine at the film's center was so obviously trans that I knew her identity within about ten seconds of seeing her on screen. And yet, cisgender moviegoers, including plenty of gay men and lesbians, were shocked, *shocked* at her unveiling. Even now I don't understand the incredible earthquakes people experienced when, say, Boy George or Liberace came out as gay. I remember hearing people saying things like, Wow, not Boy George! As for Liberace, isn't there a scene in one of the Austin Powers movies where our man, unfrozen after several decades, is catching up on recent history, and says, *Liberace, gay! Never saw that coming.*)

For transgender people the question of passing is directly connected to issues of privilege, which in turn are connected to issues of economics and race. If you struggle with what people mean by *intersectionality*, this is Exhibit A: the way in which transphobia is amplified by racism. If life for trans people can be easier the more they blend in with cisgender society, then who can afford the surgeries and therapies and countless other procedures that can ensure that passage? People of economic means, of course (since so much of this, even now, is not covered by insurance). Which sadly, still can mostly mean: white people.

Even among people of privilege, though, I know plenty of transgender women who will never pass, no matter how many surgeries they have. Unsurprisingly, these women's lives can be tremendously hard, their days filled with everything from getting called by the wrong pronouns to threats of actual violence.

Other trans women I know are drop-dead gorgeous: they're fashion models, movie stars. In the trans community, alas, there's a not particularly subtle tyranny of the pretty. Sometimes our movement seems to value trans women based on their beauty, on their ability to slay, on their ability, in short, to pass. I admit that this has given me plenty of occasion for melancholy, when I realize that despite anything I may have contributed to the advancement of my people, I will never be considered one of its most respected voices at least in part because I will never have a little button nose.

Back when I was going through transition, I deliberately decided I didn't want to have some of the surgeries on my face and on my hips to make me look more conventionally gorgeous. Because I thought: well, I'm not going on this long journey in order to be a fashion model; I'm in it to become myself. As a feminist, I bridled at the idea that in order to be a success I'd have to be cute. Fuck that, I thought. I'll amaze them all with my brilliant and clever prose.

Imagine my shock when I learned that prose has less value—at least in some circumstances—than a pair of gorgeous gams. Once I walked a red carpet at an awards show in Hollywood with a group of about a half dozen authors. Among us were two Pulitzer Prize winners and a recipient of the National Book Award. And also among us was John Leguizamo, a movie star whom I had met when our children had attended the same summer camp. As our crew moved before a group of photographers, the flashes popped—for a moment or two, anyway, before Johnny Legs was detected at the back of our cluster. And then, as one, all the lenses turned away from us, and toward him. There was a brief pause as we—the writers in our rented tuxes and overpriced updos—realized, *Right, they're done with us.* As successful authors we were celebrities, to be sure: but we were the very least interesting kind.

A new generation of trans activists has pushed back on all this by celebrating nonbinary identities, by courageously staking out ground that affirms with positivity the lives of people for whom passing is not the most important thing. That's not to say that nonbinary people are glam-free: in many cases, it's just the opposite. But rejecting the gender binary is something that they do every day, and in so doing, they've also helped redefine what it means to be glamorous—although to be fair, they haven't redefined it so much that a writer like me—who spends most of her life in flannel—is considered hot.

Still, it's an inspiration. My TA at the Bread Loaf Writers' Conference in 2019 was Alex Marzano-Lesnevich, an assistant professor at the University of British Columbia and author of the amazing *The Fact of a Body,* and Alex's sense of gender, so different from my own, was (and is) nevertheless a source of joy for me.

So is their writing.

The question remaining is not, *Can some trans people pass by changing some things about themselves?* It's a trick question anyway, because those kinds of transformations aren't an option for everyone, because of economics, because of privilege, because—sometimes—of the limitations of biology. But it can be done. Plenty of people have done it.

The question is, *Should we?*

I met with my voice therapist once a week for about a year in the early stages of transition. Emma Kovacs was the voice coach at Bates, a beloved figure on that campus and a much-revered one in the Maine transgender community as well for her work helping trans women find a natural way of speaking. It was Emma who pointed out to me the fact that should be obvious, that a female voice is not so much about an increase in pitch as it is about a change in resonance. She had me do relaxation exercises which helped me become more aware of the source of my breath—my diaphragm—and what I would need to do in order to feminize my voice.

The early days of my instruction were comical, I guess, although at the time they were one more thing that filled me with terror, one more thing at which I feared I would fail. When she asked me, for the first time, to speak with what I imagined my female voice might sound like, I did, I am afraid, chirp out some breathy high-pitched birdsong that was in its own way a mournful parody of Marilyn Monroe, or Jackie Kennedy, or some other exotic girly girl. *Happy birthday, Mr. President.*

Emma herself had grown up in Budapest and had a vigorous Hungarian accent, which made me think that, if I did succeed in taking her instruction to heart, I would end up speaking like Zsa Zsa Gabor. Not that that would have been all bad. *Ve are all femmeniks, dahlink.*

My voice was not exactly James Earl Jones's to begin with, so it didn't take too much time before I was able to adapt the way I sounded. Emma had me listen to recordings of women whose voices were no lower—in pitch—than my own, but whose voices were anything but masculine.

I remember Cher was one; Meryl Streep might have been another. In the car, I would turn on NPR and try to echo the words said by Nina Totenberg and Cokie Roberts and Susan Stamberg—none of them exactly Minnie Mouse, either. Sometimes I would play books on tape, read by women, and I would try, as best I could, to repeat what I heard. I spent the long drives down to Bates College talking out loud, trying to hear myself. I also had a tape recorder, in which I would rehearse my voice, and afterward I would play it back and think about it critically.

Maybe it seems crazy for a person to have to practice how to sound like themselves. After all—or so the anti-trans screwballs have it—if you really are a woman, and you've been a woman on the inside your entire life, then what is it you need to practice? Surely your true self is just waiting to be revealed, and once you take off your mask, there she will be, all ready to go?

To such snark I might reply, I am practicing how not to get beaten within an inch of my life, thanks for asking. And that a lifetime of wearing a mask does leave its mark.

You can get so used to hiding that the mask becomes your face.

One day, driving toward Emma's studio at Bates, I found myself speaking in a voice that took me by surprise: it felt natural, familiar, something I'd grown up with. It was a breathy voice, but it was also somewhat nasal, and it had about it the distinct aroma of girls' private schools in the Philadelphia suburbs. Think of Katharine Hepburn in *The Philadelphia Story*, maybe, or Claudette Colbert. It was, of course, the voice of all the girls I knew when I was growing up on the Main Line. This, I thought! This is what I sound like, in my truest of hearts!

I waltzed into Emma's chambers and began to speak: *EM-ma! The most MAH-vellous THING has HAHppened. A BREAKthrough, I tell you, a BREAKthrough. This VOICE, this MAH-vellous VOICE, WHY— (pause)—it has just COME to me, yes, it has COME. And it feels so NAH-trull, like I was BORN, yes, BORN to speak in JUST this—*

"Stop, stop, stop," said Emma, doing everything but clamping her hands down over her ears to block out the terrible noise. "What *is* this?"

*WHY it is the voice of the main LINE, Emma, the voice I grew UP with. It's di-VINE, is it not?*

"No! No! No!" said Emma, in agony. "This voice—*it is terrible!*"

I later learned this accent is also called the Mid-Atlantic voice, a voice that (with the exception of those suburbs) does not actually exist in nature. Hollywood largely invented it in the 1930s. It's the speaking voice of Margaret Dumont in all those Marx Brothers movies; Ingrid Bergman speaks in a variation of it, too, in *Casablanca*: *PLAY it, Reeck, PLAY—asss time goss BY.*

I am not even sure anyone speaks like this in Philadelphia anymore, outside of a few women in their sixties and seventies, happily thrice-divorced women who, even at their age, are called names like Muffy and Beezie and Tinkle. My people! Oh, if only things had been just slightly different, I could be collecting alimony from a hedge fund manager named Chad (Chad, who would have left me for his secretary), and I would now have summer homes in Bimini, Newport, and West Palm Beach. Oh well.

It was a close call. But I would not be speaking like Katharine Hepburn in the days that were to come.

Emma was not the only authority I turned to when I tried developing my female voice. Like a lot of trans women in those days I turned to someone named Melanie Anne Phillips, who had a series of online videos. She sold tapes, too, and her instructional video, "How to Develop a Female Voice," was kind of like *The Moosewood Cookbook* of late '90s trans women-to-be. Melanie deserves credit for shepherding so many of us along (her website, dating back to 1994, was one of the very first, if not *the* first, trans support site on the net), and I want to resist the temptation to talk trash about people who came before me—a temptation I indulged in my memoir, *She's Not There*, when I was all tut-tut-tut about trans legend Jan Morris, and to whom I never got to apologize before she passed in 2020. I guess it's human nature to try to establish yourself by tearing down the generation before you, but it's ungenerous, and facile. Having now been on the receiving end of that snark my own self I can only say: I understand how much it hurts. None of us were trained in this work. We have been fighting our way through the dark, and it was necessary, probably, for us to make so many mistakes in order to arrive at the place we are at now.

I never really got anywhere with Melanie's tape, which was not only about pitch and resonance but affect as well. She encouraged people bent on passing to imitate some of the worst clichés of femininity. Raise your voice at the end of a sentence, for instance, she suggested, so that everything sounds like a question. *Hello? I'm Jenny Boylan?*

More discouraging, from a feminist viewpoint, was the way she recommended using little-girl words when those of an adult would do just as well. Don't say, *I got a pain in mah gut.* Say: *I have an ouchy in my tummy?*

She also advised giving food orders as if asking for permission, rather than issuing commands. Don't drive up to the window at the fast-food joint and say, *Gimme a Fatburger!* Say: *Hi? Can I please have a veggie burger, please?*

Concerning the question of whether all of this talk-like-an-idiot dialogue was, perhaps, undignified or insulting, I can't remember the exact phrase Melanie used, but it was something like, *This isn't about criticizing the cliché; this is about embracing the cliché.*

But the question of voice is one which many women have to consider, whether they're trans or not. The terrible fact is that this little-girl mush talk actually can get you what you want, in some situations, with some people, usually men.

But I just couldn't bring it off. It was depressing to me to have traveled all this way, and to have put myself and the people I love at risk, only in order to arrive at womanhood in time to be fifteen years old. If you're going to go through such incredible trouble to become a woman (as I cruelly told Caitlyn Jenner in one of our televised encounters), in the name of god, don't be a stupid one.

I can tell you that, of all the trans women I know, the most predictable indicator of success post-transition is whether they were feminists *before*.

This shouldn't be a surprise. Anyone who expects life as a woman to be all about sparkles, hot rollers, and ice cream sandwiches should probably prepare for disappointment.

Although, to be fair, I know plenty of cisgender women whose lives appear to revolve around just those things, and most of them wind up as Instagram sensations with eight billion followers. So, again: maybe I'm the wrong guy to ask.

Or maybe we should just all agree that everyone gets to live their lives according to their own lights. I do know that, even though I would be at considerable less risk in the world if I talked in the fashion that Melanie (and Emma) tried to teach me, I would also be just a little bit less myself.

In the end, my voice morphed from the sounds I perfected with Emma and became something a little more androgynous, a little more—what is the word? Nonbinary. And that's fine with me. What I feared, early on, is that if I didn't fit in with everyone else, if I seemed like someone who was less than 100 percent feminine, that my womanhood could be taken from me—that it would, like the immunity necklace Jeff Probst is always describing on *Survivor*, be "up for grabs."

Now, after all this time, my womanhood cannot be stolen from me. My womanhood is not dependent upon the proper deportment at Fatburger, or anywhere else.

Except—now and then, at the end of a long day, when I'm collapsing in some hotel room in a strange city, and I pick up the phone to dial room service, and the person on the other end of the line says, *Yes, sir, what can I get you?* It's those moments when I hurt inside, and wish that what has come so naturally to so many other women had come to me as well. It's those moments when I wonder if I am as fierce as I think I am, and I wonder whether I really have the strength to keep swimming against the current of the culture forever. I slip into Jennifer voice and say, *I'm sorry? This is Mrs. Boylan?*

That uptalk in my voice was never so sad as when I was introducing myself. As if, after this long journey, my identity was still a question. As if, after all this, I still did not know who I was.

There are, of course, other solutions. Something called *Wendler glotto-plasty* is offered at a number of clinics that perform transgender surgery; it's usually done in combination with voice feminization therapy, and many medical centers—Mount Sinai, to name one—are careful to describe the Wendler glottoplasty as but a single part of a bigger picture. Many people who come to their clinic—says Mount Sinai's website—wind up not bothering with the Wendler.

If you do opt for it, you'll have your vocal cords shortened somewhat, increasing your pitch. (Although the Mount Sinai site is adamant in re-minding potential patients that pitch is really not the most important thing.) There's an eight- to ten-week recovery period, which is itself then followed up by therapy. For those willing to risk it, and willing to endure the recovery time, it's an option.

What I wonder is, if in the aftermath, you can say *Gimme a Fatburger*.

I know several transgender women who've opted for this—and other—vocal surgeries, and the results are mixed. I think the surgery has gotten much better in the last decade, but I knew at least one woman who wound up with not much more than a whisper.

I admit that it never occurred to me to have surgery on my voice. Perhaps I was just afraid of a bad result, or maybe it was just that my voice was already androgynous enough to get me through most situa-tions. But I also wondered, on some fundamental level, if I really began to sound different, would I still be myself? It was, perhaps, the same ques-tion that I had considered when I weighed whether or not to have facial feminization surgery. I had decided in the end not to change my face—which, sure, was feminine enough already—but also because I feared that if I really looked different, my wife would no longer love me. I know this seems insane, given the things that I *was* changing—but somehow I concluded that breasts and a clitoris weren't deal-breakers, identity-wise; a cuter nose, meanwhile, would be.

It is hard for me to recapture my logic now, so I'm sorry if this all seems to make as little sense to me at this hour as it probably does to you. I think that the process of growing older does demand that we constantly interrogate the mirror, though. What does it mean to look into the mirror at age sixty and wonder who it is looking back at you? In the end, the fact that I see a woman's reflection where I once saw a man's is probably less dramatic than the fact that I once saw a young person there, and now—well, now I see someone else.

And so. All in all, I feel happy with the way I sound. When I hear my voice on tape, I still hate it. But not because I do not sound like Marilyn Monroe. What hurts more now is just that I do not sound like me, only younger.

There is only one exception to this, and that is my singing voice.

I cannot say it is a particularly beautiful voice, although I do have my moments. Somebody told me once I have a lovely voice but a very limited range. Specifically, I think he was praising my D, maybe my D-sharp and, at times, even my E. Those three notes, I am like a regular Caruso.

Beyond that, though, not so much.

Still, I have always taken great joy in singing, from my coffeehouse days in college to jams at bars and parties here in central Maine. When I sang at Wesleyan, I accompanied myself on piano and on the Autoharp, which I played Appalachian-style, with the three finger picks. It is fair to say most Wesleyan students had never heard the instrument played unironically. On these occasions I lifted my voice in song. It was, to put it modestly, not a great voice. I wanted to sound like Bob Dylan. What I got was Bob Dole.

As years went on, I got to be a better singer, in the way most people get better at anything, that is, by practice. By the time I landed in my forties, there were times I was pretty good, especially at 1) traditional Irish ballads and 2) rock and roll.

At home, on the harp or the piano, I liked to sing "Bold Riley" and "The Wild Goose" and "Arthur McBride." I had a separate collection of songs to sing when I was drunk, too: "The Dog Crapped on the Whiskey" and "Fooba Wooba John" and "That's the Way You Spell Chicken." These were more performance pieces, sung out of obnoxiousness and joy, and I didn't suppose anyone would get all teary when I reached the conclusion of the "Whiskey" song, "But I can't forgive that fuckin' dog, nine miles from Gundagai!"

But I put my heart into "Bold Riley" and "The Wild Goose," and others: "Reynardine" and "P Stands for Paddy."

*Farewell my darling, farewell my dear-o*
*Bold Riley-o has gone away.*

As Jimmy Durante once noted about his own talents, "Sometimes I sing so pretty, I make myself cry."

When I played with bands, I was usually not the lead singer, in part because I had my hands full with the synthesizer and the Hammond emulator, and also because I was fortunate to play in bands that already had incredibly talented lead singers. To succeed, rock-and-roll bands really ought to operate under a one-diva policy, same as in English departments. And that diva was not me.

Still, there was often one moment each night when I got to sing a single tune, like I was the Ringo Starr of a central Maine dive bar. I liked to sing "Gimme Some Lovin'," a song that was not without its own classic organ part, or "Let It Rock," a Chuck Berry tune that was a fine vehicle for my left-hand boogie-woogie, or "Loose Lucy," a song by the always-respected Grateful Dead. Since I didn't have my own microphone, usually we had to twist someone else's mic so it could reach over the piano (everyone in the band had a mic but me), and in so doing it was traditional that there'd be a short burst of unbearable feedback. This made my singing sound sweet, in comparison. Anyway, people would clap politely, and then the mic would get twisted back around, and Shell (who enforced the one-diva policy) would say, "Jenny Boylan, ladies and gentlemen." And then she would belt out "Dr. Feelgood," or "R-E-S-P-E-C-T," or "Superstition" in a manner so impressive that it left no doubt as to why I only got to sing one song per night.

Still, I loved singing about as much as I loved anything.

There was one thing you could not say about my singing voice, though, and that was that it was a woman's voice.

My speaking voice was passable enough—except, as I keep pointing out, on the telephone. When I was in a tight corner I could always up-shift into Jennifer voice. But one thing I could not do with anything remotely resembling femininity was sing.

There are therapies that help trans women sing *en femme* as well. But I liked my singing voice, and I didn't want to change it.

All of which was fine if I was singing "El Paso" on the porch on my birthday with my friends, a group of local bluegrass musicians. But it was a different situation when the band was on stage entertaining millworkers in Livermore Falls, and it was well past midnight. Given the peculiarities of passing privilege, I was able to rock out in my tight top and my fish-nets at Ma Ducks' Tavern, and it never occurred to any of my drunken brethren and sistren that the keyboard player had a very interesting his-tory, genderwise.

But it all changed when I opened my mouth to sing. You could feel the atmosphere in the place grow tense, as my voice outed me, once and for all, to everyone within blasting distance of my amplifier. I never sang that much with Shell's band, but I was in at least one in the later days in which I was the only person who *could* sing, and this made our public ap-pearances complicated. (Plus, my voice is not really one you want to lis-ten to at great length, it being a blessing best enjoyed in carefully rationed intervals.) With that band—appropriately named The Stragglers—the drummer had taken me aside one night and said, "Listen, you gotta stop singing. You're going to get us all killed."

And so I stopped singing, and not just in public. At home, I put the Autoharp aside, and when I sat down at the piano, mostly I played instru-mentals.

I could apparently no longer sing without outing myself. Outing my-self to whom? Well, to others, but perhaps more grimly, to myself. I would hear my man voice crooning out "Norwegian Wood," and I would think, *If I sound like that, maybe I am not me after all.*

And so, I fell silent. I stopped singing, and I gave up a thing I really had loved.

L*emme outta here*, said the voice in the trunk. *You gotta help me.*

Dude, I thought. I know exactly how you feel.

"How do you do that?" I asked the ventriloquist. "Throw your voice?"

"It's not really throwing your voice," he replied. "That's not how it works."

"How does it work?"

He looked at me closely. Sometimes this kind of inspection made me uneasy. Was it possible, if he examined me closely enough, that he could figure out I was trans?

"You're not really—" he said, slowly, "a ventriloquist, are you?"

This wasn't the question I'd been expecting. "No," I said. "I'm—a writer."

"I knew it," he said. "You're working for Candice Bergen."

Candice Bergen, the actress, had been lurking all around the ventriloquist convention, interviewing people. Her father, of course, had been the famous ventriloquist Edgar Bergen. He'd left his dummy, Charlie McCarthy, $10,000 in his will; he'd left his daughter nothing. Likewise, the dummy had his own room in the Bergen house. The dummy's was bigger than hers.

Sometimes she sat on her father's knee. "A gentle squeeze on the back of my neck was my cue to open and shut my mouth so he could ventriloquize me," she wrote in her autobiography.

That's a heartbreaking scene—but it's as good a metaphor for the relationship between men and women as I can think of. For centuries, men have put their fingers on our necks so they can make us say the things they want us to say. So perfect is this process that women have long since learned how to ventriloquize ourselves—to make our voices sound uncertain so as not to offend them, to say *tummy* when we mean *stomach* because the only kind of power allotted us is the power that comes from being a little cupcake.

Earlier in the evening, before he'd outed me as a non-ventriloquist, my bar mate had asked me, *Where's your dummy?* I'd told him at the time that I didn't have one, but now it occurred to me that a more truthful answer might have been, *I am my own dummy.* After which, I might have added, *you bastard.*

"I'm not with her, Candice, I mean," I said. "I'm just here to do a story."

"Yeah, so what's the story?" he asked.

*Ask her if she wants to come back to your room,* said the voice in the trunk. *Ask her if she wants to fuck!*

"Hey, knock it off!" the ventriloquist shouted to the trunk on the floor. "Sorry," he said to me. "He gets like that when I don't let him out of the box for a few days."

Now it was my turn to look at him harder. "You," I said gently. "You don't really have a dummy, do you?"

"What are you talking about?" he said. "You can hear him yourself!"

*Hey, if you won't ask her, I will! What do you think, Lady? Let's ditch this loser!*

"You have a trunk," I said. "But there's no dummy in it."

He supped a little of his pint. "That," he said, "is a very interesting theory."

He gave me a look. "Tell you what. If there's a dummy in the case, you have to come back with me to my room. If there's not, you have to buy me a drink."

I thought this over. "You know I'm married," I said.

"So?" he said. "I'm married, too!"

He bent down and turned the trunk on its side. And there he was: a little dummy.

The ventriloquist lifted him up and put him on the seat next to mine. "I love you, Jen-nay," said the dummy, although his mouth did not move.

I looked at the dummy. I wanted to ask him whether he thought his owner would be able to see my history, if we proceeded with this escapade.

The surgery I'd had years before was highly successful, and it was more than likely that our man was not going to be able to tell the difference between my anatomy and that of his wife. Why yes, it is that good, thanks for asking.

But since I'd never had sex with a man before, what might tip him off was the fact that I wouldn't exactly know what I was doing. What might out me, more than anything else, was awkwardness—and, quite frankly, guilt, since it wasn't entirely clear that my wife would have approved of me fucking a ventriloquist. We'd talked about a lot of stuff before we got married, but not this.

I thought about Deedie, and my children. The dummy looked at me. I wanted to say to him, *Lemme outta here! You gotta help me!*

Later, in my hotel room, I'd looked in the mirror. "*Laady,*" I said.

A few years later, I was at an afternoon jam at a pub in Baltimore. It was a rangy group of people, some of whom I'd known for years and some of whom were complete strangers. There was Isabelle, who'd been a nanny to my children; and Chris, who was a friend of my friend Tim Kreider, the writer. There was their friend Dave, who was a communications architect at NASA; and another guy whose name I did not get but who appeared to be a chimney sweep. I was playing Autoharp unironically. Lots of beers were poured, and shots of single malt whiskey. We played "Rhinestone Cowboy," and "Miller's Cave," and "Midnight Train." Dave had a number of original songs, including the affecting "Another Day Older, Another Budweiser" as well as "A Pretty Lady and Sausage Gravy."

All in all, it was pretty great. There were pipes and fiddles and banjos. Isabelle played the snare drum. Now and again Dave picked up an old accordion and honked it.

Late in the afternoon, though, when the instruments were mostly leaning against the wall, and many of us were leaning upon our fists at a table, someone started singing a cappella. I forget what the tune was, but I remember staring down into my Guinness, thinking, I used to sing like that, too.

That's when Isabelle looked over at me and said, *Sing us one, Jenny.*

I hadn't sung much at all in three or four years, and I was afraid. Most of the people in the bar didn't know I was trans, and the ones who did had kept their mouths shut about it—or, more likely, they hadn't mentioned it because it didn't seem all that important.

It occurred to me that they were right. I asked myself, Is your plan really to go through the rest of your life without singing? You're going to deny yourself this thing you love because you're afraid that this vestigial link to the person you have been will somehow make you less the person you have become? It struck me that rather than this voice being a curse, perhaps it was a gift, a reminder that my life did not begin just this morning, and that I have a history. That history is full of sadness and suffering at times, but there's no small measure of joy and blessings in it, too—and who's to say, in the end, from which one of those experiences my singing voice is descended?

I put my pint down on the table. I stood up. I sang.

# HISTORY

We were standing in line at the Haunted Mansion in Disney World, the whole family, waiting to be admitted to the room in which the paintings suddenly grow long. *Your first challenge? Finding the way out! Ha ha ha ha ha!* Then the doors opened into the embarkation area, where Deedie and the boys and I were escorted into our own private hearse.

"Maddy?" said Zach, nervously. He was seven. "This is going to be *funny*, right? Not—scary?"

"Oh it's funny," I said. "Mostly."

My cell phone rang. "Ms. Boylan," said a voice. "My name is Becky. I'm a field producer for *The Oprah Winfrey Show*."

From the innards of the Haunted Mansion came the endlessly unspooling song: *When you hear the knell of a requiem bell. Weird glows gleam where spirits dwell.*

Zach covered his face with his hands. "Maddy!" he screamed. "You *promised* it was going to be *funny*!"

A couple of weeks later I was on a plane to Chicago. I looked out the window. There below me were the green cornfields of Indiana. I felt my heart pounding in my breast. I was on my way to Oprah, to talk about my gender change on national television. I was so hopeful that the words that I had written would open people's hearts, at least a little.

But did the Oprah people really want me for my words? Was that what this was about? Or would it devolve into the kind of spectacle I'd seen again and again, growing up, some terrified trans woman sitting as if on trial, as Jerry Springer or Morton Downey, Jr. or Sally Jessy Raphael grilled them. "What would you say to someone who says, 'God doesn't make mistakes'? Well?"

What I would say is that the people insisting that god doesn't make mistakes more often than not are wearing glasses, or hearing aids, or pacemakers.

Somewhere over Bloomington my fear ascended into a full-blown panic attack. I'm not going to make it, I thought. When we land I have to tell the publicist at Random House, I'm sorry. I just want to go home.

My pounding heart made my blouse quiver with each pulse. Sweat began to trickle down my temples and onto my cheeks.

What could I do? I thought I might distract myself by reading, but the only thing I had to read was *She's Not There*, the very book that had gotten me into this terrible situation in the first place.

But what the hell, I thought. I might as well reacquaint myself with the particulars.

*There they were*—one chapter began—*two young women standing by the side of the road with their thumbs out. They weren't warmly dressed, considering that it was December, in Maine. One of them had green hair. They looked to me as if they were in trouble, or about to be. I pulled over, thinking, better me than someone else. The world was full of characters.*

Hey, I thought. This is good.

The pilot announced that we would be landing in Chicago in twenty minutes. I thought, All right, fine.

What could I do in the end except trust my words and the story that I had told? I was overflowing with doubts, from what I believed to be my ridiculous appearance to the damage I'd caused my family by exposing us all.

But I trusted my story.

It put my heart at ease, a little, to know that I had done the best job with it that I could. I looked at the epigraph to the book, which was from *Huck Finn. Providence always did put the right words in my mouth,* it read, *if I would only leave it alone.*

I n *She's Not There* I had mentioned, at one point, that whatever being trans is, one thing it surely is not is a "lifestyle." *When I imagine a person with a lifestyle,* I wrote, *I see a millionaire playboy named Chip who likes to race yachts to Bimini, or an accountant, perhaps, who dresses up in a suit of armor on the weekends.*

*Being transgender isn't like that. Gender is many things, but one thing it is surely not is a hobby. Being female is not something you do because it's clever, or postmodern, or because you're a deluded, deranged narcissist.*

*In the end, what it is, more than anything else, is a fact. It is the dilemma of the transsexual, though, that it is a fact that cannot possibly be understood without imagination.*

It is fair to say that the discourse around trans bodies now, almost twenty-five years later, isn't anything like that. The medical model for talking about trans lives sounds dated, and quite frankly, more than a little weird. And I have met many people since then for whom gender really *is* a hobby, although the word *hobby* feels dismissive. But here in the twenty-first century, messing with gender brings plenty of people a kind of disruptive, subversive joy. There is surely an oppressiveness to the "gender binary," by which I mean the rigid restraints of masculinity and femininity that chain all the boys to one side of the room eating raw steak and all the women to the other side eating little salads. The thing that is most striking to me now is how many trans and nonbinary people love to occupy that middle zone, to embrace androgyny and gender fluidity, not because they're "hardwired" that way, or because their neurology demands it, but because doing this brings them a sense of elation and fun.

As I look back on *She's Not There* now, it is impossible for me not to notice what feels like an air of apology to the whole thing. In so many ways, the author of that book is begging the reader—*Please, don't hate me. I'm so sorry.* The book sets out to justify what I then presumed was a situation the average reader would struggle to comprehend.

And this is, perhaps, the biggest change from 1998, when I first began to come out, to the present. People coming out as trans now aren't apologizing for who they are. They aren't begging for forgiveness or understanding. They don't feel any particular need to explain. If straight or cis people are uncomfortable with who they are, their sense is, Good. You *should* be uncomfortable. Maybe that sense of discomfort is something you might think about, and learn from.

There's a Bob Dylan song: *I cried for you. Now it's your turn, you can cry awhile.*

One of the struggles people have with the advent of trans visibility is that it seems like a new thing. "I talk about transgender, everyone goes crazy," noted Donald Trump in 2023. "Who would have thought? Five years ago, you didn't know what the hell it was."

I don't know, Donald. Five years ago I was pretty sure I knew a lot about it.

When I hear alarms about gender transgression being some sort of newfangled social contagion, it is impossible for me not to think of the movie *Harvey*, in which Jimmy Stewart has a friend who is a giant invisible rabbit, a "pooka," in fact—a Celtic word for a mischievous animal spirit. "Pooka?" a woman asks Jimmy Stewart. "Is that something new?"

"No," says Jimmy, aka Elwood P. Dowd. "That's something very old."

Humans have been messing with gender since, well, since there have been humans, in fact, and anyone who thinks that transness is something new has simply not been paying attention. Roman emperor Marcus Aurelius Antoninus, known as Elagabalus, preferred to be known by female names and pronouns, wore wigs and makeup, and tried to find surgeons who would transform his nether bits into a working clitoris and vagina. In the Middle Ages, Jewish philosopher Kalonymus ben Kalonymus wrote a poem lamenting that he had been born a boy, and referred to his male unit as a "defect." In colonial America, Jemima Wilkinson renamed themselves the "Public Universal Friend," and shunned their birth name and female pronouns.

The Friend preached throughout New England, opposing slavery and advocating free will.

Jesus, in fact, provides some counsel on the proper response to transgender people: "For there are eunuchs who were born thus from their mother's womb, and there are eunuchs who were made eunuchs by men, and there are eunuchs who have made themselves eunuchs for the kingdom of heaven's sakes." He concludes, "Let anyone accept this who can."

It is clear enough that transness is not something new. It is, like the pooka, something very old indeed.

What is new is calling people "transgender."

This is perhaps a good moment to point out that *transgender*, or *trans* for short, is best used as an adjective, as in *transgender man* or *woman*, or *trans person*. It's not a noun—so don't be saying things like, *Look at all those transgenders over there.* Sometimes, I even see *transgenderize*, or *transgendering*; I don't know what those are, and I'd counsel against them. *Transgenderize*, to me, sounds like something you'd do to a steak, to make it more tender. Or less.

Yes, the language has changed swiftly, and it can be hard to keep up. How fast does it change? In 2003, when *She's Not There* was first published, the most common term was *transgendered*, and that's the word I used to describe myself then. But just as a person can't be *gayed* or *lesbianed* (as if this was something that was *done* to you), a person can't be *transgendered*. I changed that word in the tenth anniversary edition of *She's Not There* (itself now published over a dozen years ago), and who knows? If *Cleavage* is still around in ten years, maybe there will be different language *then*, reflecting what I hope will be an even newer understanding of what makes us all tick.

*Trans*, or *transgender,* is an umbrella term, including a wide range of gender-variant people. The word itself is relatively new, having been (allegedly) coined by activist Virginia Prince in 1969. It is easy enough for us to look back across history now and to use the term to describe Joan of Arc, or author Radclyffe Hall, or for that matter, Marcus Aurelius Antoninus, aka Elagabalus.

But we use contemporary terms to understand historical figures at our own peril; it seems more honest, and more fair, to understand them first and foremost for who they were in their own time.

Trans history also depends on who is telling it. The first trans person I remember being aware of was Jan Morris, the glorious travel writer whose

1974 memoir, *Conundrum*, blew my world wide open. I remember coming downstairs on a Sunday morning, age fifteen, and seeing her photo on the cover of the *New York Times Book Review*; I felt the floor disappear beneath me. It was a preview of the feeling I'd have two years later when Mickey drove the Volkswagen off a cliff, and I stared up into a blue sky as a voice called out to me, *Son? Son?*

I had seen female impersonators (as they were then called) on the *Mike Douglas Show*, but even then I sensed that people like Jim Bailey (a celebrated female impersonator of the time) didn't seem to be searching for the thing that Jan Morris—and I—were searching for. Bailey's femininity was about performance, about being an amazing Judy Garland, or Liza Minelli, or Carol Channing. But what I wanted was to be *myself*.

Two of the most important figures in the modern trans movement are Marsha P. Johnson and Sylvia Rivera. Johnson—she said the *P* stood for "Pay it no mind"—was associated with the Stonewall Riots of 1969, although she later made it clear she was not present when the riots began. But on a subsequent night she threw a shot glass at a mirror in the bar, shouting, "I got my civil rights." Later she called it "the shot glass heard round the world."

Marsha P. Johnson actually told more than one version of that story, and it's hard now to know the exact truth at this hour. What we do know is that she spent a lot of her life as a street queen. She liked to wear flowers in her hair. Edmund White later wrote that she lived in "the interstice between masculine and feminine."

In 1992, she was found dead in the Hudson River. Police said it was suicide. Her friends said it was murder.

Marsha P. Johnson met Sylvia Rivera in 1963. "She was like a mother to me," Rivera said later. The two of them started the Street Transvestite Action Revolutionaries (STAR) in 1971, a group dedicated to support the trans community in New York. It's another measure of how fast the language around gender issues has changed that now, just a little over fifty years later, the word "transvestite" is considered a slur. As is the even more gruesome "tranny."

The language matters. But what might matter more is the thing in the hearts of the people being described. As I said, none of this is new.

What *is* new is that now, as a result of the work of people like Sylvia Rivera and Marsha P. Johnson, people like us refuse to be erased.

What's new is that our desire—indeed, our right—to live our lives by the light of our own stars can no longer be denied.

What's new is that trans people—by whatever name—are determined to live with dignity and with grace.

Our lives are not a thing to be ashamed of, or apologized for, or explained. Our lives are a thing of wildness, and tenderness, and joy.

In the years since transition I have sometimes wondered whether it is my sense of history itself that has been most affected by my change of gender. How often I have turned to Zero, or to Link, and reminded them of a poignant moment that we shared, and survived, only to have them look at me and say, I don't know what you're talking about. Remember that time I hitchhiked to your house—I'll ask Zero—and we planted sunflowers in your garden? And you had the tune "Salt Peanuts" by Stan Getz playing on the stereo? You had the speakers pointed out the window as we dug the earth with beat-up trowels and hand rakes. A crow landed on the arm of the scarecrow. That scarecrow was wearing one of the shirts you'd worn at Haverford.

Zero just gives me a curious look. If you say that happened, I believe you, he says. But I don't remember that at all. You're saying you came to Syracuse? While we were planting the garden?

Yes. I hitchhiked from New York. One of the drivers who picked me up played John Valby on the stereo. You know, the pornographic piano player? He played the "William Tell Overture." And then he sang, "Waltz Me Around by My Willy."

Zero just shakes his head. How is there room in your head for all this stuff? he asks me. What I do not say, but which I sometimes feel, is, How can there *not* be room in yours?

It is entirely possible that I have a uniquely weird memory—after all,

I can recite the names of all the American presidents, in reverse order (the tricky part is the Buchanan-Pierce-Fillmore-Taylor-Polk chain, although my sense is that you really can recite those five in any order you like). But the things that I remember are not merely the stuff of barroom trivia contests; what really makes me remember are the emotions around them. And so *of course* I remember hitchhiking up to Zero's house in Syracuse that spring; I was so lost, so unhappy. I was searching for an emotional recharge, the sentimental equivalent of Captain Scott, lost in Antarctica, desperately trying to get his dogs and his men to the next supply depot before they froze to death.

There was a copy of the *Village Voice* lying in his living room by the wood stove that same trip, an issue that had a long essay about Candy Darling, the trans woman who'd been part of Andy Warhol's Factory. There was a haunting photograph of her on her death bed. She lay on her side, her hands tangled up in her hair. There was a rose upon the sheets.

What I wonder is whether men and women experience memory in different ways. The boys I know seem to live in the present, striving and smelting their experience in order to bring about some new creation. The women, though, seem to be weaving the present moment into what has come before.

Does estrogen affect the way you experience time? I don't know. Maybe it's just me.

But whenever I'm with my male friends, they're always telling me, *I can't believe you remember that.* To which I can only reply: *I can't believe you forgot it.*

In the wake of *She's Not There,* and Oprah, I became the media's go-to person on trans issues for a decade or more. In addition to appearing on the *Oprah Winfrey Show* five times, and on *Larry King* twice, I was on the *Barbara Walters Special.* I was the subject of documentaries on the History Channel, and on CBS's *48 Hours,* and *Rock Center with Brian Williams.* I served as a consultant on the series *Transparent.* I was even a cast member on Caitlyn Jenner's docudrama series. In each case, I did my best to tell stories of trans experience with dignity, although there were times—like when we all went disco roller-skating on the Jenner program—I wondered whether I was just fooling myself. I had hoped to have a good influence on Caitlyn when she came out; it was my sense that a little loving care might help to open her heart to the experience of trans people other than those who live on a mountaintop fortress in Malibu. I know that Caitlyn initially meant well, and I was grateful for the friendship that we had, during those days. But in the end I fear I did not make much difference. She has gone her own way since then, and I have gone mine.

And then there was the night I was watching *Saturday Night Live*, when the cast did a sketch about me appearing on *Larry King Live*. Cast member Will Forte appeared as me, wearing a blond wig. My agent later told me, "He even did that thing you do with your lip." I said, *What thing do I do with my lip?*

Among my friends there were two very different reactions to the *SNL* skit. West Coast pals were all like, *You're famous!* Those on the East Coast, though, wondered whether my feelings were hurt, being portrayed by a man.

*That's okay,* I told them. *A man played me for years.*

I was surely not the first transgender person to appear on a talk show—I remembered catching glimpses of people like me in the media over the decades before. One time, on a Sally Jessy Raphael show, I saw a mother who was told, right then and there as the cameras rolled, that her son was becoming a woman; the mom had no idea. And then they brought the son (sic) out on stage wearing a dress with sequins while the house band played music that sounded sort of like "Who Let the Dogs Out." What, Sally Jessy asked, did Mom have to say about that? Mom, understandably enough, broke down and wept.

That's what it was like, back in the day. Everything was played for maximum shock value, maximum horror at the whole idea of difference. In college, my friend Thad had shown me a *Newsweek* story on transsexuals, and he said, *Don't you think these people are really fucked up?* And what could I do, except say, *Yeah, I guess*, which is what I supposed someone who was not one of them would say. That was the kind of person I was trying to imitate, anyhow.

Later, Thad became a plastic surgeon, specializing in what he called "breast work."

The Oprah show that I was on, when *She's Not There* was published, was different from what had come before, in part because I was able to be fast on my feet, and to speak about what was in my heart with what I hoped was grace. And yet, when I was asked about my sex life, or what was in my underpants, and so on, I still politely answered Oprah's questions. It never occurred to me to tell her that these things were, in fact, none of her business. I'm ashamed, now, that I was so eager to participate in the sensationalizing of my own story. At the time I felt like, *Well, it's her show.*

My feeling was that I had to be the Jackie Robinson of trans people; I had to keep my head held high, to answer every insulting question with grace and humor, to never let anyone see me sweat, or flinch, or cry. There are no dumb questions! I'd say, in hopes that being excessively forthcoming might do the necessary work of educating people.

But just because a question is not dumb doesn't mean that you have to answer it, every time.

This is how trans people were portrayed in the media up until about 2014. And by trans people, I really mean trans women, for at that moment in history, trans men were pretty much off the radar. (In 1994, author Amy Bloom published a piece in the *New Yorker,* "The Body Lies," in which she basically explored, all wonder-struck, that there actually *are* trans men in the first place! Who knew?!) This changed in January of 2014, when Carmen Carrera and Laverne Cox did an interview with Katie Couric. Katie interviewed Carmen first, and right on cue, started asking about "all the surgery you had to go through." Carmen demurred and focused on the fact that "after transition, there's still life to live." Later, Laverne came on. They talked a little bit about *Orange Is the New Black*, but then it was back to the surgery question, and what was in Laverne's underthings. She replied that the preoccupation that cis people have with our bodies objectifies trans women and intrudes on our privacy. "By focusing on bodies," she said, "we don't focus on the lived realities of that oppression and that discrimination."

It was May of that year that *Time* magazine put Laverne Cox on their cover with the headline, "The Transgender Tipping Point." It's easy enough to think that this was about the way Laverne brought a sympathetic and complex portrayal to the character of Sophia Burset on *Orange Is the New Black*. But the tipping point was not then; it was that moment with Katie Couric, when Laverne and Carmen had said, with poise and grace, *We're not talking about that anymore. There is a difference between what is secret and what is private.*

I remember watching that moment on television. From now on, I thought, a little wistfully, things are going to be different.

I only wished that I had had the courage to behave with the fierceness and valor that Laverne and Carmen had shown.

Later, I sent an email to Laverne, whom I knew through my work at GLAAD, as well as one to author Janet Mock, who, like Laverne, represented a new generation of trans spokespeople. I told them how grateful I was for their work, and that I wished I had been able to be a little more like them. Unsurprisingly, they both responded with kindness and love. But I was left with something not unlike the melancholy of late-stage Frodo Baggins: *We set out to save the Shire, and the Shire has been saved. But not for me.*

There's something called an Amazon ranking. On Amazon, every single book is ranked, from number one to number five million, based on how many copies it has sold that day. On the morning of the day of the *Oprah* show, *She's Not There* was number 200,000 or so. By the evening, it was number eleven. All of that happened in a single day.

I was grateful to Oprah Winfrey for featuring my book on her show, and for giving me the chance to talk about it. It was Oprah, more than any other single person, who gave me a career.

But there was something unsettling and sad about the whole experience.

I had wanted to be the transgender Toni Morrison. Instead, I was Moms Mabley.

On the plane, on the way back to Maine, and my family, I looked out the window at the clouds. I had seen them from both sides now. I thought, in wonder, about what had just happened to me. I had been struggling as a writer for decades. Now, after all these years, I was, at last, the author of a bestselling book.

I looked at the clouds, and cried.

# LOVERS

My cousin Colleen and I were in a little boat. This was in something called the Ghost Ship, in an amusement park called Playland in Ocean City, Maryland, summer of '69. There was a monorail and an Alpine Sky Ride and a roller coaster called the Monster Mouse. Colleen and I entered a long tunnel. There were black lights that made the faces of the skeletons and pirates glow all green. The smell of that place! Sweet like a graveyard after rain.

Her white shirt glowed in the black light. Then we banged through a set of swinging doors and everything was dark. Colleen leaned her head against mine. For a few seconds we lay like that, our heads together. We could not see ourselves.

My father and Colleen's father had been best friends in high school. So my Uncle Jack wasn't really my uncle, and Colleen wasn't really my cousin. They had a house in Rehoboth Beach. Every summer we'd spend a week there. There was a room with bunk beds for the boys, and another one for the girls.

Uncle Jack woke us up each day at dawn, and we rode bikes in the early-morning light—me, Colleen, my sister Cyndy, cousin Donna, cousin Edward, cousin Binny. We rode our bikes along the boardwalk, wind blowing in from the sea. There was a store with a salt water taffy machine, churning that goo around even at sunrise. The air smelled like beach tar, hot peanuts, yellow mustard.

After we got home, we all changed into our suits. The ocean would raise you up, the ocean would put you down. Sometimes there were terrible, terrible jellyfish. When there were jellyfish, you just had to lie there in the sand. If my ear was against the sand, I could hear the sound of footsteps, approaching and receding. There was a sharp *whack* as people played with Kadima paddles. Or you could look up into the puffy clouds. One time I had a box kite.

If I was lying face down, sometimes the unit would get hard and then you had the dilemma. There was no hiding a thing like that if you rolled back over. You had to wait for it to go away. Or else you had to wrap your towel around yourself and run toward the ocean and dive right in. The cold water, and the horror of the terrible jellyfish, would shrink things back down.

Then you were okay for a while. But not forever.

They had an outdoor shower at the house, and when you got back from the beach the boys all crowded into it to wash off the sand. Then the girls would do the same. It was a tight space—me, Uncle Jack, my father, cousin Edward, cousin Binny. I don't know how we all fit. It was the first time I remember seeing so many units. The adults' all hairy and tired looking, like elephants' trunks; the boys' tiny and pink, like newborn hamsters. The water rushed down our bodies. Sand trickled in little rivulets down the drain.

There was a hammock near the outdoor shower. After I dried off and changed, sometimes I lay in that hammock, swinging back and forth, reading.

When I got sunburned my mother rubbed Noxzema cream onto my shoulders and my back. It smelled like coconuts and cold alcohol. Sometimes the sunburn hurt so much it made me sob out loud.

One time, back at the beach house, I found Colleen's bikini hanging in the bathroom. She didn't have any more breasts than I did. Why would she? We were just kids. I slipped into her swimsuit, looked at myself in the mirror. It was damp, the suit. What I saw in the mirror was an idiot. I took off the suit and said, *What did you do that for, never do that again.*

At night, as I lay in my bunk bed, I could still feel the waves lifting me up. Then they laid me back down.

Can I describe the things I felt, when I was a child, as things that boys might feel? Or were the things I felt the things a girl would feel, if she'd been forced to wear a disguise?

It is hard for me to say, this is what boys felt, this is what women feel. Because, well, you see. When I was a boy, there was a woman inside me. And as a woman, even here late in life, the boy that I once was has never entirely vanished.

But back then I was aware that my peers and I seemed to want different things. At the end of eleventh grade, Dylan Edwards and I were smoking reefer down by the pond one day. He looked at me with satisfaction and said, *Now that we're seniors, one thing's for sure. We're going to get* all *the pussy!*

I could not even imagine what it was he was talking about. *Getting pussy* was pretty far down on my list. I mean, getting *a* pussy, that was way up top, although not really. Because how could you get such a thing? How could you go through such a transformation and survive? Who would I even be, if I got the impossible chance to be myself? The whole idea was impossible. The thing I wanted was not pussy. And I didn't especially want any balls or dicks around the place, either. Asses male or female were neither here nor there to me. What I wanted, Reader, was to be in love.

That meant making out, to be sure—huggin' and a-kissin', slippin' and a-slidin'.

You know. *A wop bop a loo bop, a lop bam boom.*

But all of that was part of being loved—being safe, protected, desired.

The algebra of it worked like this: I knew I was a girl and had known this from childhood. I also knew that this was an insane desire, and if I didn't stop being haunted by it, I knew my life would be a ruin. And so: How could this desire be suspended? By getting outside of myself, by having my own love for someone else outweigh the desire my own heart had for transforming itself.

In some way, maybe, I had looked upon the example of my father, who had put his own dream (of studying medieval history) aside in order to care for others—my sister and my mother and me. There was true peace to be found by devoting one's life to others, by devoting yourself to making someone else happy instead of endlessly feeding the insatiable monster inside you. Because in the end, clearly, we are not here for ourselves. In the end, we are here for others.

Is that what I thought being in love would be like? A chance to have my own desires eclipsed by the kindnesses I could bring to someone else?

I don't know.

But I was never half as interested in fucking as I was in being in love. To tell you the truth, that's still true. Which is not to say a word against fucking. Fucking, when it finally came around for me, turned out to be a ton of fun. Oh, how I *loved* the fucking. It turned me inside out.

But fucking was the icing on the cake. I never wanted the fucking for the sake of the fucking, any more than I'd want to eat a big bowl of chocolate frosting all by itself. The fucking was the way I could show the thing I felt. How much do I adore you? *This much*. I have this very precious, rare thing, that I only share with people who have touched the most vulnerable part of me. Here: I give it to you.

You can say that this is a very feminine way of approaching this topic, and I guess you wouldn't be wrong. But I know *tons* of women who love the fucking just for the fucking. I remember, as a young man, getting all sweet on someone the morning after we'd rolled off each other, and telling her how much I loved her! And she kind of rolled her eyes and said, *Whatever*, as she put back on the clothes she'd worn to my apartment the night before. I'll call ya, she said, as she stepped out into the daylight, still dressed for cocktails at eight in the morning. Did she call me? No, she did not.

Why didn't she call me? What aspect of me might have raised the wee red flags? How could it not have been the hunger so self-evident in my eyes? *Please fall in love with me,* I said, without words, to every girl I fucked. *If you do, I'll stop wanting to be like you, and I'll be able to stay like me.*

Maybe you can see how this would get complicated real fast.

I don't blame those women for rolling their eyes at me. It wasn't too hard for them to see that when I reached out for them the thing I was reaching out for was not their own good selves but some kind of cosmic life preserver.

Let's fall in love, I might have suggested. That way I won't have to kill myself.

The sad thing was that I *did* fall in love, lots of times. Sometimes we'd fuck, and sometimes not. But in every instance, the certainty that I was female remained constant. The only time it ever disappeared was in my late twenties, when I fell in love with Deirdre Finney, the girl I married. With Deedie, for a long, long time, I had no desire to be anyone with her except James Boylan. At long last, the thing I had always prayed for had come true. My heart had finally been transformed, and had come, at long last, to rest.

For a little while, anyhow.

In high school, my sister tried to set me up with a friend of hers, the captain of the field hockey team. She arranged for me to meet this girl, Maryelise, after school. Maryelise was beautiful but tough—a real jock. She looked me up and down and then quickly turned away, just like Fermina Daza erasing poor Florentino Ariza in *Love in the Time of Cholera*.

*"No, please," she said to him. "Forget it."*

At the time I was doing all I could to make sure that no one knew what was in my heart. But it all leaked out anyway. Some girls thought that my gamine appearance was intriguing. I looked like a little aspen sapling. Others, like (apparently) Maryelise, looked at me and thought, *Poofta*. It was the kind of thing that could wear you down.

Would it have been easier if I'd been attracted to boys? There was no shortage of gay men at Haverford, either in the student body or on the faculty. I was constantly being courted by men, young and old, who thought that I was like them. But incredibly, I was just oblivious to them. All I wanted was to be a lesbian.

I met Katie Strawbridge under a weeping willow. Its trailing limbs and leaves created a green curtain. I was coming home from ceramics class on a hot summer day, that summer between tenth and eleventh grade.

I got off the bus in Villanova and walked up to that big tree and then parted its thick green scrim. It was like a whole other world in there—dim sunlight filtering down through the leaves. Katie was waiting for me. She leaned against the trunk.

I showed her some of the things I'd made in ceramics class. A coffee mug. An ashtray. A bowl for rosebuds. I kissed her and she kissed me. I don't know how long we were in there. The whole world had disappeared! What would we know about the passage of time?

She put one hand on my cheek and whispered to me, *James Boylan, I love you. I've never met a boy like you before. You're so different.*

But by fall I had ditched her. Maybe I was bored. But how could I have been bored with someone who parted the green curtain of that willow? Was it really that she'd just gotten too close, and sooner or later I'd have to tell her the truth? Which, please: I was not going to do. Would you?

I remember one night the two of us lay on the bed in my room listening to Bob Dylan sing, "Tomorrow Is a Long Time." As I lay there, I felt the thing that Bob was describing. I felt her heart a-softly poundin'. Katie had told me before that she didn't like Dylan. But *now*, she said. She sure liked him now!

I kept getting crushes on people, going out with them a little, then ditching them. Years later, when I saw the movie *Aladdin* with my children, I remembered the boy I had once been as our hero sings about having to constantly elude his pursuers. *One jump ahead of the slowpokes, one skip ahead of my doom.*

I had wanted love to save me, to enable me to get outside myself forever. But it was impossible to forget myself. In the most electric throes of passion there was always a ghost with one hand on my shoulder, pulling me back. That ghost's identity wasn't hard to figure. She was the person I was commanded to become—but whom I knew I could never be.

Some years later, a writer named Phraze pulled back from an embrace and looked me in the eyes. *Who are you?* Phraze asked. *Who's in there?*

What do you mean? I said. It's me?

I'd spent six months in London during college, fell in love with a girl from Plymouth, Mass., the night before she had to get the flight back home. We wrote letters to each other after that. They were pretty hot, those letters.

There was a street market in Chinatown, near the West End. I walked through there one day and saw a blue silk robe with a dragon on the back. It was a thing of such beauty. I decided I'd buy it for my girlfriend, but not right away. Because I was set to travel around Europe with Link and Zero after the term ended, and I didn't want to haul that robe all the way to Scotland and Ireland and France. I had to reserve space in my pack for stuff like canteens and gorp.

She wrote me letters. Julie was an illustrator, going to RISD, and the letters she sent me were full of her wild drawings. One night I sat by a campfire on the bonny bonny banks of Loch Lomond with the boys. We were so far north that the skies were lit up, even at midnight. I let Link read the letter. He just shook his head. *She's a live wire, isn't she,* said Link.

We threw a few more logs on the fire. It was dark for a little bit, then it was light again.

I took leave of my friends somewhere in Ireland, about a month later. I put my thumb out and got a ride to Dún Laoghaire. I got on board the Sealink, got as far as Holyhead, and took an overnight train to London, where I arrived just after dawn. I took the Tube to Leicester Square and walked over to the site of the street market, in hopes of buying Julie one of those dragon robes.

But, of course, at that hour the market was closed. The place where the vendors had been was now just a vacant lot, lined by barbed wire. A lot of old trash was blowing around the lot. An old poster advertising the *Daily Mail* blew against me, and I untangled it from my shins. On the poster were two words: "Bhutto Hanged." He had been the prime minister of Pakistan. Not anymore, though.

I thought of the end of James Joyce's story "Araby." *Gazing up into the darkness I saw myself as a creature driven and derided by vanity, and my eyes burned with anguish and anger.*

We were watching a play about infidelity, Rachel and me. By my midtwenties we'd been living together for a couple of years, in an apartment one floor above an S&M dungeon. We had descended the sixty-odd blocks to see Tom Stoppard's *The Real Thing*, at the Plymouth Theatre. "He loves me," Glenn Close said. "He wants to punish me with his pain, but I can't come up with the proper guilt. It's so tiring and uninteresting. You never write about that, you lot."

"What?" Jeremy Irons said.

"Gallons of ink and miles of typewriter ribbon expended on the misery of the unrequited lover!" Close replied. "Not a word about the tedium of the unrequiting."

Rachel was the one who waited me out, as I learned all the things that most other men had learned a decade earlier. It wasn't a good relationship; I was most definitely under her thumb. I guess the easiest way of understanding it is to know that I was a writer, and she was an editor. In that kind of situation, it's hard for the writer not to wind up with a lot of important things getting crossed out in red pen. Every now and then, I'd say the equivalent of *stet!* That's when we'd have a fight.

I'd never had fights with anyone I loved before. My parents had yelled at my sister sometimes, and every once in a while, at me, but never at each other. Rachel's family, on the other hand, was just everyone yelling at one another all the time, people storming out of the room, leaving their dinners uneaten on their plates, doors slamming, people weeping. And then, a little later, everyone came out and everything was back to normal.

I don't know what's stranger—that kind of family, or my own. In any case, Rachel and I fought a lot. Usually, in the end, I'd just let her have her way, in the interests of peace. Rachel thought this was a little strange. It put me in mind of Harry the Haggler, in *Life of Brian,* who refuses to simply let Graham Chapman purchase a gourd. *Come on. Do it properly. Haggle!*

The sex was good, plentiful, joyful. Sometimes we'd have a big fight, and afterward there was make-up sex. I began to suspect that sometimes Rachel would pick a fight simply so we could have make-up sex later. I still don't know what she saw in me, but Rachel really loved me. She was a sweet, smart, kindhearted woman, opaque. Surely, she deserved someone less translucent than me.

In time we left the apartment above the S&M dungeon and moved over to the East Side. There was a Mexican restaurant in Yorkville, not far from our flat, with the inevitable name of Margaritas, where Rachel and I would go after sex and drink frozen tequila drinks and eat enchiladas. I'd get so drunk on margaritas that sometimes Rachel would have to carry me back to the apartment in her arms. There were times I'd jump into her arms even when I wasn't too drunk to walk, just so she could carry me. I guess this was my equivalent of provoking a fight just to have the make-up sex afterward.

People are funny, is my conclusion.

I don't know how she managed to carry me in her arms for two or three blocks, but she did. Rachel said I didn't weigh anything at all.

I went to a party in an artist's loft in SoHo, back when that was a thing. Rachel wasn't there. There were a hundred shady characters all packed into the space. It was filled with sculptures of things that looked like tree trunks but which had human arms, raised up to heaven. There was a mirror on a spool table with a dozen lines of coke on it. In the kitchen was a big pot of mac and cheese. Someone had made spanakopita.

All the phyllo dough had been shattered by the rough handling from oversize spatulas. From the stereo came the sounds of the Clash, the Talking Heads, the Ramones, even the Shaggs. *Who are parents?* Everybody was high, everybody was dancing. We were all immortal.

A woman wearing mirror shades slipped a photocopied piece of paper into my pocket. I looked at it later, as I rode the number 6 train uptown.

*You are an amazing looking man,* it read. *We want to take your picture for our new book.* It had a title like, *Sex Gods of the New Generation.* I just looked at this and laughed and laughed.

I crawled into bed next to Rachel, who was awake, waiting for me. I told her about the flyer the mirror girl had given me. She didn't say anything.

In the morning I looked for it, but it was gone. I thought it'd be cool, to be a sex god of the new generation.

I asked Rachel about the flyer. She told me she'd thrown it away.

One night we had a fierce argument about Diana Ross. I said I thought she was beautiful. Rachel was furious. How can you say that? What's wrong with you? she yelled. She stormed into the bedroom, slammed the door. When I finally went to soothe her, she was weeping. I just think she's so ugly, she said.

That night there was a terrible thunderstorm. Lightning flashed against the window in our bedroom. I lay there watching the rain hammer against the glass. I don't know if Rachel was awake or asleep.

In the morning the rain had stopped and the window was wide open. We opened the bedroom door and found our wallets on the floor. All the cash was gone. The front door was unlocked.

I looked out the open window and saw a thick rope, attached to a pipe on the roof, that unspooled all the way down to our second-story apartment. During the storm, a thief had descended the rope, opened the window of our bedroom as we slept, and slipped into our apartment. He'd looked for our wallets, of course, taken the cash, and then rushed out the door.

But before that, surely there'd been a moment when he looked over at the two of us, lying there asleep in each other's arms. Sometimes I wonder, when the stranger looked upon us, what it was he thought he saw.

Eventually I went to grad school, in part so I could break up with Rachel without having to have a fight about it. It was very sneaky of me, to go off and do something that would transform my life, and to do it as an act of cowardice.

The first week at Johns Hopkins, I found myself on a couch with an Irish writer named Jean, listening to a piano piece by Mussorgsky, *Pictures at an Exhibition.* During a movement called "Catacombs," the music grew dark. I looked over at Jean, and she looked at me, and at that moment we came to an unspoken agreement about the trouble we were about to cause. In the weeks to come, I would take care to wash my sheets.

Jean had a cat, and Rachel was allergic. I knew Rachel would realize something was up the first time that she sneezed.

My relationship with Rachel didn't last more than another year after I kissed Jean. But then, my relationship with Jean didn't last after I kissed Sandrine, and after her, Samantha, and Nancy, and Minnie. I kissed all those women, each time knowing that I was betraying the woman before, but also hoping that somewhere, in one of these relationships, I would find the courage to let myself be known.

In Stoppard's play, there's a moment when Jeremy Irons's character comes to a realization. "I remember how it stopped seeming odd that in biblical Greek *knowing* was used for *making love,*" he says. "Whosit knew so-and-so. Carnal knowledge. It's what lovers trust each other with. Knowledge of each other, not of the flesh but through the flesh, knowledge of self, the real him, the real her, in extremis, the mask slipped from the face."

That was the strangest thing about being a twentysomething. I had grown up thinking of myself as unlovable, an aberration, a freak. Girls had laughed in my face; the prospect of sex had filled me with terror. But by the time I arrived in my late twenties, I was adorable. I was *AN AMAZING LOOKING MAN!*

Dylan Edwards wasn't all wrong. The seniors *did* get all the pussy.

Minnie and I had made out a bunch of times. She was very quiet. She wrote nonfiction.

I asked her, What would we do if you got pregnant? What choices would you make? I figured this was a good thing to know about in advance, in case what she'd want to do was to have a baby. Because I was definitely not doing that.

She looked at me in wonder, a little confused. "No man has ever asked me that before we had sex."

This surprised me. "Ever?" I said. She shook her head. "Ever." I can't remember what she said she'd do. I'm pretty sure she said she'd have an abortion, but I don't know for sure. I never did sleep with her, though. Something always came up.

I know people who were attractive when they were young, even if only fleetingly, who now are pretty much hideous, and not only because of how they look. But they continue to think of themselves as the cat's pajamas. For how many people is the opposite true? All those years of people literally laughing at your face can leave you feeling hideous and unlovable, even when you've emerged as a *sex god of the new generation*. And so we continue on our journey, endlessly yearning for a sense of completion that always remains just beyond our grasp.

Which sounds terrible, I guess, but I wonder whether it's so wrong that some things remain beyond our grasp. In the metaphor of the carrot and the stick, we all have a few laughs at the donkey's expense. The carrot dangles before him, kept just out of reach by the stick, and the donkey plods along, pulling his donkey cart, a kind of perpetual motion machine powered by nothing more than hunger, and hope.

The conclusion being, *Ha ha, stupid donkey! Doesn't he ever realize he can never have the thing he wants?*

But I suspect that the donkey is smarter than that. It can't take too long to understand that the entire situation is a cruel charade. Even a donkey knows when he's being had.

And yet he keeps on trotting down the path, even after he realizes he's never getting that carrot, even after he realizes everyone thinks he's stupid. Why?

Is it possible that desire is its own reward? That wanting the thing that is always just out of reach is its own form of bliss? It's better than a carrot, anyhow.

The book my father gave me, H. A. Rey's *The Stars,* has a broken back now. The binding is held together with tape. I'm sure there's a new edition, but I like the one I have. On the first page, Rey writes, *The space age is upon us. Rockets are leaving the globe at speeds unheard of only a few years ago, to orbit earth, moon, and sun. Any day now men may visit the moon, or may have done so as you read this.*

In the back of the book I wrote down the names and the dates of a particularly good stargazing session. The first names I wrote down were those of boys—Ben, Tugger, Kenny. But then I started to write down the names of the girls whom I loved, the girls with whom I had ventured out on a cold night to look at the heavens.

There they are—Julie, and Rachel, and Minnie.

Finally, just as I turned thirty, I wrote: *Deirdre.*

At our wedding reception, we drank champagne. A waiter was walking around with little snacks. We were talking to a friend of my sister's, a young woman named Lauren, whom she'd met in grad school. They were studying medieval literature together.

Several years earlier I'd thought about dating Lauren, but it never quite happened. What with one thing and the other.

The waiter approached us. On a platter he had some hot baked goods. "Would you care for a roll?" he said.

Deedie looked philosophical. She knew what was coming.

"Don't mind if I do!" I said, handing my flute to Deedie, dropping to the floor, and then rolling all around. Then I got up, dusted myself off, and took back my champagne flute. "Thanks!" I said. The waiter wandered off thinking, *Asshole.*

Lauren looked at me, and then at my bride. "Deedie," she said, shaking her head. "You're going to have—a funny life."

It sounded good, a funny life. Who wouldn't want one?

But the way Lauren said it, it sounded a little sad.

We moved to Maine, and I took the job teaching English at Colby College. We found a farmhouse out in the country. Behind the house was a broad field. The night was full of the sounds of crickets.

My love and I lay down in the field and looked at the stars of summer—Cygnus the Swan high overhead. Pegasus and Andromeda, back-to-back, forming the Great Square. Low on the horizon, the Scorpion and the Archer.

Deedie rested her head upon my stomach. With one hand I touched her hair.

After a while I turned the flashlight off. Then we turned away from the heavens, and toward each other.

Thirty-six years later, we are still turning toward each other.

Who are we, now that we are old people, instead of young ones? Does love mean something different to me—or to her—now that I am female?

I don't know. Maybe I'm the wrong guy to ask.

It feels indecent, at this late hour, to write about my most intimate relationship—because part of what makes a relationship intimate in the first place is the idea that there are things you know about each other that no one else will know.

So what can I tell you?

I can tell you that she still likes roast potatoes, and Bruce Springsteen, and Irish whiskey, and me.

I can tell you that many of our friends use the same phrase that I use, "the Deedie light," to describe the glow of the sunset on the far trees across the lake.

She's all that.

I know that there is a certain cohort for whom the life of a couple like Deedie and me is almost unimaginable, people who say things like *I want to hear Deedie's side of the story, she's the real hero!* as if there can only be one hero in our story, or more accurately, as if either of us, in choosing to love each other, is heroic.

But honestly, it's not like that. On a good day, we're pretty boring.

When I wake up in the morning, Deedie is already outside, walking around the neighborhood with her friend Julie and Julie's dog, Walter. When she gets back, she brings me a cup of coffee, which I drink in bed while reading the newspaper. Then I come downstairs and we eat breakfast together. Eggs, toast. She does *Yoga with Adriene* via YouTube in the living room, and I go downstairs and do stretches for my terrible knees and follow this up with a half hour of tai chi. She's in Mountain Pose, the Crow, and Downward Dog; I'm Parting the Wild Horse's Mane, Picking the Needle Up from the Sea Bottom, and Waving Hands Like Clouds. When all of that has safely blown over, I will try to write, and she'll dig in the flower garden. We come in for lunch and read more of the news off our glowing devices, and then we take a walk together around the neighborhood: the lake is beginning to melt, or to freeze; the leaves are turning yellow, or green, or coming into bud, or falling on the ground. When we get back, we will sit in chairs and I will read or grade papers or prepare for a class. Maybe one of the kids will call us on the phone? How we miss them, those two! Sometimes Deedie and I talk about that: how much we miss them. Eventually we start thinking about the evening's cocktail: A Boulevardier? An Old-fashioned? An Aviation? The Naked and Famous? I build a fire and then we sit there with the cocktails or maybe we walk down by the water. There's Deedie light on the far trees, burning bright, and then slowly fading as the sun sinks down behind us.

Like I said, I am not sure I know how to make our lives seem interesting. Or, worse: a kind of smugness wrought from privilege drips from my prose when I try to write about it, like maple syrup oozing down a stack of pancakes. Meanwhile: every day I read the story of transgender people driven from their homes, or literally throwing themselves in front of trucks, as Republican legislatures spend their valuable time in the wells of their various statehouses coming up with incredible new ways of making our lives impossible. Every few weeks I hear about a trans woman who's been murdered.

And so I'm not so sure how the story of my wife and me drinking cocktails helps anybody. I think that my life has been made possible, among other things, by a tremendous amount of luck. It might just as easily have been very different for me, for us. I know lots of people who are genuinely suffering, and for no other reason than that their luck was different from mine. Don't they, too, deserve to Wave Their Hands Like Clouds? Don't they, too, deserve to watch the sunlight on the far trees? Doesn't everybody?

The first half of my life was defined by a sense of yearning: I wanted to be loved, and I wanted to be my actual self. I had always assumed that if the latter came true, the first would never happen. So instead, I hoped that if the first came true, that the lack of the second would not hurt so much. I've written about this before—the way many of us hope that we might be "cured by love."

But love is not the same as penicillin.

And this is true whether the thing you hope to be cured of is being trans or something else entirely. Is there anyone who has never hoped that being in love would somehow make them into a better person?

There aren't many people who hope to be worse, anyhow.

I can tell you that before I met Deedie, I felt incomplete. I had hoped that being her lover would complete me, in every possible way that a person can be completed—and indeed, I felt blissfully whole for many years after we were first married. But little by little the hard facts of my soul again made themselves clear to me—quietly at first, and then with blistering urgency. And so then I had to figure out what to do next.

Eventually, I had to share with her the thing I had always kept hidden—which was, like most conversations about sex, or gender, not a single conversation but a series of them, each one more heart-wrenching than the last. She spent a year or so considering whether she'd be happier with me, or on her own. There was a while where it seemed like all we did was weep. She could either abandon the person she loved at the moment of his greatest need, or she could help the person that she loved become someone else entirely. What kind of choice was that?

In the end, incredibly, she decided that the love she felt for me transcended the body in which my soul was contained. How on earth, you wonder, did she make this decision?

I cannot tell you. I mean, I can be pretty fun, on a good day. But I'm not *that* fun.

*How can she be happy with me?* I ask myself now and again. Now and again I'll catch a far-off look in her eye, and I'll want to say—*It's okay. I understand if I am not enough.*

When I put this into words, she says, *Marrying you was the luckiest thing that ever happened to me.* And then looks at me, her eyes aglow with that Deedie light.

And I'll think, *Was it?*

# THE UNIT

On the way home there was a dispute in the car about whether I had a big one, or what. This was in the days Before, long Before. I didn't think it was anything special. But Dan had seen mine one night the boys in our comedy group got naked at some radio station, and so he held his ground. For their part, Maggie and Tom were curious, I guess. I don't remember Peter weighing in, but it was a whole thing, the conversation rising and falling. I kept hoping they'd move on to something else, but you know how people are with a thing like that.

Finally I told them to pull the car over, and I whipped it out in the breakdown lane. This was on Route 101, the two-lane road that leads from Olympic National Park to Bainbridge Island, where we were going to catch the ferry back to Seattle. We'd been in the wilderness.

Everybody got a good look. Then I pulled up my pants and returned to the back seat, where I was jammed in between Peter and Maggie. We got back on the highway. Nobody said anything for a while.

Dan said, "I think it looked cold."

Everyone nodded. Maybe it *had* been cold. That could have explained a lot of things.

Freud figured everybody wanted one. *It consists in attributing to everyone, including females, the possession of a penis, such as the boy knows from his own body.* And: *The boy's estimate of its value is logically reflected in his inability to imagine a person like himself without this essential element.*

There's a lot, as they say in grad school, to unpack there. But the phrase that I come back to is *a person like himself.* Freud assumes that men and boys are the *default human.* If you're female, you must spend your days in lamentation that you somehow arrived on earth without the factory settings. And that, penis-wise, we're like the playthings in *Toy Story. If you don't have one,* counsels cowboy Woody, *get one!*

That women might consider *ourselves* the default human, or, god forbid, that in fact there might not even *be* a single way of being human, seems not to have crossed Freud's mind.

Since penis envy is a concept with its supposed roots in childhood, though, it is worth noting that the only default humans I ever encountered in elementary school were bullies and assholes. Most of these were boys, but there were a few girls in that cohort, too. They always got their way, those characters.

I didn't hate the one I had. It was pleasant enough if you wanted one, which I didn't. I guess the thing I would compare it to, really, was like having a St. Bernard dog for a pet. There were times when it made demands, and then there was the problem of what we might refer to as the *drool.* Other times, it was adorable: a big, sloppy, goofy presence that merely wanted, as they say in Ireland, "to live a life given over totally to pleasure." In the years since, I've known a lot of men, and more than a few women, who have wanted to live their lives like that, too: like penises. They do just as they please. Are they happy, people like that? I don't know. A lot of them *look* happy, anyhow.

Anyway, most of the time mine just lay there like a St. Bernard puppy, exhausted, sated, fast asleep.

*All this seems to show,* Freud writes, *that there is some truth in the infantile sexual theory that women, like men, possess a penis.* And: *They develop a great interest in that part of the boy's body. But this interest promptly falls under the sway of envy. They feel themselves unfairly treated.*

I *did* feel myself unfairly treated. There I was, with a penis that I did not want. I didn't hate it, or write it angry poems in which I told it *you are a caul that blinds my sight.* It just didn't make any sense. I was clearly a girl; I mean, as they say in psychoanalysis, *duh.* I'd known this from the age of five or six, from the languid afternoon when I lay beneath my mother's ironing board, and she said, as she steamed my father's shirts, "Someday you'll wear shirts like this," and I thought, *What? Seriously?*

Unlike lots of trans girls today, it never occurred to me back then to say out loud the thing that was in my heart. These days, I look at young girls out and proud, taking puberty blockers, wearing dresses to school, buying *My Little Pony* lunchboxes. It just amazes me. The closest I ever got to that was one time when I got frozen, sledding at Woojee Trousdale's house, and I started crying because of the cold. Her mother took me in, set me down by the fire, dressed me up in her daughters' clothes until I warmed up. When at last I'd thawed, she suggested it was time for me to go home.

But I didn't want to go home.

I guess it would have been easier for me if I'd been born later, or if I'd had the courage to state the truth when I was a child. But what's the point of this kind of thinking? It's kind of like saying, *Life would have been different if I had a time machine.* Maybe that's true, but I don't know if it would be better. Mostly I'm grateful for the life I've had, even with all the trouble.

Sometimes, I'd see men naked in locker rooms or skinny-dipping in a pool, wreathed in careless contentment. Back in the late '90s, when I'd taught at University College Cork, I'd seen huge men standing nude before the mirrors at the gym, shaving the thick cream from their pink faces as steam from the showers drifted around them like fog. On these and so many other occasions I would look on in wonder, and try to imagine what it might be like to be a creature such as this.

I don't know cis women who've ever experienced penis envy as Freud described it. But as a woman born with one, all I can say is, I know exactly what he meant. Why yes, I did feel myself *unfairly treated.*

In the movie *Zelig,* the title character says, "I worked with Freud in Vienna. We broke over the concept of penis envy. Freud felt that it should be limited to women."

We stood backstage at the Met Breuer museum, the poet Sharon Olds and I. This was just a few years ago. We were part of a festival called "The In-Between," which the Met was staging in the museum that had formerly been the Whitney, and which the Met was now taking over. The festival was taking place after the Whitney moved downtown but before the Met moved in. Everywhere you looked there were sawhorses, ductwork, big piles of trash. The place was in transition.

That title, "The In-Between," had irritated me a little bit, given that, post-transition, I didn't feel particularly liminal. Still, it was good company: not just Sharon and me, but Isabella Rossellini, too. They'd wired us all up with those remote headphone microphones, so we could hold forth wirelessly at the podium. As we waited to go on stage, it occurred to me to ask Sharon about the poem she'd written some years before, "Outside the Operating Room of the Sex-Change Doctor," a work in which a tray of displaced penises take the measure of their situation.

It's got a wow finish, that poem: *Only one is unhappy. He lies there weeping in terrible grief, crying out Father, Father!*

I'd always revered her work. She was my favorite poet. But that piece hurt my feelings. Even now, I get sad just thinking about it.

I imagined myself clearing my throat and saying, *Sharon, listen, can I ask you about something?*

Onstage, we heard the person before us wrapping up his speech. I think this was Ricky Jackson, a man who'd spent thirty-nine years imprisoned for a crime he did not commit. I've never been behind bars, but sure: his story spoke to me, as a transgender person. I hadn't committed any crimes, either.

Maybe, I thought, if Sharon heard the piece I was going to perform, her heart would open. I was doing the story of my trip to Nova Scotia, that time I didn't think I was coming back.

In the auditorium, the audience applauded, and the stage manager pointed to Sharon and said, "You're on!"

The third penis in that poem says, *I am a caul removed from his eyes. Now he can see.*

She stood up.

"Break a leg," I said.

We'd wound up in Olympic National Park, my friend Peter and I, at the tail end of a long road trip that had begun at my parents' house in Devon, Pennsylvania. Summer 1982. We'd taken the blue highways the whole way, stopping en route at places of interest to stoned-out goofballs, which, let the record show: we were.

Before I went out West with Peter, I'd spent June of that summer house-sitting my mother's house, back in Pennsylvania, while Mom was off in Germany, where she'd lived as a child. It was the first time she'd been back since the war. I spent those weeks *en femme*, day after day. It was the first time I'd really been able to be myself without interruption for a long time. It had been glorious, and deeply frightening.

I'd shaved my legs for the first time that June, a process that turned out to be a whole lot less fun than you'd think. A month later, I was faced with the awkward experience of having to keep my friend Peter from noticing the fact that I'd shaved my legs. One day, in Yellowstone, I'd jumped into a swiftly moving stream, and found myself briefly borne off by the current. When I got myself back on land, I was afraid Peter was going to notice, all at once, that his friend had legs like Sharon Stone.

But Peter didn't notice. The hairiness of my legs wasn't a topic that concerned him.

I'd broken things off with my psychoanalyst just before I left New York to house-sit Mom's place. He had a practice in one of the tenement buildings on Broadway and 125th Street, right where the number 1 train emerges from the tunnel. Once a week I'd walk up there and lie down on his couch. The very first time I went there it took me virtually the whole session to say this sentence out loud: *I have juh juh juh juh gender issues.* Sweat poured off me. My whole body shook, like I was riding the Wild Mouse in Ocean City.

It was just like in the cartoons, me lying on a couch, my analyst—let's call him Dr. Fernweh—staring at his notepad from his chair adjacent. He held a pen to his lips. Sometimes he licked its tip. Dr. Fernweh had cold blue eyes and a gray goatee. I wish I could say he had a Viennese accent, but he didn't. Actually, there were long, long minutes in which he said nothing at all. He did that thing where he waited me out, like someone fishing for marlin. Eventually I just started talking, but only because I was embarrassed. I felt bad for him, not having anything to say.

*Was my mother overbearing?* he asked. No, she was sweet and literary—a bookseller in the days before she met my father. *Would I describe my father as remote?* No, he was an all-around good guy, gentle and loving. *Would you describe yourself as depressed?* Not really. Only when I'm sad.

The doctor licked his pen. My condition didn't fit any of the theories.

Freud, for his part, wasn't exactly hostile to transgender people, although the reasons he dredged up for our existing in the first place are kind of adorable in their ridiculousness. One famous psychoanalyst allows as how psychoanalytic treatment is a "transgenderization" process, *as any psychoanalysand goes from a phallic position in the beginning of their psychoanalysis towards a feminine position at the end of it.*

To which I kind of want to say, yeah, that's kind of clever, but the thing you're describing there isn't exactly analogous to the moments where, for instance, I had to lie on my back screaming as every one of the thirty thousand beard follicles on my face was fried with a burning hot needle. But all of that came later. I had stood there with my hand on the doorknob for all my life; but I was forty years old before I actually walked through the door.

My psychoanalyst's ears pricked up when he heard about my sister, who rode horses. Our family's lives revolved around her when I was young. *Were you jealous of your sister?* he asked. I said, *Yeah, I guess.* I could almost hear him thinking, *Aha!*

*Did you ever feel like you wanted to* be *your sister?*

I lay there, dumbfounded. Be her? Why would I want to be my sister?

*Perhaps you wanted her life?*

Even now, forty years later, I would like to push a baked bean up his nose. My sister is a lovely person; she lives in England now and is a scholar on the history of books. But I have never wanted her life. The life I wanted was my own.

But I was convinced by Dr. Fernweh that this was my problem; somehow, bereft of love, I wanted to be my sister.

How could I have known back then that being trans isn't the result of envy, or loneliness, or you know: *polymorphous perversity*. It is, instead, a thing that god has given us: like the blue potato, or the duck-billed platypus. As such it is not a complex for theorizing. It is a wonder of nature.

That's what makes me sad about psychoanalysis. My doctor didn't want to make me happier; he wanted to lower a complex superstructure of behavioral speculation over my head, like I was a toucan and he had the world's most fascinating birdcage. Never once did he say, *Well, here's what you might do in order to find solace.* Maybe that wasn't his job; I don't know. But that's the thing I needed. Instead, in so many ways, psychotherapy set me back years and years.

Once, in frustration, I asked him, Well, what *about* transgender people? What are some of the paths people have followed in order to find their happiness? He licked his pen. Then he suggested I might take out some books from the library.

In 1854, Drs. James Bovell and Edwin Hodder injected a forty-year-old man with twelve ounces of cow's milk. They had a theory: milk would transform, within the body, into white corpuscles. Dr. Henry Cotton, a half century later, also had a theory: mental illness was the result of infected teeth. In order to help his patients, he pulled them all out.

History is full of bright ideas: bloodletting leeches, drilling holes in the skull.

My thought is that if you have a theory that does not bring kindness and compassion to people who are suffering, what you really need, more than anything else, is a new theory.

After the long trip West, Peter and I wound up at my sister's house in Portland, Oregon, for a few days. She was then living in an apartment one floor above a guy who played the bass for Frank Zappa and the Mothers of Invention.

After a few days at my sister's, Peter and I headed up to Seattle, where we met up with friends from college: Tom, and Maggie, and Dan. Tom had worked in a factory that made replicas of old flintlocks; Maggie played the mandolin. Dan, with whom I'd had a radio show back in the late 1970s, was just getting started now in the world of video production. We were all twenty-five, plus or minus: a bunch of misfits casting around for whatever came next. One day, in Seattle, Tom and I wound up at a grocery store, where the video game Frogger was brand new. Hour after hour we poured quarters into that machine, making the frog leap from lily pads onto the swiftly moving logs. When the frog died, a big skull and crossbones appeared on the screen.

In the evenings, we went to a place called Dick's for hot dogs.

Then we went out to Olympic National Park. We hiked in on a boardwalk through the tropical rainforest: huge trees, shiny moss, slugs the size of hamsters. As we walked, blackness descended on me. It was clear enough that I was never going to be able to do anything in this world unless I dealt with the transgender business: I would never be able to write, I would never be able to be in love. But what could I do? I'd tried psychoanalysis and it had left me more miserable than when I began.

What I thought, as we trudged west through the deep forest, was that I'd gone about as far as I could go.

As we walked, somebody came up with a funny bit of business about the size of the one I had. They slapped their inner thighs to indicate its length. They spoke my name: *James—slap! slap! Boylan!* Then, my friends would laugh, but only because it was clear, maybe, how much I hated this. I guess it was pretty funny, if you were not me.

At a ranger station in the lush wilderness I saw a young woman in a ranger's uniform, a Smoky the Bear hat. She looked so much like me, if I had been born female, that I was stunned into silence. Even my friends noticed it. *She looks more like your sister,* Peter said, *than your sister!* The ranger showed us a hand-drawn map of that part of the park. There was a place on it marking the location of an old cemetery on the banks of a lake. The location was marked with the same skull and crossbones we'd seen in Frogger a few days before, after the frog died.

Some of the early settlers were buried in that graveyard. "Could we go and see them?" I asked. The ranger-girl looked at me funny. "Why would you want to see the cemetery?"

"To see where they wound up," I said. "Those early explorers." Considering that she looked so much like a nether-me, that ranger-girl was strangely oblivious to the way I identified with those people. But they'd come all this way. Then they couldn't go any farther.

My friends weren't interested in finding any overgrown graveyard, either. And so we continued walking west.

We arrived on the beach near sunset. The Pacific Ocean crashed before us.

Peter and I pitched a tent not far from the North Ozette River, a broad creek that emptied out onto the sand. Later, as I lay in my sleeping bag, I heard the sound of its clear waters, rushing toward the sea.


The average penis is between 5.1 and 5.5 inches; 85 percent of people who have one think that the average size is bigger.

In 2015, a man named Roberto Esquivel Cabrera was certified by something called the World Record Academy as having a penis 18.9 inches long. "Look where it goes, it goes beneath the knees," he said miserably, after the official measurement. Mr. Cabrera said his penis had ruined his life. "I cannot do anything," he said. "I cannot work."

He had hoped, in going public, that he'd be certified by the more-prestigious Guinness World Records. But Guinness had told him it had no category for penis size.


In June of 2020, J. K. Rowling posted an essay in which she explained her reasons for speaking out about gender issues. "Woman is not a costume," she wrote. "Woman is not an idea in a man's head. Woman is not a 'pink brain,' a liking for Jimmy Choos, or any of the other sexist ideas now touted as progressive." She concludes: "Biological sex is real."

I agree with all of that. I am not female because of an idea or a costume. I don't own any Jimmy Choos, which I am told is a kind of shoe. And my brain is gray, same as hers. The thing that makes me female is the same thing that makes her female: a sense of self, deeply rooted in neurology and experience. Being female is not an idea for me; it is a fact. But it is a fact that cannot possibly be understood without imagination.

It would be nice if the line between male and female were simple. But gender, like the universe itself, is all gnarly. Clownfish can change their sex. So can reed frogs, green sea turtles, slipper limpets, and central bearded dragons. These creatures—like me—do not change sex in order to hurt Ms. Rowling's feelings. We do so because nature demands it. Because we are, like so many things on this earth, wonders of god's creation.

I'm going to believe in a better J. K. Rowling, not the one that she is, but the one she might still become. As one of my favorite authors once wrote, "It matters not what someone is born, but what they grow to be."

Who wrote that? J. K. Rowling, of course.


In the morning I woke to the sound of the ocean, and crawled out of the tent to find the horizon gray in the early light of dawn. I had lived on the East Coast almost my entire life; the Pacific Ocean filled me with wonder. It still does, actually.

The ocean was filled with crags; off to the right was a huge outcropping of rock with a cave on one side. The waters of the North Ozette River glided across the sand.

I stepped into the water. It was cold. A few steps in, the ocean floor disappeared beneath me, and now I was swimming in those blue waters. I headed straight out, toward Japan. Big swells lifted me up then fell again. I banged my knee on a submerged rock. It hurt.

I treaded water for a moment, and then turned to face the shore. All of my friends were standing there, watching me. Dan gestured with his hands. *Come in, James. Why don't you come in.* Another wave picked me up.

When I finally got back on land, Maggie gave me a towel. "I don't think it's safe to swim here, James," Dan said. "The undercurrents. You might get swept away."

I couldn't tell him that getting swept away would have suited me just fine.

Later that day we got high and waded out to the crag with the cave. It was a big womblike space, with an arching ceiling, tide pools on the floor. Dan and Tom and I sat down on the rocks and looked at the sea anemones and hermit crabs. Everything echoed in the cave. Now and again a wave would crash through the entrance. Light rippled on the ceiling.

"The anemone of my anemone is my friend," I said.

"Hey," said Tom, in glee. "I made a hermit crab change its shell!"

*Och,* I thought sadly. *Lucky hermit crab!*

Tom was a small man with merry eyes, his head shaved nearly bald. Tom and Dan sat there for a long time playing with the anemones and the hermit crabs. They watched the crabs scamper around; they tricked them into wrapping their pink tentacles around their own fingers.

They were so entranced, those boys. What would it be like, I wondered, as I looked upon my friends, to be able to lose yourself in something other than yourself? Were Dan or Tom so much happier than I? I was pretty sure they didn't spend hours privately agonizing over the fact of their own embodiment. But what did I know? They had problems of their own.

The thing they had, and I did not, was not a penis; it was the ability to be in love. Dan once told me that, when he was single, having sex was just about the best way he could imagine of getting to know someone. But that was the very problem: I was too frightened to allow myself to be known.

I was twenty-four, and for all intents and purposes, still a virgin. It was pretty clear by now that the thing that was wrong with me was not a thing that could be solved.

The tide was coming in. If we waited long enough, it was possible the entrance to the cave would be underwater. But Dan and Tom weren't concerned. They were exactly where they wanted to be. Their voices echoed in the cave. *Yo,* said Tom, with delight. *It has a mouth in the middle!*

I looked at those men with envy and sadness, and an anger burned in my heart.

Later, as I walked on the beach with Peter, we ran into a ranger from the Ozette Reservation just a few miles to the south. "What do you do?" Peter asked.

"I control the tides," he said, matter-of-factly, and then roared. It was a deep, hearty laugh. I had never heard anything like it.

"Did you see the eagle?" he asked us. "There was an eagle flying."

I shrugged. I hadn't seen any eagle. "I was looking down," I said. What I was kind of thinking, actually, was *fuck you. Fuck the eagles. Fuck the tides.*

"Well," said the ranger. "If you always look down, you won't see the eagles."

I wanted to tell him, I don't always look down. But then I wondered whether this was true. I was so consumed with trying to solve the mystery of my own impossible life that I was pretty much blind to everything.

In the meantime, the ranger had turned and walked away. A moment later he'd faded into the forest and was gone.

Twenty years later, I was wheeled off to surgery on a gurney. My wife and my friend Rick were at my side. *"I'm going to wash that man right out of my hair!"* I sang. *"I'm going to wash that man right out of my hair!"*

The intern wheeling me away looked entertained. "She's singing," he observed.

"Is that—typical?" asked Rick.

The intern shrugged. "We get all kinds of reactions," he said.

A few years later I was watching some movie on cable TV. I forget which one. But all at once, there was a naked man on television. I hadn't seen one for a while. I looked upon his junk and thought, *Will you look at that!* It struck me with wonder: the penis, and the scrotum, swinging around like the giblets you'd yank out of a Thanksgiving turkey.

The new unit, mysteriously wrought by my surgeon out of nothing more than pixie dust and marzipan, was something entirely different. Everything looked just like it was supposed to. I'd been to two different gynecologists in the days since surgery who—at least at first—did not know and could not tell. Yes, I can have an orgasm, thanks for asking. As my friend trans legend Kate Bornstein likes to say, *The plumbing works and so does the electricity.*

Now and again, catching a glimpse of myself in the mirror, I'll think— *Well hello, Jenny Boylan. There you are.*

As I gazed upon the unexpected junk on the television I did not feel myself *unfairly treated.* What I felt more than anything else was a vast sense of relief. It seemed like a long, long time ago, when I was sad.

We struck our tents and hiked back through the rainforest to our car. We didn't see that ranger-girl again, although as we passed the lodge, I looked around. I thought to myself, Someday I'll come back here, as a woman, and I'll hike through those woods and find that cemetery. I'll stand by those graves and say, *Thank you.*

I said that to myself that summer, August of 1982. But I've never been back.

Twenty-five years later, walking through Morningside Heights, I saw Dr. Fernweh walking south on Amsterdam, not far from the Hungarian Pastry Shop. He hardly seemed to have aged a day: same black glasses, same gray goatee. I was thunderstruck. Here he was, after all these years! I wanted to rush up to him and say, *Doctor! Doctor! It's me, Jenny Boylan! I did it! I'm happy!*

Which I am, most of the time. Although, like anyone else, I have my bad days, too. But most of the trouble I find in the world doesn't have anything to do with being trans. It comes from being female, a soul who, even now, some individuals see as something other than the *default human.*

It is hard being around people without imagination. But it is not really my problem, that I am someone for whom others have no theory.

*The programme of becoming happy,* Freud writes, *which the pleasure principle imposes on us, cannot be fulfilled, yet we must not—indeed, we cannot—give up our efforts to bring it nearer to fulfilment by some means or other.*

Dr. Fernweh looked at me.

I waited for him to find the spark of recognition, for him to see his former patient, now an older woman, at peace at last.

But he just walked on. It didn't matter to him whether I was happy, or not. What did he care? I was no one he had known.

# SONS

It hurt less than I thought. But maybe I was in shock? I feared the pain would spike if I moved. So there I lay, looking up at the blue sky. Fingers of mist billowed up and over the crest of Pamola Peak. That mist was cold.

The Knife Edge trail, from which I'd fallen, was still in sight. I could see the blue blazes on the pink granite. It was still morning. Maybe some other hiker would come along, someone who might help me up, call in the rangers, tell Deedie I was okay. I was okay, wasn't I?

*At this point, we don't know!*

Every summer, I'd read about these stupid people who'd broken bones on Mt. Katahdin, men or women who had to be medevaced off the summit by helicopter. I always had contempt for these people. You wouldn't get into trouble, I figured, if you were prepared.

It was 2001. I was a year into hormones. It was clear that something was happening to me, but I hadn't told anyone at work exactly what. People thought I had cancer.

I looked down at my leg. Blood was running down the right calf. I could see a few inches of my tibia, the white of the bone shocking and stark against the red blood.

I lay my head back down. A hard wind rushed over the stone, and again I felt the chill as the mist passed through me. There was the soft sound of water trickling down the sides of Baxter Peak toward Chimney Pond. It was so quiet where I had fallen, as quiet as heaven.

I thought: *I'm in trouble.*

The effects of estrogen were gradual at first. My skin got softer, and more sensitive. I felt more aware of changes in heat and cold. The fat on my body moved around—away from my face and neck, and toward my hips. My breasts started to hurt, and the nipples rose up like soft hills. Slowly but surely the rest followed. Soon enough I was taking after my grandmother and mother and sister, with their generous tops and slim hips. I grew my hair out. One day, a waiter called me *miss*. This felt like an accident at first. Then it happened again, and again. One evening I went into the men's room in a restaurant, and a fellow at the sinks looked at me and smiled. "Wrong room," he said, kindly.

I turned around and entered the other one. A woman standing before the mirror looked at me and then back at herself. There was nothing about me, she seemed to have concluded, that suggested I was in a place I did not belong.

One day, as I was driving the boys around in our minivan, I talked to my children about what was happening. This was far from the only conversation we had about my transition, but I remember this one because their friend Finn was in the car, too. Finn lived down the street, an adorably wicked boy who was always getting them into trouble. As we drove along the banks of the lake, I said that my insides and my outsides didn't match. I asked them, *Did you ever feel that way, like there was something inside of you that other people couldn't see?*

Finn sighed deeply. "All the *time*," he said.

*I've always felt like a girl inside,* I said. *And now I'm taking some medicine that is making my outsides match my insides. That means I'm going to start looking more and more like a girl outside. I know it might make you sad, but you should know that I'm still going to be me, and that I'll still love you just the same.*

"Why would that make me sad?" Zach asked. "If you're still going to love us the same?"

"I don't know," I said. "Change can be hard, I guess."

"Some of my friends think you *are* a girl," said Sean.

*The main thing,* I said, *is that you should know that boys turning into girls is very rare. It's not contagious. And it's not going to happen to you.*

Finn looked at me with an excited smile. "This is gonna be wicked!" he said.

Now I lay on the pink granite of Mt. Katahdin, looking up at the blue sky and the blowing mist. I tried to get up, but it hurt.

I thought, *God, if you'll just get me out of this, I'll stop with the woman business. Whatever that desire is, I'll quash it forever. I'll flush my hormone pills down the toilet. You'll see. If you'll just get me off of this mountain, I'll go back to being a man again.*

"Are you all right, miss?" said a voice, and I looked up. There was a woman about my age. Short hair. Big pack.

"I fell," I said.

"You sure did," she said, and climbed down to where I lay. She took off her pack and, just like that, whipped out a first aid kit. "What's your name?" she said, as she dabbed the wound with a cotton ball.

"Jenny," I said.

She looked at my leg carefully, then nodded. "You're going to be okay, Jenny," she said.

"Am I?" I asked the stranger.

"You are," she said. "Nothing's broken."

By Christmas that year, I was presenting as female most of the time, at least while I was at home, anyway. Deedie got me some earrings for Christmas. I got her some whiskey.

We gave Sean tracks and cars from the Thomas the Tank Engine show, which he adored. His favorite was number 5, James the Red Engine. "He's a *tender* engine," said Sean.

Finally Zach opened one of his presents. Inside was a toy shaving kit, with an assortment of plastic razors.

I touched my own face. After the months and months of electrolysis, it was nearly as smooth as Zach's now.

It wasn't clear what was going to happen to us as a family. Deedie and I were doing our best to hold on to our children, and to each other. But it felt at times as if we were standing on the edge of a precipice, being blown toward the edge by very strong winds. We did not know whether, or for how long, we could hold our ground.

I worried constantly about my sons, about the effect that my transition was going to have upon them. Who's going to be protecting them now? I asked myself. Who's going to teach them the things that Dick Boylan had taught me?

"What's this?" said Zach, with an unexpected tinge of disappointment.

"It's a toy shaving kit," I said to him. "For your very own!"

But Zach just burst into tears. For a while he was unable to speak, just completely inconsolable.

Finally he caught his breath. "I didn't want a *toy* razor," he said. "I wanted a *real* one!"

Time passed. One night, Deedie and I came home to find Sean alone at the kitchen table. From construction paper, he had glued together a sphere of interlocking pentagons and triangles.

Hi, Seannie, we said. What's this?

Sean didn't look up. *Rhombicosidodecahedron,* he said.

Deedie and I looked at each other. A what?

Rhombicosidodecahedron, he said. It's a sphere of twenty triangles, thirty squares, and twelve pentagons.

We looked at the thing he had made. The triangles were orange, the pentagons green. He looked up at us for a moment. *It's an Archimedean solid,* he added by way of explanation.

"This is so cool," Deedie said, beaming with pride. "Is this for a project you're doing for school?" Sean was in sixth grade.

Sean looked at her like she had said the strangest thing ever spoken by a parent. "School?" he said, as if remembering distantly that there was such a place, and that there were people not unlike himself who occasionally went there. "No," he said, and laughed quietly to himself. *"School."*

More time passed. Now Deedie and I sat beside each other in a dark theater, watching our older son on stage. Zach spread his arms.

"If I were king of the for-rrrr-rrrr—esssst! Not queen. Not duke. Not prince."

We sat there stunned. Five minutes earlier, I'd cut the umbilical cord that had tethered him to his mother. Now he was the Cowardly Lion, and a damned good one, too, at least as far as these things go.

*"If I, if I, were king."*

Sean, at that moment, could have been found in South Africa, spending a semester at a school in Cape Town. Every couple of days we'd check his Facebook page, and learn, for instance, that he'd been shark cage diving. Then he went mountain climbing. And bungee jumping. And skydiving. He sent us a video of himself jumping out of an airplane. His hair blew wildly all around his head as he plummeted toward the earth.

One time a journalist had come up to Maine with a film crew and watched as I made pizza. When I brought it out of the oven, I sliced it up and we all stood around eating the pie as the cameras rolled. "What's the secret?" asked Harry Smith, from NBC News. "What do you all know that other families don't?"

Sean had lifted his slice into the air. "Our family," he said, "is bound together with cheese."

By the time we were in our fifties, almost every other couple we knew that had gotten married, like us, in the late 1980s, had gotten divorced. Which is no shame: not every marriage is designed to last forever, and surely everyone deserves to find their own happiness, wherever it lies. But sometimes, when asked in some public setting what the secret of a happy marriage might be, I'd smile wickedly and say, "Well, gentlemen, if you want your marriage to be like ours, you know what you have to do."

I even wrote a book about how transition had affected our family, titled *Stuck in the Middle with You*. It also contained a dozen interviews with writers I knew, conversations about their experiences of being a parent, and a child. Edward Albee talked about being adopted. Ann Beattie talked about being an only child. Richard Russo said, *The thing about having children is that suddenly you have something that under any circumstances you cannot afford to lose. Suddenly you have something that is more important to you than yourself.*

That book had contained a line, "Having a father who became a woman has helped to make my children into better men."

It was a good line, summarizing neatly the sense of pride I had in the family we had become. I hoped that having me as a parent had taught my boys something about having an open heart, about accepting difference, about fighting for the underdog.

But late at night, as Deedie slept, I still wondered whether this was true. Had I really helped them become better men? Or was the jury still out?

Looking back, I wished I'd had a little more insight into the pressure I was putting on my sons to succeed as men. Look at them, I suggested to the world. Look how straight they are, how normal, how exceedingly well adjusted! It was as if I was trying to use my sons as evidence that I was not a bad person. That each of them, in his own way, represented a second chance for me, one last shot at getting the man thing right.

You don't have to hold on to that strap," said Zach, as we screamed around a corner. "I know what I'm doing."

"Of course you do," I said. "I trust you!" We were on the college tour. We'd already visited Brown, Vassar, Colby, Bowdoin, Amherst, Dickinson, the University of Maine, and Johns Hopkins. Still ahead were Oberlin and Gettysburg. Zach was behind the wheel.

At Hopkins, we had had lunch in the faculty club with my old mentor, John Irwin, the chair of the Writing Seminars. In so many ways, John had made my own career possible, had even published my first collection of stories, *Remind Me to Murder You Later,* at Johns Hopkins University Press. I had adored him as a professor; he was just a complete lunatic. In his seminar on Poe and Borges he had given us many lectures on what he called the *mutually constitutive bipolar opposition of spectral doubles.* Most of my classmates were terrified of Professor Irwin, and not without good reason. But I just loved him. You never knew what insane thing he was going to come up with next.

In addition to this, Professor Irwin, a native of Houston, was full of odd Texas slang like, *As long as I got a biscuit, you got half!*

We'd found ourselves reunited, after twenty years, in the fancy faculty club. It was like something out of Mycroft Holmes—dark leather chairs by a fireplace with professors emeriti reading *The Wall Street Journal*; an *actual harpist* not far from that same fireplace, softly plucking out works by Bach and Mozart.

Zach sat there, eyes wide, mildly terrified. He'd been brought up in rural Maine, spent his birthdays at bowling alleys and Red Robin. There'd been endless towers of books in our house, of course, and he'd read everything from Homer to Faulkner at his school. But still: this was not that. Professor Irwin and I talked merrily about the way the roman numeral X was really just two *V*s, inverted one atop the other, just as ten is itself twice five, a perfect example of the way our lives consist of mirror folds, one thing reflecting another. In just this way men and women are inverse reflections of one another, just as children are reflections of their parents, just as all of humanity represents an imperfect reflection of an idea that exists deep within the mind of god. Zach looked over at me, his eyes flickering with fear, or disappointment, or anger. I thought back to our time in Disney's Haunted Mansion: *You told me it was going to be funny!*

I had tried to prepare him for the world ahead, as best I could. But I had not prepared him for a dark chamber of slumbering, bearded men, pipes falling out of their wet mouths, a harpist serenading them. Again I wondered whether the trauma of having me as a parent had wounded my boys on some level beyond my ability to heal?

The waitress came over to our table. "We don't have the crab cake," she said. "And also, today's special is the Seizure Salad."

After she walked away, I turned to my mentor and my child. "You know what a Seizure Salad is?" I said, almost unable to contain my joy. "You take one bite and then you go like this." I crossed my eyes, stuck out my tongue, and said, *Hyeallchhh!*

Zach covered his face with his hands, mortified. John Irwin leaned back in his chair and laughed. "My god, Boylan!" he shouted. "You haven't changed!"

Then he looked at Zach, still mortified. "Don't worry, son," he said. "Your momma's a goofball. *But she's smart as a hoot owl!*"

One day I came downstairs to find Sean working on a series of complex equations at the dining room table. "What's this?" I asked.

"I'm thinking about the problem of time travel," he said.

And I thought, *Of course you are.* "The problem? Like it's not possible, you mean?"

Sean ran his hands through his big head of curly blond hair. "Going *forward* in time isn't possible," he said. "But theoretically, going *backward* could be done. If you could only . . ."

He trailed off.

"If you could only what, Sean?"

He just gave me that smile, like, *I could explain it, but you'd never understand.* I recognized that smile. There were times, when people asked me about my history as a woman, that I gave a smile just like that.

I went outside, took a walk down the dirt road beside the lake. There was a great blue heron standing at the end of the dock. I watched it for a while, then tried to sneak up on it. But it just flew off.

When I got back inside, Sean was gone. On the table where he'd been working was a diagram of a timeline, an $X$ representing the present, and an arrow pointing back. This was surrounded by a series of algebraic expressions.

Sean was nowhere in the house, although his wallet and keys were right where he'd left them. "Seannie?" I called out. But my son had disappeared.

To be a parent means making peace with the fact that the people you love most in the world are destined to leave you. In fact, if they *don't* leave you, and set out in the world to find their own adventures, you've probably done something wrong. Zach went to Vassar, and then moved to Washington, D.C., to try his luck as an actor. Seannie, for his part, had gone to college at the University of Rochester, and then later at the University of Michigan.

It was strange to think how very, very slowly the days had seemed to pass when the boys were small. And how very, very swiftly all that time had disappeared.

I kept the diagram that Sean had sketched out, the one investigating some of the mathematics behind time travel. I taped it to the refrigerator, in fact. Sometimes, in the morning, I stood before the fridge waiting for my coffee to brew, staring at that piece of paper. I put my finger on the $X$, and thought, *This is the moment I am experiencing right now*. But I looked at the arrow pointing back, and thought, *Those were the days when my boys were young*.

Fourth grade—about five years, more or less, after my transition— had been particularly grueling for Sean. There were mornings when he refused to get out of bed and go to school. Instead, he lay there in his bed, softly weeping. We arranged that year for him to see the counselor at school, a woman who reported back that Sean was a complex boy indeed. "Very, very smart," she said. "But with a very deep sense of self."

I could only assume that I was the cause of whatever was making my child sad. Surely having a parent who'd come out as trans—and thus making her children ripe for ostracism and bullying—was a very heavy burden to have laid upon them.

It was during this era that Ranger had arrived. We'd been talking about getting a dog ever since the previous one, Lucy, had given up the ghost. When at last we came home with the adorable black Lab puppy, it was clear that Sean, of all of us, had the most intimate friendship with him. Those two seemed to share an unspoken private language.

Each day, after school, they practiced soccer in the front yard together. Later they lay in the dog bed in front of the woodstove, side by side, as Sean did his homework. Ranger lay on the floor of Sean's room as he folded his origami cranes, as he practiced the French horn, as he lay in his room with a Skype link open to his friend Olivia. For a couple of years Sean and Olivia traded first and second places in their high school academics.

We sang Ranger's praises together. We said that he was *Brave*. That he was *Noble*. That he was known for the *Impeccability of his Character*. But the truth is that Ranger was an easily frightened dog. He seemed to worry a lot.

I don't know, maybe he'd taken one look at our family, and decided that, between the four of us, he had his paws full.

But Ranger watched as Sean came into his own—as a scholar, as a musician, as an athlete, as an all-around fountain of mischief and invention. He became a soccer star. He played the French horn in the Maine Honors Orchestra. He won medals in the Math Olympiad. He was chosen to play big parts in a series of musicals: *The Pajama Game, Carnival*. As the dog stood watch, our son emerged from whatever cloud had enveloped him when he was small, and began each year to shine brighter and brighter.

Some years later, he was finally able to talk about the thing that had made him weep in fourth grade. "It was my teacher that year," he said. "She treated us like idiots."

"Oh," I'd said. "I was afraid—it was because of me."

Sean just looked confused. "You?" he said. "Why would I be sad because of you?"

"You know," I said. "Because I'm trans. Because I made your lives so weird."

Sean smiled at me. He had the most wonderful smile—full of joy and devilry. His whole face lit up. Just looking at him, you could tell Sean Boylan was a rascal. "Oh no," he said. "Weirdness!"

Back when I'd been most worried about Sean, that fourth-grade year, I'd come home from a speaking engagement at some college with a life-size black Lab toy. I'd seen it for sale in an airport bookstore. You'd think the dog was real at first, if you didn't know any better. When I left it in the front hallway, Ranger barked at it for a while, before lying down next to it and thumping his tail on the floor. When Sean came home from school that day, he'd patted Fake Ranger on the head, and then lay down in front of the woodstove with the real one.

"Now we have two Rangers," he said, and smiled that smile.

It had been hard to tell the two apart when I first got the stuffed Ranger, but as the years went by one of those Rangers slowly turned gray, first at the muzzle, then around the neck, and then his tail. By the time the dog was ten, the same year Sean graduated from high school, it had become hard for Ranger to climb the stairs. Some nights we carried him.

I was aware that if that dog was turning gray, I was, too. Sometimes Deedie and I would look at the old dog, and at each other. "Why Jenny Boylan," Deedie would say. "I do believe you're starting to get a little gray around the muzzle."

At the end of Sean's senior year, there was a music night at the school, an evening when anyone who wanted to could perform a song. There were classical violin performances, and rock-and-roll bands, and musical theatre tunes. At the end of the night, Sean Boylan came out and sat down at the concert grand piano. He played a haunting and familiar set of chords. He began to sing.

*Ground control to Major Tom . . .*

That fall, as Sean packed up his car, Ranger stood in the driveway, watching. It was pretty clear by then that Ranger wasn't long for this world. The old dog, now twelve, was stiff. A lot of the time, once he was down, he could not get back up on his four legs without someone lifting him up.

Finally, Sean's car was ready to go. The leaves at our house by the lake in Maine were just starting to turn golden. Loons called from the lake.

Sean hugged his parents. Then he went out to the driveway. Ranger stood by the car. Sean opened the door.

For a moment, I thought the old dog was going to make one last leap and settle into the front passenger seat. I imagined him heading down the Maine Turnpike, the window down, his ears flapping in the wind.

Sean knelt down. "Goodbye, Ranger," he said. "You're a good boy." He wrapped his arms around the old dog and hugged him.

Then our son stood up and got into his car, and drove away.

How had Sean gone from one self to the next? There were times, when I looked upon the confident, brilliant young man, that it was hard for me to find the deeply private boy he once had been. But of course, he was still the same person. Who else would he be? It occurred to me, and not for the last time, that I was not the only person in our house who had been through a transition.

In the end, Sean's eccentricity had helped him on his way. Perhaps, as one of the virtues, weirdness should be held in higher regard. Sometimes I think about the words of Edgar Allan Poe: *There is no exquisite beauty, without some strangeness in the proportion.*

Sean finished his masters the same spring that the pandemic hit. That summer he returned to Maine, moving into his old bedroom, as he waited for a security clearance on his first job, helping to design the systems for a new generation of nuclear submarines. He'd be off to New London, Connecticut, as soon as the clearance came through—but the security check was slowgoing.

By the fall, he was still stuck at home with his parents, as well as a dog we'd adopted, Chloe, a sweet black Lab/flat-coated retriever mix who was very sweet, but dumb as a bag of hammers.

Then one day I came downstairs to find him wearing that smile again. "The Department of Defense," he said, "has decided I am not a security risk."

"Oh, I'm so glad," I said. It had been six months. "I was afraid that they were delaying because they found out who your parent is."

Sean thought this over. "Wait, what?"

"You know, like they learned your Maddy is some famous transgender warrior, and they feared you might be, like, a troublemaker."

He just shook his head. "Maddy," he said, "someday you're going to learn that not *everything* is your fault."

A week or two later, he was off again, this time to New London, where he'd found an apartment online that was not too far away from the vast facility where the nation's submarines are designed and built. He'd taken a few things to get himself started—an inflatable mattress, a sleeping bag—but he'd arranged for the rest of his belongings to be transported by a moving company a few days later.

Chloe didn't watch as Sean drove off. But this wasn't out of character. She didn't have much of an attention span.

When the moving company arrived the next week to carry off the rest of our son's belongings, it didn't take them long to load up. He wasn't taking that much with him. There was a chair and a lamp, a couple of boxes of books, some camping gear. As Deedie reviewed the checklist with the movers, I went up to Sean's now-empty room and lay down on the bed. I felt the emptiness of the house, now really and truly bereft of the children. I looked over at his dresser. His soccer trophies were still there, along with a giant knife he'd purchased in Japan. School textbooks. His fencing equipment.

I thought, with wonder, about the swiftness of childhood. One day you're holding a baby in your arms. *Zach raises his hands from the crib, and asks, Can I hold him?* The next you're standing next to an old dog, watching your child drive away. I thought of my own parents, Dick and Hildegarde. Had they felt this way, the day I'd packed my things into a knapsack and headed down the street to catch a train to New York City? Had my father ever come up to my room in our haunted old house and lain down on my bed?

My eyes fell on the Fake Ranger in the corner.

I picked it up, went down the stairs, and then carried it out to the van. I lay that Ranger down upon the rest of Seannie's things. A moment later the mover came out, lowered and locked the rear door, and then drove off, leaving Deedie and me standing in the driveway. Later that day, Sean would receive Fake Ranger, in Connecticut, along with the other things he'd decided to keep from his childhood home. Who knows? In the years to come, it still might come in handy.

Deedie and I wrapped our arms around each other. I cried softly.

Sean was right about time travel. You *can* travel into the past. Any fool can do that. The future, though. That's harder.

Prince Hal bowed before the king. *I shall hereafter, my thrice-gracious lord, be more myself,* said he.

This was at Vassar, where Zach was majoring in theatre. My son was not Prince Hal, or the king, or even Hotspur. He was, you know: *an attendant lord, one that will do to swell a progress, start a scene or two, advise the prince, etc.* I was proud anyhow. It was a gift to see my boy lit up by spotlights. I couldn't believe it: here he was, all grown, performing in *Henry IV, Part 1.* Against all odds, I was still here, too.

Later, Zach was slain in a swordfight. It was all I could do to keep from leaping out of my seat, trying to save my boy. *If you want to slay him, you're going to have to slay me first!* And so on.

After the swordfight, members of the stage crew, wearing black, rushed out to haul my son's corpse away. But his belt buckle got stuck on an old steam grate on the floor of the stage, and as they pulled on his dead arms, his pants came off.

My son was dead. We were all trying not to laugh.

In the spring of 2014, I got an email from the president of Barnard College, in New York. *I don't suppose you'd ever want to be part of our faculty, would you?*

That fall, after twenty-five years on the Colby faculty, I took a new job as the writer in residence at Barnard. The moving man who had driven all my stuff from my office at Colby down to Morningside Heights had come up to me after he'd moved the last box, asked me to sign the paperwork, and then gave me a look.

"Listen," he said. "Are you sure about this, Prof?"

The new job at Barnard meant that it was a little easier to visit my boys during their college years. There was a train from Penn Station that took me to Poughkeepsie, and another one that could take me to Rochester. I'd see Zach in plays—*Henry IV, Part 1,* and *Prometheus,* and *The Servant of Two Masters.* Another weekend I went up to Rochester to see Sean perform in an improv troupe. It amazed me that he had time for this while he was busy studying solids and fluids and thermodynamics and robotics and heat transfer. I met Sean at his dorm, and there he was: twenty years old, his hair still blond and curly, his body still taut and lean.

He walked me all around the campus, showing me where his classes were, showing me all the cool things there were to see. There were libraries and laboratories, big green lawns, the Genesee River. Then he said, *Maddy, let's go in here.* And then he led me down some stairs and into a concrete building filled with the sounds of people practicing their instruments. He opened a door, and there was a room with two pianos, one nested into the other.

We noodled around with "Norwegian Wood." A minor into D major and back again. Waltz time.

I was so glad I had this way into Sean's heart, and he into mine. *She told me she worked in the morning and started to laugh.* It was such music—my son and me! Those old pianos rang like a bell.

Later that night I watched as Sean and his improv group leapt from one ridiculous idea to the next. He was a castaway on a ship at sea. He was a monster with one leg. He was on a date while eating an invisible turkey leg with one hand. It was all so fast, so strange! My heart surged. I could feel it. I wanted to stand up and shout, *That's my son! Do you understand? My son! My son! He lived!*

We had Thanksgiving that year in the Barnard apartment, a place overlooking Riverside Park with a big living room and a grand piano in one corner. Zach and his fiancée, Terry, were coming up from Washington, D.C. Sean was coming down from Rochester.

Since graduation, Terry had begun a grad program in plant biology at George Washington. Zach was working for a health care company while playing a few roles in a theater company started by some Vassar grads.

Deedie and I heard the door of the apartment open and close, and my son and his lover came down the hallway and dropped their bags in the living room. There were hugs all around. Deedie opened a bottle of prosecco, and put some cheese and crackers on the coffee table.

I remember thinking, *So this is what it's like, to have grown children! Here he is, supporting himself in the world, trying to make art! Here he is, in love with someone who loves him back!*

But then I caught a worried glance, exchanged between Zach and Terry. They joined hands.

Zach took a deep breath. "Listen," she said. "There's something I need to tell you."

# II

# MOTHERS

Two years after our child came out as trans, on a fierce December day, Deedie and I were screaming down the Maine Turnpike, the Bruce Springsteen channel blasting on the satellite radio. Deep, dark snow blew past us as our windshield wipers slapped back and forth. *The kids round here look just like shadows!* The car spun, briefly, but Deedie, teeth clenched, pulled us out of it. The highway was down to a single clear lane now; ahead of us in the early dawn we could just see, through the gray whirling storm, the taillights of a snowplow. We began to spin again and I reached up for the Jesus handle.

*Better be careful.*

"Deedie," I said. Her eyes were fixed on the road ahead. My beloved muttered softly to herself. *Fuck fuck fuck.* "Deedie?" I said again.

Bruce was bellowing. *Down in Jungleland!* I remembered seeing him play this song live at the Philly Spectrum, back when I was a boy. Sixth row.

"Deedie?"

"What, what, *what*?" she said. On the other side of the highway now we saw cars off the road, one of them facing the wrong direction. Cop lights were swirling around, turning the snow red. Frozen people were talking to a frozen policeman. The back doors of an ambulance were wide open.

"Maybe we should go back?" I said.

We spun left, then right, then came back to center. Deedie drove on. Clarence Clemons was playing his famous sax solo now. It was terrible to listen to.

"Back?" she said. *"Back?"*

I looked at my watch. "We're not making this flight anyhow. If it even takes off."

Deedie's hands gripped the wheel like she was holding a rope suspended over a yawning black precipice. "The app said flights were leaving on time."

"Yeah, I know," I said. "But this—this is nuts."

She looked over at me and gave me a hard, piercing glance. "Tell me," she said, looking swiftly back at the dark, frozen highway. "What about this *isn't* nuts?"

I opened my mouth, then shut it. She had me there.

"There's no point in us getting ourselves killed, just to be with her," I said. "If we wind up dead first."

Clarence was still playing saxophone. It was heartrending.

Deedie's eyes were fixed upon the road ahead. "We've seen worse."

"Have we?" I asked. Offhand it was hard to think of a moment during our thirty years of marriage that had seemed more desperate. We'd driven through blizzards before, of course, spun the car around, collided with deer, wound up in one ditch after another. But this felt different.

"*I* have," said Deedie.

After Zach came out as trans, after she told us that she was already on hormones, that she was deep into transition, that her new name was Zaira—in the wake of this Deedie and I had both reacted as if we'd been struck by lightning. I think I even jolted in my chair in the first few seconds after my child—now my daughter—spilled the beans. I thought of the lines in the movie *Gettysburg*, when dying General Armistead learns that his friend General Hancock has also been wounded in battle.

*Not—both of us! Not—all of us!*

We'd rebounded in the days after, sort of. Deedie set about trying to figure out, once again, how she could best help a member of her family with the complex business of transition. It took longer for me, perhaps because I spent no small amount of time convinced that, whatever my child was experiencing, it was all my fault. I had hoped that my position as a very public trans person had given people hope, had let them know that they—and their loved ones—were not alone.

But my heart felt heavy, too. *Is it possible,* I wondered, *that I made this look like fun?* Could my daughter have possibly looked at the intricacies of my life—of our lives—and not seen how hard it all had been, how there were times when I'd felt like I was clutching for dear life onto a tiny life preserver in the middle of a swirling, freezing sea?

Deedie's love for me had literally saved my life. Her devotion and affection, as well as that of many other friends, had given me a sense of euphoria and gratitude that I'd never have known had I stayed closeted forever.

And yet, it all was something I'd never have wished on anybody, especially someone whom I loved.

If my sense of guilt had paralyzed me, had made me unable to help my own child, it was also true that Zai seemed to have no particular interest in asking me for counsel. She was going to come out as trans according to her own lights, not mine. Sometimes, as you might imagine, this hurt my feelings. I wanted to shout at her—*You know your mother is Jenny Fucking Boylan, right? You think I might know a thing or two worth knowing at this juncture?*

But Zai just smiled at me, in exactly the way the young smile at the old. *I've got it,* she said. *Really.*

But you have to let me help you! I'd say. There's so much that I know!

Zai smiled. *You know how you can help me? Just support me, and tell me that you love me. That's really all I need.*

Six or seven months into her transition, they'd even arranged for a kind of summit meeting on the phone. Terry and Zai wanted us to know that what they didn't need—what they increasingly resented, in fact—was *advice.* In no uncertain terms, they gently but firmly asked us to *back off.*

Now we were driving through a historic blizzard in the predawn hours of an arctic December day. We were going to spend Christmas in New York in a hotel, as Zai recovered from surgery at Mount Sinai's gender clinic. We'd ceded her the Columbia faculty apartment for her recuperation; in those chambers she was going to be attended to by a loyal crew of her friends and lovers from Vassar. And not us.

A huge plate of ice blew off the roof of a truck on the opposite side of the highway. It spun through the air and then shattered on the front hood of our Subaru, leaving us, for a few terrifying moments, blind to the world.

For my eighth birthday we were supposed to go to Aquarama, in South Philly. They had a three-story tank: manta rays, sea turtles, the works. They even had two pilot whales from Nova Scotia: Willy and Winky. Four times a day a clown named Flippy would come out to feed the fish; four times a day Flippy lost his footing and fell into the tank.

A pod of dolphins swam to rescue him. "Hang on, Flippy!" the announcer shouted. "They're coming to save you!"

My friend Buddy and I were waiting for my mother to come downstairs so we could drive in to Philly and Aquarama. We were psyched about Flippy. "Okay, boys!" she called to us. "I'll meet you in the car!"

"Race ya," said Buddy to me.

And we were off, tearing down the back stairs into the basement, running past the washing machine, past my father's workbench, past the hamster's cage.

Buddy was a lot faster than I was, though. He got to the back door first. It was made of glass. It swung closed behind him, as I reached out my arm to grab the handle.

My mother heard the screams—first mine, then Buddy's.

A few minutes later we were driving toward the Bryn Mawr Hospital. My aunt Nora was behind the wheel. She wasn't a great driver. My mother was pressing a towel down upon the place where I'd been sliced open.

"Can you please drive faster, Nora?" she said to my aunt.

"You know," said Aunt Nora. "Wouldn't it be good, if there was something you could put on your car, which would let everyone know that it wasn't your fault you were breaking the law! You know, that would just excuse you!"

I had passed out for a few seconds before my mother found me lying there in the driveway in a pool of blood. I looked out the window, everything rushing by in a blur, and felt dizzy again. Maybe I wasn't going to get to see Willy and Winky, or Flippy, or the sea turtles. Maybe I was going to miss out on a lot of things.

"Mom," I asked, "am I going to die?"

"No," she said. "You're going to be fine."

Later that day, ten stitches in my arm, I sat in the audience as Flippy toppled into the dolphin tank. "Hang on, Flippy!" said the announcer. "They're coming to save you!"

I was waiting in line at Katz's Deli. I figured this was what Zai might need most, two days after her surgery, a couple of big pastrami sandwiches with mustard. When I got to the counter, I put in my order, and the deli man cut a sample of the pastrami and handed it to me on a plate to taste, like a sommelier pouring a little wine into your glass before you order the whole bottle. The pastrami was the color of a soft rosé, marbled with fine lines of juicy fat. There was a black crust on the outside. It crunched.

"That's good," I said to the deli man. "Two on rye, with mustard."

It took him a while to make the sandwiches. As I waited I looked around the huge old room, with its brown paneling and pictures of celebrities on the wall. There was Mikhail Gorbachev and John Glenn, Mr. T. and Cyndi Lauper, Cornel West and Sarah Palin. Above a table to one side was a sign indicating the spot where Meg Ryan faked an orgasm in *When Harry Met Sally.* The table was full.

I was given a choice of pickles. I went with the full sour.

Sandwiches in hand, I made my way to the cash register, where I surrendered my ticket and paid fifty dollars, which is a lot for a couple of sandwiches, if you think about it.

I stepped back outside, where the winter wind howled down Houston Street. It took a while to get a cab. I felt the cold on my ears. The paper bag with the sandwiches in it was warm.

Finally a taxi pulled over and I hopped in the back. "Mount Sinai," I said. "The one on Second Avenue." The car pulled away from the curb, and the meter started counting the minutes. I looked out the window. The world was gray, although a few Christmas lights glowed in the windows of bodegas and tenement buildings.

I remembered the days after Zai had come out. I'd been offered solace and strength by my pastor, Amy Butler. I'd gone up to see her in her office, high atop the tower of Riverside Church, where I wept and prayed. Afterward, I'd headed back to the tower elevator and pushed the wrong button. A few moments later, I found myself among the bells. They hung down on their yokes.

The clavier for the carillon in Riverside was inside a little glass booth. I walked in. There was nobody up in that tower besides the pigeons and me.

I punched down the rod of the lowest bell, and it rang, *Onnnggggg,* a sound so loud it made the fillings in your molars shake back and forth. I punched it again. *Onnnggggg.*

What kept me from showing my own child the same love my mother had shown me? I remembered standing by Zaira's crib, Baby Sean in my arms, as my child reached up toward me. *Maddy,* she said. *Can I hold him?*

Yes, I'd said. You can hold him.

"You get the sandwich?" said the cabbie, looking at me in the rearview mirror. The aroma of pastrami and salt and mustard and pickles was rising.

"I got two," I said. "One for me, one for my daughter."

"How much that sandwich cost?" The light ahead of us turned green, and he leaned on his horn. *"Asshole!"* He looked back at me. "You see this guy?"

"It's about twenty-five bucks for the pastrami."

"Twenty-five!" said the cabbie. "That's too much!"

"Normally, I'd say yes."

We drove on in silence for a few moments.

"They make that movie there," the cabbie said. "That girl who fakes the sex!" He smiled. "Crazy stuff!"

I nodded. "It's a classic."

I reached into the paper bag and pulled out a pickle. I bit into it: sour, crunchy, incredible.

We drove on. Soon enough we were at the clinic. The cabbie waved at me as he drove off, like we were best friends.

"Crazy stuff," I said, then turned to find my child.

It's true that, the night I came out to her, my mother took me in her arms and said, *Love will prevail.* But in the months after, she tossed and turned at night, wondering what was going to happen to me, blaming herself for whatever this was, fearing that I was about to destroy my life as well as hers. *I have to fix this*, she thought.

But this was something she could not fix.

She'd come to this country as a child, fleeing East Prussia with her mother and five siblings, settling in New Jersey for a few years before heading back, just in time for Hitler. My grandmother gave birth to child number six, my uncle Alfred, while they were back in East Prussia. Then they fled Germany for good. She had one more child after the return to New Jersey. But little Wilhelm did not live.

My mother left me a small book of stories of her childhood—about begging for food in Williamsburg; about getting felt up by the man who delivered their coal; about her mother who, after the death of her seventh child, traveled to Philadelphia to get an abortion before she had an eighth. *I cannot feed the children I have*, she told her daughter.

Sometimes, Hildegarde said, she would find her father, Emil, in the pigsty in the morning, where he'd fallen asleep the night before, drunk. It was her job, and my aunt Nora's, to haul him out of the sty. Before the pigs ate him.

Finally, he disappeared for good. Years passed. Then, in high school, while Hildegarde was working at a soda fountain, a disheveled man appeared at her counter. *"Hildegart,"* he whispered. *"Ich bin dein Vater."*

He wanted her to go away with him, to Detroit. That's where he was living then, working in an auto body plant.

She never said it to us directly, but my sister and I wonder, sometimes, if our grandfather ever abused our mother, or if he tried to. I asked her about this once, gently, but Mom just looked at me with shining eyes, and said that she didn't want to talk about it.

Years later, when he died homeless on the streets of New York, Aunt Nora and my mother told the city's medical examiner the family didn't want him. Bury him on Hart Island, they said. The city's potter's field.

My mother said that she would never get married, because she thought that men were *Dreck*. It was a promise she kept until she was forty years old, when my father, twelve years her junior, somehow won her heart.

Those years before her marriage, and after she left her own family, were what she later thought of as the happiest years of her life. At last she was away from the farm with the child-abusing coal man, with her father in the pigsty. She moved to Philadelphia and became the manager of the book department in a big retail store, Snellenburg's. She got to meet famous editors and authors. When we were growing up, the house was full of signed books.

There was *Aku-Aku,* signed by Thor Heyerdahl. And *Victory in My Hands* by Harold Russell. This was the memoir of a man who'd lost both of his hands in an accident in World War II, and later went on to win two Oscars for his performance in the 1946 film *The Best Years of Our Lives.* He'd signed it with his hooks.

And then there was *Francis,* a novel about a talking mule. *For Hildegarde Scheffler,* the inscription reads. *Whom Francis says is quite a gal!*

She had, in so many ways, fixed her own life, through force of will, and through her ability, even in that terrible house, to dive into her studies. She'd graduated as the valedictorian of her class, and it was in an adult education class twenty years later that she'd met my father. (It was a class on economics, and my father was the teacher.)

She'd also found the strength to fix her life because she had a profound sense of faith, her certainty that all the suffering she'd been through was not the only thing that life held in store. *These three remain*, she'd say, quoting one of the Scriptures that she knew by heart. *Faith, hope, and love. But the greatest of these is love.*

It astounds me that my mother's response to the abuse and suffering she went through as a child was to become the most loving, forgiving person I ever knew. Of the six siblings who survived, two became alcoholics and one was diagnosed with schizophrenia. My aunt Erna wound up living above a liquor store, playing—with her extremely long fingernails—one of those organs that makes its own percussion. My uncle Roland, the milkman, eventually got out of dairy products and became a night watchman.

My uncle Al died on board one of the trains he'd spent his lifetime riding between the East Coast and the West. The VA sent his ashes to my aunt Erna on a Greyhound bus. "His whole life he was riding freight trains," she said. "Now he comes home by bus!"

Hildegarde put great store in her ability to change the world through force of will, to repair whatever it was that was wrong with her love. I think it broke her heart that she could not fix me. I think it hurt her even more that she had never known how much I hurt.

"I thought you wouldn't love me anymore," I'd said when I came out to her, by way of explaining why I'd kept the facts hidden from her, for all those years.

"But I would never turn my back on my child," she said. "I will always love you, no matter who you are."

It hurt my mother that her love could not now change the situation I'd plunged us all into. Or so she thought. But my mother's love did save me—just not in the way that she had expected. For months after I came out to her, Hildegarde thought that her love would make it possible for me to somehow remain a man.

But it was her love, in the end, that made it possible for me to become a woman.

When I took her out for dinner, on her eighty-fifth birthday, I had said—still apologizing for the fact of my existence—that I was deeply sorry about what I called "the whole woman thing."

"I'm not," she said, and raised her wineglass. "I am so proud of you. I am so proud of my beautiful daughter."

Her love, quite literally, saved my life. But then, this was not the first

time Hildegarde would do just this. There I was, forty years old, drinking
wine with her at the Mile Post Inn. But at that same moment I was also
eight years old, sitting in the back of a Buick, as my mother pressed a
towel down upon the gash in my arm.

*Mom? Am I going to die?*

*No. You're going to be fine.*

At the end of that long week of Zai's surgery and recuperation,
Deedie and I had stood by as she returned, tenderly and tenuously,
to the apartment, where she settled at last into the fold-out couch in
front of the television, ready to spend the next few weeks resting up and
watching *What We Do in the Shadows*. She was guided in this process not
only by her parents and Terry, but by a pair of devoted friends, Caeden
and Merry, as well. After she got settled, I'd spent a few hours reading to
her from *The Princess Bride*, as she fell asleep and woke, and fell asleep
again. She was dressed in loose pajamas. A catheter ran from her nether
parts to a plastic bag. Now and again, the young people who adored her
detached the bag from its tubing and emptied it in the bathroom.

Soon enough it became clear that the young people had things under
control, and Deedie and I prepared to take our leave. Again I found
myself moved by the elastic love and compassion of the new generation.
I wondered what my own life might have been like, if I'd have been surrounded in my youth by the kinds of ambidextrous souls that Zai had
found in hers.

As Deedie and I packed up our bags and prepared to head out, though,
I was left with one lingering wistful thought. I wished that at that moment she needed Deedie and me, her parents, as much as she needed her
friends. But then, I remembered all the Christmases when I'd left my
parents' house after dinner and driven off with my friends, to do bongs or
to go down to the Jersey Shore, or to do god knows what without them.
What had Hildegarde and Dick thought, as I kissed them goodbye at the
Christmas table and jumped into a friend's Camaro? *See ya!*

My father had never seemed bothered. *Goodbye, old man.*

In the end, I guess, it was a sign of health, that there were more important people in Zai's life than her Mommy and her Maddy.

I leaned down to kiss her cheek, softly, and Deedie did the same. "We love you," she said. "Call us if you need us."

"We will," said one of the friends. The television was on. Vampires were making jokes.

"Bye-bye," said Zai.

We walked down the long hallway toward the front door. Deedie put on her coat. We pulled up the handles on our Rollaboard bags.

"You good?" Deedie asked me. I nodded, and then the two old people hugged each other.

"I'm good," I said. I put one hand on the doorknob.

And then, from the other room, Zai screamed.

The scream went on and on. She gasped for breath, and then she screamed some more. Other voices were screaming, too. One of them was saying, *I'm sorry I'm sorry I'm sorry.*

Deedie and I rushed back down the hallway. There was Zai, still on the couch, her friends gathered around her.

The catheter running from Zai's nether parts was gushing with dark blood. One of her friends had leaned in to give Zai a hug, but had somehow tripped and fallen heavily, and bluntly, right on Zai's crotch.

The friend who had fallen got back up on their feet. Then they ran down the hallway and collapsed on the floor, sobbing. *I'm so sorry I'm so sorry I'm so sorry.*

Deedie got down on one knee and held our daughter in her arms. I knelt down by her side.

*Hang on, Flippy. We're coming to save you.*

# SHADOWS

**D**onald Lugar had been on his way to see his therapist. Since they let him out of prison, he'd been trying to be good. But goodness really wasn't his strong suit. "I really don't want to just be turned loose," he told the cops later. "You know, on my own, I don't do very well."

The prison in Utah had paroled him in March of '03, sent him home to Maine to live with his parents in Vassalboro. One day, while he was cruising around, he ended up at a campground. That, he said later, was when *the littlest seed started*. There was a car in the parking lot with a pocketbook in the front seat. He broke in and grabbed it. Then he saw another one.

A week later he tried to burgle a house in Oakland. But then the people who lived there came down the stairs while he was in the living room, and Donald took off. Later, he went back to the same house to try again. But he couldn't find it.

Instead, he wound up on the Rice Rips Road, which leads from Oakland to the Colby College campus. At the bottom of a hill it crosses over the Messalonskee Stream, right at a point where the water is retained by a dam and then sucked through a vast wooden tube into an old hydroelectric plant.

*I found the dam and that's when I decided that would be a good place to do something, if I was gonna do it.*

**M**y cousin MJ led me forward into the dark space, the two of us as naked as newborn sparrows. She and her girlfriends were serious about sauna. How serious were they? They pronounced it *SOW-nuh*.

The sauna was an outbuilding behind her friend Suzi's house in

Lanesville, Massachusetts, a Gloucester neighborhood dotted by quarries and settled by stonecutters from Finland. We'd driven over there from MJ's house in East Gloucester, a comfy old place with hissing radiators and a dog named Emma Woodhouse. We'd checked in at Suzi's house first. A man with a crinkly face was reading a newspaper in front of a woodstove, an enormous German shepherd asleep on the floor by his feet. He nodded at MJ and me, pointed with his thumb toward the gray clapboard structure behind the house, as if to say, *They're out back.*

To get to the sauna we'd driven through Gloucester, a town where, for decades, men and women have taken to sea. As we drove past the bay, I caught a glimpse of a statue of what looked like a woman and her children looking anxiously toward the horizon. There was something haunted about that statue. It scared me, a little.

MJ Boylan is my fourth cousin. We didn't really even know about each other until one day when something I'd written provoked a conversation among the members of her branch of the family. Surely this Jenny Boylan is related to us, isn't she? It's not a common name, at least not around here it's not. So MJ went onto Ancestry.com, and lo and behold, found an entry Sean had made as part of a genealogy project back in middle school. His great-, great-, great-grandfather was Owen Boylan, late of Golden Ball, Dublin. MJ's forebears, for their part, were descended from Owen's brother Murtagh.

And so MJ wrote me an email. *Sorry to bother you, but I think we're related?*

In short order MJ and I were swapping emails back and forth as if we had known each other all our lives. She introduced me to the whole crew: there were nine cousins in all, whom I called the *Nazgûl.* It was remarkable, the overlap between these Boylans and my own: they were producers, musicians, writers, book editors, a poet. My cousin John is Linda Ronstadt's manager and had produced several of her albums. He had produced records by Commander Cody, and the Dillards, and Pure Prairie League, and Charlie Daniels. My cousin Terence, also known as Boona, was a celebrated folk musician; I had owned one of his albums when I was a teenager. My cousin Molly worked for *Sesame Street*; my cousin Anne had been married to the man who'd written "Rubber Duckie."

All of these strangers welcomed me as one of their own, right at the very moment I'd been in mourning for my own extended family. My parents were dead. My sister lived way across the ocean. I hardly ever saw her anymore.

Maybe that was the source of the twinge I felt when I saw that statue gazing out across the waters. Sometimes I felt that way about my sister, I guess.

But now here was all this new family, parachuting into my life. The Nazgûl were full of beans. And, since they'd never known me during the Before times, there was no trouble with anyone stumbling over pronouns, no awkward self-justifications like, *Well, you know I knew you for so long before*. Which I understood, of course, but after twenty years you'd think folks would get the hang of things. It was exhausting, always forgiving, always understanding.

MJ worked for the State, representing public housing authorities, mostly keeping them safe from gangs and thugs, as well as repairing tenancies of people who simply needed patience, understanding, and another chance. The work hadn't made her rich, but it had brought her a sense of having done something good in the world. She was just a little older than me, with salt-and-pepper hair, a pair of big glasses, and a quick and crackling laugh. We called each other 1S1R, short for First Sister, Once Removed.

Now we were naked. It was a long way from Golden Ball, but here we were. *Now I'm in the Land of Liberty, a fig for all me foes!*

MJ led me forward. The place was lit by the dimmest of lights. An iron woodstove crackled in one corner. A woman with a wooden ladle was pouring water from a bucket onto the surface of the stove, sending a hot cloud of thick steam into the air. There were long wooden platforms in the sauna upon which a dozen women of all ages were splayed, oh so naked, like one of those languorous nineteenth-century paintings of *Ladies in the Turkish Bath,* the kind Mycroft Holmes and company surrounded themselves with in the smoking room of the Diogenes Club.

"This is my cousin," MJ said, as we worked our way forward into the steam. "Jenny."

The women called out to me. "Welcome," they said. "We've been waiting for you!"

I knew what they meant, that they'd been waiting for us for like ten or fifteen minutes. But as I settled onto a bench in the hot and languid sauna, I could only think, *Well, I have been waiting for you, too, waiting for you all of my life.*

A woman with shaggy fair hair was at my side. She turned toward me, her breasts heavy and veined and amazing. "Hey girlfriend," said she, with a laugh. *"Welcome to sauna."*

Many years after the murder, Chloe and I walked along the dark banks of the Messalonskee Stream, where Donald Lugar had left the girl's body.

It is worth stating clearly that Donald Lugar isn't his real name, nor is the name I'm using for his victim. I've changed them here in hopes of providing their families a belated veil of privacy, a veil they surely did not have back in the fall of 2003. But you could look it all up if you wanted; those names aren't hard to find. No one who was part of the Colby campus that autumn has ever forgotten those terrifying days, when it seemed absolutely plausible that the murderer might be one of us.

Chloe paused to sniff the air, and to look at me uncertainly. *Are you sure about this?*

Crickets thrummed. On the stream's opposite bank was a Central Maine Power substation. Electricity buzzed in the transformers.

*No,* I told the dog. *I'm not sure about this.*

Ahead of me, at the end of the gravel road, was the old hydro plant. To the right was the decaying wooden tube, held together with metal restraining bands, like a barrel. Water gushed out of it in places where the staves had come loose. I could hear the water dripping onto the earth beneath the pipe, forming a small rivulet of runoff that trickled back toward the stream.

I took a step down the bank, then stopped. Chloe sniffed the air.

I had asked my friend Sam to join me. He'd been one of the detectives back in 2003. But Sam had refused to come. No, he'd said firmly, when I asked. I don't think so.

And so there we were, Chloe and me. The wooden pipeline smelled like creosote and tar.

Before me was a tree where they'd found the hand-drawn sign. On one side was a map.

On the other, the words: *The World Will Never Know.*

I stood there for a long time. At my feet was some trash other trespassers had left—a package of sparklers, an empty can of beer. A blue jay shrieked in a pine tree.

Chloe raised her head. Some of the fur on her back rose up like a mohawk.

"It's okay, girl. It's nothing." I said this as if I were an authority, as if I knew anything.

Why had the detective—my friend—turned down my request for him to accompany me on this trip? Why had he left me to explore this dark place all on my own?

"I know it was sixteen years ago," he'd said. "But I just can't, Jenny. That place—the leaking wooden tube, the dark waters of the stream. Even now I have nightmares about it."

A soft rain fell on the morning of September 16, 2003. The parking lot in back of the Colby dorm was shadowed by tall trees. At 7:20 Dolores Leverdiere walked toward her car—a red 1993 Mercury Sable.

She dropped something as she approached her car, and she bent down to pick it up.

A stranger drew near. It was no one that she knew.

Dolores lived in Anthony-Mitchell-Schupf, a Colby College dorm nestled between the shady parking lot and another dorm called Hillside. One side of the dorm looked out on the sloping hill that led up to the college chapel, which is where I met her, the day our paths crossed.

In those days I struggled with faith, wrestling with my sense of rationality and doubt (on the one hand) and my desire to be what I described, annoyingly, as "an instrument for the love of god" (on the other). I often wandered over to Lorimer Chapel after lunch at Colby, and sat in a pew in prayer, or in meditation. There was a beautiful Steinway concert grand there, too, and if the chapel was empty, I'd sit down on the bench and play.

I'd looked up one morning, and there she was: a young woman sitting quietly in a pew. I felt embarrassed at having played the Steinway while someone was trying to pray. If pressed, maybe I'd have tried to explain that playing the piano was a form of prayer, too. But mostly I just felt ashamed at having intruded on what I assumed was a stranger's hope to have a private moment with god.

I got my purse and my jacket and headed up the aisle. Her eyes were closed, but as I passed the pew she opened them and looked at me. One of her eyes wandered. She had blond hair, parted down the middle.

"I'm sorry," I said, as I walked past.

She didn't say anything back. I wasn't even sure she was looking at me. As far as she was concerned, I might have been a ghost.

A few weeks after Donald Lugar laid eyes upon Dolores Leverdiere in a parking lot at Colby College, I found myself giving a reading at the Odyssey Bookshop in South Hadley, Massachusetts. That night I read from the second chapter of my memoir, the one in which I find myself with my aunt Nora in Surf City, New Jersey, as a hurricane approaches and the island is evacuated. At one point in that chapter I described myself standing on a jetty, looking out at the churning sea, trying to figure out how I'm going to survive my life. I think, *Maybe I could be saved by love?*

I reached the final line of that chapter, in which my aunt turns back to me as we drive away in the storm, and says, *Don't worry, we're going to be safe now.* And right on schedule, my throat had closed up, and the tears rolled down. Then we moved to the dreaded question-and-answer session.

A woman stood up and said, *Listen, I don't really get it. I've suffered my whole life being female, been on the receiving end of threats and violence from men and boys of all kinds. And now, it's like you arrive in my neighborhood by helicopter or something, expecting me to welcome you when just like five minutes ago you were part of the crowd of people making me feel unsafe. Why should I welcome you? What have you ever done to merit inclusion in my world?*

I had tried to explain that I had not arrived in order to take anything away from her. And that, technically speaking, her neighborhood was pretty large, and it did not belong to her alone. Maybe I explained that being trans was a medical condition, at least in part, and that my desire to be whole was not a plan to make her feel unhappy.

I don't really remember what I told her, exactly. It was a long time ago. But what I know is that I went to bed that night thinking about her. It was the first time I'd ever encountered a woman who was hostile to the idea of my transition, who seemed to feel that something about it was unfair.

She was, I know now, my very first TERF (short for trans-exclusionary radical feminist). This is a term coined by the TERFs themselves to refer to a group of left-leaning feminists whose sense of womanhood is essentialist, which is to say, something fixed and innate. People like me, in this view, are like wolves in sheeps' prom dresses. Double agents. Creatures whose struggle to find a sense of peace and wholeness is seen as a threat.

Since then, I've encountered a lot of TERFs, and occasionally tried to open their hearts. You can't be a woman if you can't get pregnant, they say. I point out that lots of women can't get pregnant. You can't be a woman if you've never had a period, they say. I point out that my aunt Erna never had a period. You can't be a woman if you don't have a double X chromosome!, they say. I point out that there are plenty of women who have XXY chromosomes, or other genetic mosaics, or a Y chromosome and never even know it.

They tell young people, *You can't transition because you're just a child, and you need to wait until you're older so you can be sure!* Then, when we're older, they say, *You can't be a woman because you didn't live your whole life as female—it's too late now!*

And so on. They have all kinds of objections to the fact that we exist. But I keep coming back to that thing the woman at the Odyssey said— that she'd spent her life on the receiving end of threats and violence from men and boys. That her experience of womanhood was one of opposition to men, and that this opposition is born from the very real ways in which men can make women feel endangered.

Maybe I'd be reluctant to embrace a trans woman as a sister my own self, if all I knew about trans people was who they once appeared to be, instead of who it is they have become.

But I also wonder if a woman like that would be more likely to think of me as her sister if she knew how often I have been threatened with male violence myself.

If she knew about the time a man followed me home from a bar, tail-gating me, with his bright lights on.

If she knew about the night Lefty jammed his tongue down my throat.

If she knew about the night in Hobart, Tasmania, when I got lost on the way back to my hotel, and I heard the footsteps approaching behind me, getting closer and closer.

Would these stories have made me more female in her eyes?

I suspect not.

But surely there is more to female experience than horror and fear. Is it really so wrong to think that a woman's experience is also about joy, and delight? And sure, some of that joy is about the big stuff: nurturing a child; sharing tears with a friend. But is it so wrong that it might be about the goofy stuff, too? Am I really such a monster if I love eyeliner, and earrings, and Key lime pie?

In the end, what TERFs, and other trans-resistant souls might all have in common is a lack of moral imagination. By which I mean, the ability to con-ceive of what the experience of being human might be like for someone else.

It's possibly the hardest thing about being trans: making cis people understand that your life has been dominated by something that, for them, has never even once been a problem, something that, quite frankly, they've never even heard of. Which is not the same as saying that women, or for that matter, men, are always thrilled with the role that society calls upon them to play. I don't know any woman, or any man, who hasn't occasionally thought that their particular gender has given them a bad deal.

But that's different from wanting to sail across the cruel gender ocean and take up life on the opposite shore. It's a different thing entirely.

The biggest obstacle to trans equality? A lack of imagination.

Donald Lugar was forty-seven. Since he'd turned sixteen he'd spent at least part of every year in prison, jail, or reform school. His record was long: disorderly conduct, larceny, kidnapping, burglary, robbery, automobile theft. He didn't really have a good explanation for it all. *I'm a sick puppy,* he said.

The counseling hadn't helped.

Driving toward his therapist's that morning there had come a moment when he hadn't made the turn toward the highway and the road that led south toward Augusta. Instead, he drove up toward the college, and as he drove he saw the dirt road that ran parallel to the stream and the leaking tube that fed the hydro station. He observed that no one was there. It was raining.

*Then I went to Colby and then I seen the girl.*

One day, early in my own transition, I put on makeup and a wig and a green twinset. I put water balloons in my bra. If you looked real close, you could see nipples poking through. I made those with Advils. And thus bedecked I got into my car and drove to Freeport, Maine, where I spent the day shopping and eating lobster rolls and feeling the cool air upon my stockinged legs.

I was, I can now admit, something of a spectacle.

Would you have been wrong, to have looked upon me then, and concluded, there's a very bookish-looking drag queen?

Late in the day I tried on some jeans in a Gap. As I left the store, I crossed paths with a mother and her young child. The boy looked at me in wonder and confusion. "Mom," he said, urgently. "Mom! What was that?"

The mother did not pause. "That," she said, "was a human being."

It had been raining, Donald Lugar explained later. He drove up to Colby and saw Dolores. He parked his car nearby. She dropped something as she headed to her car. He drew near.

They got in her car. He made her drive down to the hydro dam. Tied her up with her own bra. Then he got a rock and hit her on the head. He dragged her to the water, and then held her face under. There were bubbles at first. Then they stopped.

I had stepped forward into the sauna with my cousin MJ and taken up residence among the dozen or so sisters gathered there. Some of the women's bodies were young and perky. Others had stretch marks, mastectomy scars, age spots. There were a lot of different female experiences in that room. No two of us had traveled the same road to get there.

Finally, when all was said and done, we wrapped ourselves up in towels and got dressed once more. The air outside felt cold against my warm skin. I felt happy and complete. As Tracy Chapman once sang, *I had a feeling I belonged. I had a feeling I could be someone.*

Later, as MJ and I headed out, I saw, through the farmhouse window, that lone man I had seen before, his German shepherd still at his feet. He seemed deep in thought, so much so that he did not look up as the women from the sauna went their separate ways.

It looked to me as if he was thinking over a difficult problem, considering the possibility of one solution, and then another.

I wondered if one of the answers to whatever question he was pondering was the possibility that he might be cured by love.

MJ and I drove through Gloucester, back to her house with the hissing radiators and the dog named Emma Woodhouse. We didn't say anything as we headed home, but we didn't have to. There were lights on little boats out on the ocean. I thought of that movie, *The Perfect Storm,* about a Gloucester swordboat crew. Again I saw that statue, a woman looking out to sea. I thought of my sister, far away in England.

Later I learned that the monument had been built by the Gloucester Fishermen's Wives Association. When it was dedicated, the president of that organization had made a speech. She said, *The memorial serves as a testimonial to what wives, mothers, sisters, and children of fishermen of the world have endured because their men chose to be on the water. They had no choice but to stand on rock, to be on land.*

Chloe the dog and I looked down at the place where Dolores had been murdered. Everything was very still. Then the dog growled, softly.

A car was coming down the dirt road. The engine died, and the driver got out.

I remembered the night they apprehended Donald Lugar. I was in the greenroom of a television show called *207,* a newsmagazine on the NBC affiliate in Portland. On one wall was a monitor showing the live program.

A mug shot appeared on the screen, suddenly, a huge man with a face of burning fury. I knew who it was, and what he had done, even with the sound off.

I was just moments away from stepping in front of the cameras and talking about my book. How I'd gone from male to female with the help of my colleagues and friends. How in the end, just as my mother had foretold, love had prevailed. And love, I was just about to say, can prevail for you, too. You just have to believe in the goodness of humans, and the kindness locked inside each and every soul.

Donald Lugar's face stared out at me from the monitor. *And then I seen the girl.*

Looking at that face I felt a sheer terror I had never known in the times Before. For the first time I understood that, for the rest of my life, I would be at risk for violence, for rape, for murder. Not because I was trans—or not only because I was trans. But because I was female.

The odds of violence on any given day were small, perhaps. And the likeliest outcome was that I would spend my days safely, protected by the community in which I live and the people who love me. Monsters like Donald Lugar are uncommon. You can't spend your life worrying about people like that, any more than you might worry about an asteroid coming through your ceiling and setting your bed on fire.

But Dolores Leverdiere surely thought the same thing. All of us are safe, guarded by our faith and our own good fortune. Right up until the moment you cross paths with a stranger who's been waiting, all this time, for your arrival. *I started toward her and she was still there and there was nobody around, nothing.*

*So, I figured it was a go.*

"Okay, Professor," said the director. "You're on."

Chloe growled again. The stranger started walking toward us.

"Jenny," the stranger said.

I couldn't tell if it was a man or a woman. I felt in my pockets for my keys. I wasn't much of a fighter. But I'd seen people hold a car key in their fist and use it as a weapon. Maybe I could do that, if I had to.

But then, the fog lifted. It was no stranger—it was my friend Sam, the detective. Sam looked different to me—softer, a little careworn.

"I thought you said you couldn't make it," I said.

Sam looked down at the water. "I haven't been here since it happened," he said. "It's still—" He shuddered.

Chloe lay down, put her head on her paws.

"The thing is," Sam said. "I need to talk to you. I need to get this out."

"Okay," I said. "I'm listening."

So Sam told me about the case, remembering what he had seen that day, how it had haunted him in the years since. He talked for a long time, and as he did, I looked at the enormous wooden pipe, bound with staves. Water was leaking out of it, and running into the stream.

"Do you remember that time I pulled you over?" Sam said. "You were speeding."

"You let me off with a warning," I said, remembering. This was years and years ago, in Oakland.

"I was so nervous to meet you," he said. "My heart was pounding."

"Wait," I said. "You were nervous? To meet me?"

"Yeah," Sam said. "Because Jenny—I'm transgender, too."

The words hung between us. The water trickled in the stream.

"I've been on hormones for about a year now. Pretty soon it's going to be impossible to keep hiding."

What could I do, but open my arms and give her a hug?

"I don't know what's going to happen once the word gets out," she said. "I'm going slow. I keep hoping for the best, but—I don't know. People can be—"

"It's going to be okay," I said, but even as I said this I wondered if it was true. The words my aunt had spoken all those years ago came back to me, the ones she'd spoken as she drove us away from the storm. *Don't worry, Jimmy. We're going to be safe now.*

Was I? Were we?

I was walking home from a bar in Hobart, Tasmania, when I heard the footsteps behind me. I stopped and looked down the empty street. But there was no one there.

I'd spent that week as a guest of something called the Dark Mofo Festival. On the opening night there was a barbecue outside a vast bonfire. Whole lambs, skinned of their wool, were roasted on crosses by the flames.

That day I'd given my final reading in a theater downtown, and it had gone well enough. I walked down to the harbor for dinner and sat down at a bar and had a dozen oysters and a martini and a juicy steak and it was all fantastic. But then it was time to head back to the hotel.

I was staying in something called Hadley's Orient Hotel, in a suite of rooms once occupied by Roald Amundsen after he first visited the South Pole. There was a living room with striped wallpaper and a bedchamber with a king-size bed and a balcony that overlooked the city. A bell in a church steeple across the street had pealed the hours.

I thought I knew my way back to the hotel, but somehow, after dinner, I got lost. I had left my phone back at the hotel, so all I had now was a folded-up tourist map. I tried to figure out where I was, but I couldn't see the map in the dark.

The footsteps started again, and I stopped. There was no one else around. A few lights burned from high windows above shuttered shop buildings.

Ahead of me I saw a sign for a pub, but the pub was closed. I peered through the glass. There were empty stools along the bar, levers for the tap covered with dust. A cracked window was sealed up with duct tape.

The footsteps came again. This time I turned and saw the silhouette of a man down the block. He stopped and stood there, waiting.

Bells chimed. The sound came to me from a long way off, as if those bells had rung a whole lifetime ago and only now had reached me, like the light from burned-out stars.

There had been times, back when I was a boy, when I'd walked through a strange city, not sure where I was going. Surely there were even nights when, by accident, I'd wound up trailing some woman I did not know. Had she felt then the thing that I was feeling now?

The stranger drew near, and I wondered, if I turned to look him in the eyes, whether the face I might see was my own.

I started walking faster and faster. My shadow was close behind.

# ROGUES & PIXIES

The night his ship finally returned to America, after one hundred three days at sea, Moynihan had a dream. He and another shipmate were throwing wooden boxes off the stern. Voices were calling. *I face the wind, and stare at the bow,* he wrote later. *If I leave the well-lit stern and go down to the dark deck to the forepeak I will have it. The Voices promise—not nirvana, exactly, but some great awareness, a psychic perception.*

*In the gales, on the bow, in the dark they call, but I am too scared to go.*

He was awakened at this point by two other sailors. "You see, Mate?" one said to the other. "I told you he was asleep in his room." They looked at Moynihan, then at each other.

"We just got a report that you were drowned. The Coast Guard is dragging the river for your body."

They explained: one of the other seamen on the tanker had tried to kill himself by jumping overboard. As the ambulance took him away, he was shouting, "John Monahan is dead. He's drowned!"

In a trembling voice Moynihan then told the men about the dream he'd had, about the voices he'd heard, and resisted.

"That's fucking," said one of them, stunned. "Why that's fucking *psychiatric.*"

Meanwhile, in Middletown, Connecticut, my friend Maeve was taking a college class on Alexander the Great. Everybody had to do an oral report. An anxious young man named Nelson was doing one on the Amazons. Every time Nelson said the word "Amazon," Maeve, sitting in the front row, raised her shirt and flashed her breasts at him, and said *Voop*!

Nelson turned redder, and redder. Sweat trickled down his temples.

"The-the-themiscyra was the name of their city," he said, looking down at his index cards.

"*Wait now,*" asked their professor, one Andrew Szegedy-Maszak. He was sitting in the back row and couldn't see what was happening up front. "Whose city?"

"The—uh. The—"

"Go on, Nelson!"

He closed his eyes. "The Amazons!"

*Voop!*


Film critic Nathan Rabin coined the term "Manic Pixie Dream Girl" to describe a class of female characters whose role in many stories is to release a young man from his troubles by showing him that life can be lived with creativity and imagination. Examples of the Manic Pixie Dream Girl include everyone from Audrey Hepburn in *Breakfast at Tiffany's* (as Holly Golightly) to Diane Keaton (as Annie Hall).

My own favorite version of the MPDG is the Ruth Gordon character in *Harold and Maude*, the seventy-nine-year-old free spirit who shows young Harold (Bud Cort) how life is better than death. Which only goes to show that some Manic Pixie Dream Girls are older than your grandmother.

Criticism of these characters focuses on the fact that these women are really just male fantasies, magical creatures whose primary purpose in a tale is to set a mournful young man free.

But I have known a lot of women who've lived with creativity and invention. They've composed music, published books. Some of them have even raised children. My friend Emily is a professional dancer—even now, into her sixties. My friend Zoe became a singer-songwriter at about the same age. One Sunday morning, I heard one of her songs on WXPN while I was washing dishes.

These women's lives have not revolved around setting anyone free except, perhaps, themselves.

But for women, finding that kind of freedom can sometimes come at a very high price. I think of Amelia Earhart, or Janis Joplin, or Candy

Darling, women whose dreams of fierceness cost them their lives. Often, stories of women like that have a kind of moral judgment built into them, as if the fact that many of these pixies died an early death only proves that defying the laws of the culture is business better left to the menfolk. Amelia Earhart is a beloved, tragic heroine: Joni Mitchell (a pixie in her own right) sang hauntingly of her in the song "Amelia." *Like me, she had a dream to fly . . .*

Once, in speaking about Earhart with a slightly drunken male friend, I heard another conclusion: *You know how Amelia Earhart could have avoided death?* he said. *She could have fuckin' stayed at home.*

Maeve was my friend, and when I think of her now, I like to think of her flashing her breasts at poor Nelson every time he said the word "Amazon." It'd be nice to imagine her immune from the cruel realities that constrict what women can and cannot do. But for Maeve, being a free spirit came at a very high price.

In college she went for a few weeks during her sophomore year when, on principle, she only ate doughnuts and only drank beer. This went on until she finally wound up at the college infirmary. What was wrong with her?

What was wrong with her was *scurvy.*

The doctors said it was the first case of scurvy they'd seen in twenty years. She was embarrassed by this, but to the boys in our circle, it only deepened her legend. Maeve had contracted scurvy, the same disease as *actual pirates.* For what purpose, or for whom, had she contracted scurvy? *She had done it for us.*

Many years later, Gillian Flynn had this to say, in her novel *Gone Girl,* "Men actually think this girl exists. Maybe they're fooled because so many women are willing to pretend to be this girl. For a long time Cool Girl offended me. I used to see men—friends, coworkers, strangers—giddy over these awful pretender women, and I'd want to sit these men down and calmly say: You are not dating a woman, you are dating a woman who has watched too many movies written by socially awkward men who'd like to believe that this kind of woman exists and might kiss them."

I did believe that these women existed, and I did kiss them.

There's a male equivalent to the Manic Pixie Dream Girl—the Rogue, the Scoundrel, the Scallywag. Moynihan was a man like that. Like Pixies, Rogues—like Harrison Ford (as Indiana Jones) or Humphrey Bogart (as pretty much anything)—live outside the rules of the world. They are mavericks and cowboys, bank robbers and pirates. Unlike their female counterparts, they usually get away with their various capers. In fact, the more outrageous their antics, the more we love them.

Errol Flynn, for his part, actually wanted to title his autobiography, *In Like Me!* His editor, George Putnam, said no. Instead, they settled on, *My Wicked, Wicked Ways.*

It's hard to think of many women who've been celebrated—loved, in fact—for their wicked, wicked ways. Mae West, maybe? Madonna? Catherine the Great?

Perhaps what we love most about scoundrels is that we suspect, deep within those strapping chests, what they long for above all is the chance to put the bullwhip down for good. Transformed, as it were, by love.

At the end of the final Indiana Jones movie—the *Dial of Destiny*— seventy-year-old Karen Allen arrives at the apartment of eighty-year-old Harrison Ford. They've separated after the death of their son in Vietnam, but here she is, ready to take care of the old scallywag. She's brought some groceries. His adventures, at long last, appear to be over.

In theory this scene should have rubbed me the wrong way—*Please,* I thought, sitting in the darkened theater, *don't turn Karen Allen into a simpering mommy figure.* After all, her character—Marion Ravenwood— was once something of a pirate her own self, outsmarting Nazis, running her own bar in Nepal.

But there I was with the tears rolling down my face, as I watched them reenact, as an elderly couple, the scene we'd first seen in *Raiders of the Lost Ark*, over forty years earlier. *Where doesn't it hurt?* he asks her, referring to the aches and pains of old age.

She points to her elbow. *Here*, she says, and he kisses her. *Here.*

I thought I was alone. That was how Moynihan liked it, catching you with your guard down.

I was reading *Gargantua and Pantagruel*. I was twenty-one years old, a Wesleyan student, a creature as lissome as a willow tree. *Seeing how sorrow eats you,* Rabelais suggested, *defeats you, I'd rather read about laughing than crying. For laughter makes men human, and courageous.*

Something creaked behind me. I had just enough time to look up from my book when I felt the point of a sword at my throat.

"Avast," said Moynihan.

He was wearing an elaborate costume, kind of a cross between a pirate and one of the three musketeers. He had a hat with a plume, a black cape, a mask.

"What time is it," he said.

I knew what time it was, because when Moynihan snuck up on you, it was always the same. "Time to walk the plank," I said, irritated. It was *always* time to walk the fucking plank.

"This is the map," he said, pulling a scroll out of his jacket. "Trust no one, mate. Not even yourself!" He stuffed the map into my hands, then he went to the window. With a single gesture he threw up the sash. "Look to see me," he said. "No more!"

Moynihan pulled one end of his cape with his hand, and then, with a velvet flourish, jumped out the window.

I lived on the first floor. But still.

I suppose it's important to note that he was the younger son of Senator Daniel Patrick Moynihan, although he'd be irritated with me indeed for mentioning it. His famous father had taken his family around the world—to India when he'd served as ambassador there in the early 1970s; to Manhattan when he'd been the U.S. Ambassador to the United Nations; to Washington when he'd been elected Senator. It was Moynihan, Senior, who'd said, "I don't think there's any point in being Irish if you don't know that the world is going to break your heart eventually. I just thought we'd have a little more time."

My friend, John McCloskey Moynihan, did break my heart eventually.

He was absolutely gorgeous. You'd notice the eyebrows first. They waggled around wickedly, promising trouble. God, he was beautiful.

Even now the world is full of people who traveled in his wake. He was my generation's Neal Cassady, a beloved character who drew people toward him with his charm, then drove them away with his caprice. Like Cassady, he published only one book. It came out posthumously.

When we heard that he was dead, my first thought was that it was one more of his stunts, a piece of theatre he'd brought about in order to bring his many friends together at the graveyard, only to pop out of the coffin like Finnegan in the old Irish ballad, shouting, *Whirl your whiskey around like blazes, Thundering Jesus do you think I'm dead?*

But he was.

A couple years after I graduated from college I arrived in Boston to visit him. I woke up in the apartment one morning to find Moynihan standing by my bed, holding a bottle of India Pale Ale. "Breakfast of Champions," he said, and handed it to me. Alas, there was LSD rubbed generously around the rim. Of course there was. An hour or so later the whole world was made of softly pulsing rubber. Yellow lines floated and expanded on the floor, like ripples on a pond.

"Okay, matey," Moynihan said. "Now we gotta explore the world."

*"Werp,"* I said, like tape running backward in a reel-to-reel. Sure, I was ready to explore the world. Moynihan gave me a piece of paper.

"Here's your first clue," he said. It appeared as if we were going on a scavenger hunt.

The first clue instructed me to beware of falling glass, and to look for a frozen man. I didn't know exactly what this meant, but falling glass, in the Boston of that day, meant the Hancock Tower, whose windowpanes had become famous for blowing out of their sashes in high winds and shattering on the sidewalk.

We got ourselves to Copley Square, where a statue of John Singleton Copley sat frozen on his pedestal. Pasted to the side of the pedestal was the next clue, which, once deciphered, sent me on to Old North Church. From there I was off to the Federal Reserve Building down by the harbor. And so on. Hours passed in this manner, finding clues, deciphering them, heading off to the next incomprehensible destination. In some ways it was a little bit like grad school.

In a Cambridge bar, the Plough and Stars, we were joined by another half dozen friends. It was a big crowd by now—struggling musicians, struggling illustrators, struggling journalists. We drank a couple pints of Guinness and Moynihan told some dirty jokes and we sang some songs and the *craic* was good. I kept hoping Maeve would show up, but there was no sign of her. I'd heard that she'd spent a while in McLean, the psychiatric hospital Susanna Kaysen wrote about in *Girl, Interrupted*. I'd lost touch with her after that. I hoped she was okay, wherever she was. It made me feel bad, that being a spirit of wildness and invention seemed to have nearly broken her in two.

After a while I went to the restroom in the bar. There I found another clue, written in marker above the john.

In short order we were off to the old Granary Burying Ground, and the grave of Mother Goose. Her headstone had an ornate skull etched into the top. It was a creepy boneyard, as these things go, but it was also full of celebrities: Paul Revere, Samuel Adams, John Hancock.

The clue at Mother Goose's grave directed me back to the street— where a car was waiting. Moynihan's girlfriend Sarah was behind the wheel. "Now," she said, "we're off to Walden Pond." The others followed in a half dozen vehicles of their own.

The drive to Concord took at least a half hour, maybe more. When we got there, the dozen of us did what to us seemed like the only logical thing, which was to take off all our clothes and dive into its peaceful waters.

Thoreau called Walden Pond—and lakes like it—"the landscape's

most beautiful and expressive feature. It is earth's eye; looking into which
the beholder measures the depth of his own nature. The fluviatile trees
next to the shore are the slender eyelashes which fringe it, and the wooded
hill and cliffs around are its overhanging brows."

I did not know whether I was gazing into the pond, or being gazed
upon by it, when I got naked. The main thing that surprises me, looking back, is that we were so cavalier about stripping, not only because
I hated being naked but even more so because Walden is not exactly
an unpopulated public space. Were we just unaware of the likelihood
we'd be busted in the altogether? Was it that we just didn't care? I don't
know.

My friends were better swimmers than I was, though, and before we
reached the midpoint of Walden's waters, they were swimming away from
me. They were all on drugs, too, of course—but it still hurt my feelings,
being left by those I loved to die.

My heart pounded. My feet felt like Smithfield hams. I was short of
breath. I got a mouthful of water, coughed, flailed a little bit. Did my
whole life pass before my eyes? Maybe. What I remember most clearly is
being scared.

My head sank beneath the surface, and again I choked on a throatful
of the sweet and peaceful water.

Then there was a woman next to me in the water. *James*, said Maeve.

Where had she come from? She hadn't been part of the scavenger
hunt. She was naked, too.

I stopped thrashing. The two of us treaded water for a little bit.

"*Werp?*" I said, my voice full of tears.

She looked at me with love. *Werp*, she said, and looked back at me
with my own sad eyes.

Just like that, I was her, and she was me.

"You're going to be all right," I told the sad young man before me.
For a few terrifying seconds, I was a Cool Girl, treading water. It was a
lot harder than it looked. For the first time it struck me how very hard it
was for her to live in this world.

I also remember that having breasts wasn't that big a deal. In my pre-transition days, I'd thought it'd be amazing, having them. But they weren't amazing, not really. They were just a fact.

Moynihan would call Deedie and me on the phone, every year, on Halloween. Sometimes, we'd hear his voice—he always introduced himself as "Agent 46"—as he gave us complex instructions on executing *Plan XK-7*. Other times, he'd play a recording of William Shatner singing Elton John's "Rocket Man." (He loved William Shatner, in the same way that other people love the Beatles.)

But the Halloween after I came out as trans, in 2002, he just wanted to talk. I'd felt self-conscious telling him the news of my unveiling, perhaps because he always had a short fuse for anything that felt like malarkey, and in those days, what other word would most people have used to describe my condition? No one knew anything.

I was afraid he'd think, as the Irish say of a rugby player who's allowed a score against the team, that I'd *let down the side*.

But Moynihan would have none of this. I told him that I'd lost a few friends in the wake, and that I was sorry I hadn't told him the truth years ago. "Listen, Boylan," he said, in as unironic a voice as I ever heard him use. "Anyone who has a problem with you now, isn't your friend."

There are lots of parts of the story I don't know. There was a marriage to a girl from Alabama, followed by a divorce. There was a stint at film school at NYU. And then he was in Balmain East, Australia, a place that seemed to have provided him with the sense of solace he'd been searching for, but about which it was impossible not to wonder: What? Why *there*, for fuck's sake?

It hurt my feelings that he'd found his peace in a place so far away, a place that did not include any of the friends of his youth.

But who was I to object? It seemed as if all I could say in the end was, *Anyone who has a problem with you being Australian isn't your friend.*

My friend Beck was the one who told me he was dead. It happened in Key West. He'd been in love with a zookeeper, but his love was unrequited.

Tylenol poisoning was the story we got.

Later, there was an elaborate memorial service that took place in the Rainbow Room at Rockefeller Center. John's father, Daniel Patrick, had died just months before. John's brother, Gus, stood at a podium and said, *Well, it hasn't been a very good year for the Moynihan family.*

John's sister, Maura Moynihan, was dressed all in white. She closed the program with a few words, and then introduced the piece of music that "she knew John would want played in his memory."

From the speakers came the opening chords of The Who's "Baba O'Riley." *Don't cry. Don't raise your eye. It's only teenage wasteland.*

In 2014, I gave a reading in New Hampshire for a community group that supported LGBTQ youth. In the audience at the reading were a number of young trans and nonbinary people. It still amazes me, to gaze upon those young faces. What would my own life have been like, I wonder, if I'd had the courage to come out at twenty? Or fifteen? Or ten?

It's a trap, though, to fall into this kind of subjunctive thinking. Is there really any point in trying to live your life backward? I had come out when I could—at age forty, in fact. I know this means that some of my life was wasted in sorrow, but on the other hand, being a boy was not only about sorrow. There were times when it was pretty fun. But even on the best days, manhood was always something I had to sustain through an act of will. Womanhood, now that I have crossed the valley, is simply there; the strangest thing about finally being myself is how little time I spend now thinking about what a miracle it is to be female at last. Maybe I ought to, but I don't. In the morning I just open my eyes, and shake off my dreams. Then I put my feet upon the floor.

As I looked out into the audience that night, I saw a familiar face. It had been a long time, but she still had those apple cheeks, the look of mischief in her eyes.

In the morning, Maeve and I sat down by the quiet waters of a lake in New Hampshire with *kpanlogos*, a pair of African drums bedecked with beads.

Incredibly, there was an abandoned steamboat moored in the lake right by the place we'd chosen to drum. I don't know if it was just berthed there because it was the offseason, or if this was its final resting place, or what.

It was hard not to think, as I gazed upon the pilothouse of the wreck, of the *Walter Scott* in *Huck Finn,* the boat upon which Jim and Huck discover the corpse of Huck's father—even though it's not for several hundred pages that Jim finally reveals the dead man's identity.

I suppose I will always be drawn to stories like that, tales in which someone's secret self is kept hidden until the moment when it is at last safe to reveal the truth.

I'm not all that good at drumming, to be honest, because in spite of being a very entertaining personality, I don't have a very good sense of rhythm. As I drummed away, under Maeve's instruction, I saw her wince a little bit, every time I missed a beat. Was it possible, there in my fifties, for me to finally learn how to keep time?

I hoped that my old friend did not miss the person I once was. Just as Jim said to Huck, concerning his father, *He ain't comin' back, Huck.*

But then the person that she had been was gone, too.

There we sat by the peaceful waters, drumming on our drums. I closed my eyes. When I opened them again, I'd return to the present, to the wrecked steamboat and the fallen world in which we had become two older women. But for a moment longer I kept my eyes closed, and there we were: two young people in love and in trouble, swimming across the waters of Walden Pond. It seemed like a long time ago.

I had read *Walden* when I was in high school, but I don't remember it having any particular impact upon me. Maybe I had to wait until I was an older person, before I really understood exactly how hard it is to live outside the law.

Or maybe it's that my own idea of freedom had taken me in the opposite direction from the woods at Walden Pond. I had hoped to build a temple. But I was going to do it in New York.

*I went to the city because I wished to live recklessly, to front the nonessential facts of life, and see if I could not defy what I knew to be most true, and not, when it came to live, discover that I had never tried to die.*

It was in the waters of Walden Pond that I had been saved from death by Maeve. Not because she was a Manic Pixie Dream Girl, but because she was so profoundly real. I had seen, through her eyes, that being the kind of woman I had imagined I might become was no easy thing. I had seen that womanhood would come with its own burdens, and that bearing these burdens, for a free spirit, might be unsustainable. That it might crush me, just as it had nearly crushed her. That it might even take my life, just as it had nearly taken hers.

But with a little luck, love might well prevail.

She laughed, and started drumming again. I remembered that laugh from when we were young. It was a clear and joyful sound.

It made me so glad to be alive at that moment, female and unfettered. I was glad for every mountain I had ever climbed, glad for every one I had since descended.

I'd spent so many years when I was young trying to learn how to become a writer. But maybe, during those hard days, I was writing something other than stories. Maybe the thing I was writing was really my own body, trying, paragraph by paragraph, to transform my flesh.

"Every man is the builder of a temple," writes Thoreau, "called his body, to the god he worships, after a style purely his own, nor can he get off by hammering marble instead. We are all sculptors and painters, and our material is our own flesh and blood and bones."

*Voop!*

The night before I married Deedie there had been a rehearsal, and then the rehearsal dinner, and then a party at the National Aquarium, where we held forth among the penguins and the jellyfish.

Finally, there was a late-night debrief thrown by Moynihan, at his parents' house on Capitol Hill. We stayed up all night, forty or fifty of us, dancing and drinking and telling stories. As they say in Ireland, *the craic was ninety.*

Sometime toward daybreak, twisted on the drink, we found ourselves outside, my old friend and me. Moynihan was wearing some sort of English vicar's costume, with long black tails and a minister's collar. I was still in my suit from the rehearsal dinner, a wilted boutonniere on my lapel.

"Good on ya, Boylan," he said, raising those crazy eyebrows. "Ya figured it out, haven't ya."

But he looked off into the distance as he said this, and his voice sounded wistful, as if for once I had the advantage. He'd always been a little in love with Deedie his own self. Perhaps he felt it was slightly unfair that I'd stolen the woman he'd hoped might someday save him from the wicked, wicked ways of his own.

Deedie and Moynihan had met in a Capitol Hill bar, in fact, the week after she and I were engaged. *All these years, I was in love with you,* he said. *All these years I was going out with Sarah. Now, I'm finally single! And you're marrying Boylan!*

There he was, earthbound. Against all odds, I was the one transformed by love.

That was the last time I saw him. I threw up the sash, and jumped out the bedroom window with my sword. *Look to see me*, I said, *no more.*

# THE HEISENBERG VARIATIONS

## 1. Aria

Hermann Karl von Keyserling, for whom J. S. Bach wrote the *Goldberg Variations,* was once described as "a cheerful man of sin, [who] kept a harem of ladies, had 354 bastards, whose chief mistress was a daughter, and died drunk." It's also said that he had trouble sleeping at night. Which is understandable, if you have 354 bastards. That's just eleven bastards short of one bastard for every day of the year.

You can imagine the Count tossing and turning at night, wondering which bastard was going to show up next.

## 2. Allegro

Being a Count, Keyserling had his own live-in harpsichordist, in the same way that a wealthy person in the twenty-first century might have a nanny, or dog walker, or someone whose sole responsibility is operating the juice machine.

I've never longed for my own harpsichordist, but in thinking about it now I suppose it would be nice. That way, if I wound up with any middle-of-the-night harpsichord emergencies, I'd be covered.

What was the name of Count Keyserling's live-in harpsichordist? Johann Gottlieb Goldberg. How old was Johann when he first played the *Goldberg Variations* for Count Keyserling? He was fourteen.

The best-known version, of course, is the 1955 rendition by Glenn Gould. How old was Glenn Gould when he recorded the piece that catapulted him to stardom? He was twenty-two.

### 3. Largo

I cannot say with any certainty that I have a full understanding of the *Goldberg Variations*, or anything by Bach, for that matter. I know that there are people whose musical education enables them to see deeply into the piece's mathematical forms; I've been told that every third variation is a *canon*, and that others are *fughettas* and *Baroque dances* and *French overtures* and even something called a *quodlibet*—but to be honest most of that is lost on me. Mostly I just love the sound of it. Some of that music is mournful, some of it is exuberant. But all of it is pretty.

What I *do* understand is that the piece starts out with its *aria*, the main theme, and then that theme *transitions* over the course of its many variations. By the time we hear the main aria again, at piece's end, that music sounds different, even though it's identical to what we heard at the piece's opening.

Sometimes I long to attempt a musical stunt like that upon the page, repeating a paragraph at the end of an essay, for instance, in hopes that by the time my reader encounters it a second time, she might see how things have changed.

### 4. Pizzicato

The Heisenberg uncertainty principle comes from quantum physics. Dumbed down for popular culture, the principle suggests, in a general way, that the act of observing something changes the thing being observed. It's a handy way of describing the difficulties in knowing anything for certain. On the page, the Heisenberg uncertainty principle describes the impossibility of experiencing your work the way a reader does. By which I mean to say, that if you take your work through six or seven drafts, and you've read it, say, a hundred times, it is impossible for you to know what it will be like for someone to read your work for the first time.

The principle also describes the difficulty of knowing which self is our truest one. If we stare into the mirror long enough, our own faces become strange. I remember being a teenager, high on multiple bong hits, and staring at my reflection for so long that I no longer recognized the thing that I saw there as me. Which sounds like just another Amazing Drug Tale, except for the fact that in this I was not wrong. The person I saw there *wasn't* me, not by a long shot.

I would spend many of the years that followed resorting to one desperate measure after another, in the hope—always monstrously improbable—that one day, when I looked into a mirror, I might actually see my face.

## 5. Andante

Back in kindergarten, my teacher, Mrs. Bassoon, read us stories. One of them was *The Marvelous Land of Oz*, by L. Frank Baum, the second in the series of Oz books. That story tells the tale of Tip, a boy raised by an enchantress named Mombi. Tip also has a friend named Pumpkinhead, a melon whom he has accidentally brought to life, and who considers Tip his father. Late in the book, we learn that Tip is not really himself. He is really Princess Ozma, who had been transformed into a boy at childhood in order to protect her from her demons. "That," says Mombi, pointing at Tip, "is the rightful ruler of Emerald City!"

Tip can't quite get his head around this. *Seriously*, he thinks, *I'm supposed to be a girl?* "You are not a girl just now," Glinda explains gently, "because Mombi transformed you into a boy, but you were born a girl, and also a Princess; so you must resume your proper form, that you may become Queen of the Emerald City."

Tip isn't sure about this at first. He is afraid he'll miss his friends. But the Scarecrow and the Tin Woodman are good sports about it. "Never mind, old chap," says the Tin Woodman. "It don't hurt to be a girl, I'm told; and we will all remain your faithful friends just the same."

So Tip agrees to give it a go. A royal couch is piled high with rose-colored silk cushions. A curtain is suspended on a golden railing to provide Tip with some privacy. It has many folds of pink gossamer.

Tip drinks a poison which sends him into a deep and dreamless sleep. Then Mombi the Witch draws herbs from her bosom and makes a fire from them. She scatters a handful of magical powder over the fire, which gives off a violet vapor.

Then she chants a poem, seven times. At the end of this, she cries the word: "Yeowa!"

*From the couch arose the form of a young girl, fresh and beautiful as a May morning. Her eyes sparkled as two diamonds, and her lips were tinted like tourmaline. All adown her back floated tresses of ruddy gold, with a slender jeweled circlet confining them at the brow. Her robes of silken gauze floated around her like a cloud, and dainty satin slippers shod her feet.*

Ozma looks at her friends. They all bow before her. "I hope none of you will care less for me than you did before," she says. "I'm just the same Tip, you know; only—only—"

"Only you're different!" says the Pumpkinhead.

After she read us the story, Mrs. Bassoon sent us all into the playground to blow off a little steam. The girls jumped rope and sang a song. The boys wrestled on the blacktop. But Mrs. Bassoon found me by myself, looking at the pages of the book. "Why Jimmy," she said. "Don't you want to play?"

I just nodded and went outside onto the blacktop. I stood by the sliding board, watching the boys descend. There was a big pileup at the bottom of the slide, a wriggling meatball of arms and legs.

I looked back at the door to the kindergarten. Mrs. Bassoon was standing in the door looking at me, the book still in one hand.

Not far away were the girls, jumping rope. They sang, *Down in the valley where the green grass grows, there sat Janey, sweet as a rose.*

Up and down they went, rising and falling, the sweet voices all around.

## 6. Espressivo

The Ship of Theseus is a classic philosophical puzzle about revisions, and reinventions, and pentimenti. Imagine for a moment that Theseus, the great mariner, has a ship called the *Argo*. As the years go by, he repairs the *Argo* while he's in port—replacing the sails when they tear, the masts when they break, the boards on the deck when they warp. At some point, everything on the ship has been replaced, raising the question: *Is this the same ship?* If you want to get tricky, you can raise the complication introduced by Thomas Hobbes, who asked, What if all of the old pieces taken off the original ship were saved, and then reassembled, so that now, after ten years, there are two ships—one made of all the original pieces, and one which is all new, which Theseus sails. In this version of the puzzle, the question is *Which of these two is the true ship of Theseus? Which one is authentic? Which one is* for reals?

There are lots of approaches to this puzzle, many of them pointing out the difference between an object and the material it is made out of; there's another theory which divides all objects into three-dimensional time slices which are temporally distinct. Noam Chomsky even has a solution to the paradox which involves cognitive science, which suggests that the ship is not a Thing but an organizational structure that has perceptual continuity.

These solutions to the puzzle are more concerned with the question of what the ship actually is than the question of authenticity, I think. But if I were asked to cut to the chase, I'd say that the true ship of Theseus is the ship that Theseus sails.

It's like the story of the old New England farmer, who says, *I've got the world's best shovel! It's guaranteed to last forever! I've replaced the blade twice and the handle three times. Great shovel. Lasts forever.*

In 1992, when I taught for a semester at Wesleyan University, one of my students was a young writer named Maggie Nelson; in that class I'd spoken about the Ship of Theseus puzzle, and the way it models the uncertainty writers experience in revision. A few years later she wrote a brilliant book about queer lives entitled *The Argonauts*. In it, Maggie compares the person who says *I love you* to a sailor on board the *Argo*, in that each time we utter these words we have become someone new, someone changed by time.

Many years later I told Maggie I was proud that I'd introduced her to the concept that gave her book its name. "Yeah, listen, Jenny," she said. "I actually got that from Roland Barthes."

Maggie's relationship with her lover, Harry—at least as described in *The Argonauts*—doesn't have much in common with the one that Deedie and I share, except, perhaps, for the love at its center. That, as well as the difficulty other people seem to have in finding language to describe it. Harry, for his part, seems to delight in that very elusiveness. "Once you name something," he says, "you can never see it the same way again."

## 7. Lamentoso

For writers the question becomes, Which is the true draft of Theseus? The first one, that came fresh from our brains? Or the next one, the draft you arrived at after repeated readings, after the workshops, after all the ways we go about looking at our work and reconsidering it over time? Is that the draft that "Theseus sails"?

Is the revised version of a creative work always the most "authentic" version of the work? What do we do with the fact that all those repeated readings and reconsiderations of a story sometimes make us blind to what we've made? Is it possible that there's a very particular kind of uncertainty that challenges writers—that the more time you spend Heisenberging your story, the less you're able to actually improve that work, because all your effort makes it impossible to see it clearly?

It is a harrowing truth for artists that sometimes, when you try with all your heart to make things better, you wind up making them a thousand times worse.

I know trans men and trans women, too, whose revised selves, and revised lives, fall well short of their hopes.

And yet, even for those who lose everything—families, jobs, marriages, children, homes—even among these, I don't know a single soul who regrets the transition. Because of course it wasn't the transition itself that disappointed them; it was all those friends and lovers who, at the moment they were most needed, closed their hearts and vanished.

## 8. Forte

In my late twenties I arrived at the Writing Seminars at Johns Hopkins University bearing a box of books, a Kaypro word processor, and a long blond wig I kept hidden in a box in the closet.

We were encouraged to call our professor, John Barth, by his nickname, Jack, but I couldn't imagine doing this any more than I might imagine addressing Jorge Luis Borges as "Louie." The high-water mark of maximalism in American literature had come and gone by the fall of 1985; by then my peers mostly dreamed of becoming Raymond Carver, or Ann Beattie, perhaps. Still, Barth remained right up there with Borges, Pynchon, or Calvino: postmodern authors whose work combined parody, self-consciousness, and the sense that a novel might be, among other things, a comment upon itself.

In one class, Jack unveiled his theory of plot: "the gradual perturbation of an unstable homeostatic system and its catastrophic restoration to a new and complexified equilibrium." He liked drawing a parallel between the structure of dramatic action and several other things: a wave upon the beach, a piece of music, a love affair. I can see his big round head even now, smiling wickedly at me, saying, "There's a reason they call it a 'climax,' Boylan."

That year I lived a double life—female out of the classroom, male when I was on campus.

It was a complexified equilibrium, all right. In Professor John Irwin's class we studied Poe and Borges, and a literary phenomenon he described as the *mutually constitutive bipolar opposition of spectral doubles*. Most of my peers lived in terror of Professor Irwin, but I adored him, in part because he was so nuts.

That was the year I was writing my novel *The Invisible Woman*. It was meant to be Barthian in its comic self-referentiality, but in the end it turned out to be Boylanesque: a tale of a woman who had to keep herself hidden, lest the unforgiving world discover her identity. It would take me years to understand the obvious: I wasn't writing a novel, but a memoir, and the woman in hiding I was describing was, of course, myself.

It wasn't a very good novel, but Barth shepherded me through it anyway, using his abundant gifts of erudition and love. I learned a lot about writing from him, to be sure, but even more, I learned about revision. Given that survival in the world is so often about learning how to successfully "rewrite" our own selves, it may be that in the end Barth taught me less about creating fiction than how to invent myself.

It was a skill that, in years to come, would quite literally save my life. The following spring I found myself at the edge of a cliff in Nova Scotia, staring down at the waters of the North Atlantic, preparing to step off the edge and end this transgender business once and for all. Instead, I was blown back onto the soft moss by a fierce wind. I lay there staring up at the sky. I heard a voice in my heart, something that whispered, *You're going to be all right. What you imagine right now to be your unsolvable problem will one day come to be your greatest gift.*

I've imagined possibilities for who that voice might have belonged to: my guardian angel, the ghost of my father, even the specter of my future self, traveling back in time to let me know that the pain I bore was not permanent.

But those, too, might just be first drafts. Maybe the voice that spoke to me then was that of John Barth: my mentor, and my teacher, and my friend.

He did not think that he was in the business of saving lives when he told me about the *catastrophic restoration to a new and complexified equilibrium.*

But he saved mine.

## 9. Adagio

On the fortieth anniversary of the founding of Hopkins's Writing Seminars, the university staged a formal reading by the program's professors. That was the first time I heard Jack read the story entitled "Night-Sea Journey," a tale narrated by a sperm, of all things. Of course, the voice of a sperm was perhaps the last narrator I was concerned with, given the nighttime journey that I was then undertaking in the streets of Baltimore. But there still was plenty in that narrative that spoke to me, not least the part that goes, *"I've begun to believe, not only that She exists, but that She lies not far ahead, and stills the sea, and draws me Herward! Aghast, I recollect his maddest notion: that our destination (which existed, mind, in but one night-sea out of hundreds and thousands) was no Shore, as commonly conceived, but a mysterious being, indescribable except by paradox and vaguest figure: wholly different from us swimmers, yet our complement; the death of us, yet our salvation and resurrection; simultaneously our journey's end, mid-point, and commencement; not membered and thrashing like us, but a motionless or hugely gliding sphere of unimaginable dimension; self-contained, yet dependent absolutely, in some wise, upon the chance (always monstrously improbable) that one of us will survive the night-sea journey and reach . . . Her!"*

I did reach *Her* in the end. Somehow I found the very thing the narrator of "Night-Sea Journey" tries to forswear at its conclusion, the unrefusable summons of *"'Love! Love! Love!'"*

Since then, I have carried my old teacher within me in the classrooms of the places where I've taught—at Colby College, and at University College Cork, in Ireland, and even at Wesleyan, where I (allegedly) taught Maggie Nelson about the Argonauts. I have thought about him frequently, as I've tried to respond to my own students' work with the love and grace he had once modeled. Right up until his death in spring of 2024 we would exchange these lovely emails, each of his full of the old familiar linguistic pyrotechnics. As he got older and frailer, those notes got shorter. But they almost always concluded with his signature catchphrase, *On with the story!*

I've graduated authors of my own now, a whole generation of them, and some of them, in turn, have gone on to become teachers. These students, tens of thousands of them now across the country in classes taught by the thousands of writers and professors trained by Barth, these are Jack's grand-students, and he their grand-teacher.

I wasn't sure how Jack would react to the news of my transformation. While I thought of him (or at least his characters) as sexually adventurous, transgender issues in those days were still seen as exotic and inscrutable, even by the liberal and openhearted. At last, one day I got a lovely little email, in response to my memoir *She's Not There*. He wrote, "I should say she is very much there, Boylan—or should I say, Girl-land?"

*Yeowa!*

## 10. Diminuendo

In 1981, at the age of forty-nine, Gould returned to the *Goldberg Variations*. He said, of at least one of the variations he had recorded in his youth, that he could no longer recognize the person who had played it. And so, he played it again, his most famous piece, not the breakneck, perhaps show-offy version of a twenty-two-year-old, but with the cares and losses of a man approaching old age. It's the same piece, except it's wholly differ-ent: the same notes, indeed. But with an entirely different meaning, the precocious attitude of his younger self now superseded by a performance dripping with autumnal wisdom.

*"I hope none of you will care less for me than you did before,"* says Ozma. *"I'm just the same Tip, you know; only—only—"*

*"Only you're different!"* says the Pumpkinhead.

Gould died less than a year later, at the age of fifty.

## 11. Presto

In the late 2000s, Colby gave Jack Barth an honorary degree. And there we were, after all those years, together again—teacher and student, writer and writer. At a celebratory dinner the night before commencement, Jack addressed the Colby faculty, and part of his address concerned thinking of our lives as stories, the very process that had saved me, both in and out of the classroom, half a lifetime before. Reviewing his definition of plot he said, "It's—all together now, Boylan—the gradual perturbation of an unstable homeostatic system and its catastrophic restoration to a new and complexified equilibrium."

I said it word for word along with Barth. I closed my eyes and for a short, strange moment, there I was: a student again, still young, all the triumph and turmoil of life still far ahead.

He returned to the table from the podium and embraced me. "Nicely

done, Jack," I said. He replied, "Nicely done yourself, Girl-land." I should
have just let go of him then, let him return to his chair. But instead I held
him in my arms just a little bit longer, that great, kind genius of American
literature, and thought—well, what else?

*Love! Love! Love!*

## 12. Aria da Capo

Hermann Karl von Keyserling, for whom J. S. Bach wrote the *Goldberg
Variations,* was once described as "a cheerful man of sin, [who] kept a harem of ladies, had 354 bastards, whose chief mistress was a daughter, and
died drunk." It's also said that he had trouble sleeping at night. Which is
understandable, if you have 354 bastards. That's just eleven bastards short
of one bastard for every day of the year.

You can imagine the Count tossing and turning at night, wondering
which bastard was going to show up next.

# LIMINALITY

In May of 2017 I woke from a dream in which I was co-authoring a book with Jodi Picoult, a writer whom I had never met and did not know. In the dream there were two voices: a young trans woman who had been murdered and the mother of her boyfriend, who was suspected of the crime. I vaguely remember that the question of the book (in the dream) was the degree to which we can trust the people we love, whether it's possible to ever really know another soul, no matter how much you love them.

I woke up feeling more than a little disturbed. It was May, and the semester at Barnard had just finished up. I made my way to the kitchen and made coffee. As it brewed I thought about the dream some more. I thought, *Jeez, that's pretty specific.* Usually my dreams are about being lost in an infinite grocery store, or fighting a giant squid at the airport. Once, in fact, I had dreamed that I came home to find my wife in bed with Tony the Tiger. The two of them were smoking cigarettes. I said, *Deedie, what's the meaning of this.* She just replied, *What can I say, honey? He's gr-rr-rr-rr-eat!* I woke up laughing.

I got back in bed and did my morning routine—a quick glimpse at my email inbox; an inspection of the latest on Facebook. People I had known in elementary school had posted photographs of their dinners.

Then I went to Twitter, where I tweeted out: *I just dreamed I was co-authoring a book with Jodi Picoult!*

Meanwhile, in a farmhouse in New Hampshire, Jodi was online and reading Twitter her own self. Seeing my tweet, she responded: *What was this book about?*

I told her.

Moments later she wrote me back: *OMG. Let's do it!*

I replied, *You nut. We have everything but the plot.*

I've been a writer for almost all my life, and a published one for thirty-five years now, almost exactly the same amount of time I've been teaching in various creative writing programs at colleges from Cork, Ireland, to New York City. Whether my writing has changed as I morphed from male to female is probably not for me to say, although the process I go through is surely different now. As a teacher, I can affirm that when I was young and funny my students had an instant sense of connection to me—a sense of connection with my readers that eluded me, sometimes, upon the page. Back then I was, after all, no more than a decade older than most of my students, and there was the unspoken sense, I think, that they and I were in the same generation; we mostly liked the same music, the same movies, and so on. Little by little, though, I went from being something like an older brother to my students to an eccentric uncle. And then an eccentric aunt. And then—well, let's just say that an older teacher has to work harder than a younger one. You can't rely on generational solidarity as a pedagogical skill; you actually have to rely on your own scholarship and wisdom.

Which is the thing I don't have.

In my days as a man, I would perform a Barthian lecture on, say, the structure of dramatic action. "It's the gradual perturbation of an unstable homeostatic system and its catastrophic restoration to a new and complexified equilibrium!" I'd explain, using my mentor's mind-bending definition of plot. My students would write my words down in their notebooks. Meanwhile, when I told a joke, or did something just to make them laugh (one time for no apparent reason I made waffles in class), students smiled, or at the very least shook their heads like, *Thou art a real nut.*

Later, *en femme*, these same lectures were often met with—well, if not blank stares exactly, then skepticism. It was much more common for a student to push back on something I had said, echoing in their own way the words of the moving man who'd taken my things to New York when I first got that job. *Listen, are you sure about this, Prof?*

In a way, it was good that my students felt more at ease interrogating what I was saying now; that showed that they were, at the very least, more engaged with the class than when they just blindly wrote everything down without question. But it was clear enough that as a woman I was no longer an authority figure to these students. They still seemed to have a great deal of affection for me. But I was no longer scary.

Although I had been protected by the love and respect (mostly) of my colleagues at Colby, one thing that I was not protected by was tenure. Deans and chairs and things would explain that the reason I was un-tenurable was because I didn't have a "line," although whenever they started up with this, the only thing I could think of was cocaine. What was a "line"? It was this invisible thing that had failed to have been be-stowed upon my job before I even took it. It was like I'd been born, pro-fessionally, with a clubfoot. The only way to get a *line*, dean after dean at Colby wearily explained, was for me to go and get a tenure-track job somewhere else, and then bring the offer to them, sort of like bringing the recently scorched broomstick of the Wicked Witch back to show the wizard, to prove you were "worthy of the request."

When in 2014 I finally did this, bringing Barnard's offer to Colby's dean, she simply looked at the piece of paper and said, *Gee, you should take this job!*

I was probably set on leaving the school in any case by that point, but it would have been nice, at the very least, if she'd started sobbing into her hands and rending her garments first. It was sad. I hated to leave Colby. I loved that college. I was pretty sure that, whatever Barnard and New York City held for me, I'd never have the same sense of community ever again.

Not that the job at Barnard came with tenure, either. The president of the college, as I explained earlier, had invented a job for me more or less out of K-Y Jelly and marzipan, and in order to foist me on the faculty, she'd had to make sure it didn't demand any of the proctology that ten-ure appointments required. I didn't have any objection to this; arriving as the newly minted Anna Quindlen Writer in Residence meant that I would also be freed from the responsibilities that tenure demanded—like advising, and serving on committees, and doing my time as a department chair, and all of that. It was as if I had been appointed the Tom Bombadil chair of creative writing; the Rings of academia had no power over me.

I mention all of this, though, not because I'm deluded that academic politics are in any way interesting, but to point out that, in thirty-five years as an academic, I have never had tenure, and never been eligible for it. Which means that despite any of my accomplishments, there has been a penumbra of marginality that I've never quite shed.

On my glummer days, my heart has been filled with envy and contempt, not because I wanted the professional nobility of some of my more woebegone colleagues but because being trans had already made me hyperaware of my own liminality. If I had had to spend a quarter century explaining to the stupid and the cruel that *I Am So a Woman,* it surely had left me with the sense that my womanhood was something I had to win, as if everything about me was up for debate.

I had spent the heart of my working life in academia, and yet in the eyes of some of my colleagues, I was not a real and solid human being. Instead, I was something liminal and translucent. A will-o'-the-wisp. A flibbertigibbet. A clown.

I went into the photocopying room in Barnard's English department. An older woman was working the machine. "Hi," I said. "Are you Myrtle?" She'd been at Barnard forever, and at one time had been married to a famous literary critic.

She looked at me, her face ashen, and fled from the room like her pantyhose was on fire. Later, I asked a friend about this. "Oh, she's terrified of you," he said. "She's a Freudian. She doesn't have a theory for you."

I would overlap with Myrtle for the next seven years, right up until the day she retired. Never once did she speak a single word to me. Every time we were in the same room together, she would rush out the door, so paralyzing was it for her to share oxygen with someone for whom there was no theory.

Over time, the Myrtle Problem (as I called it) really wore me down. You wouldn't think that someone lacking the common decency to simply say hello would have been so hurtful, but it was.

I thought about talking to someone at HR about this situation, and I probably should have. But I was embarrassed, and I hated to cause a fuss. Instead, I quietly loathed her in my heart. Which was not as satisfying as it sounds.

I don't know, maybe I should have been more forgiving. After all, I didn't have a theory for *her*, either.

The Whitney Museum left its Midtown building and opened up a new museum down by the High Line. The Met bought the old building—the Breuer—and started to rehab it. My friend Julie Burstein told me about a series of TED Talks the museum was going to be sponsoring there while the renovation was going on—a series that eventually landed me on that stage with Sharon Olds.

"I've always wanted to do a TED Talk," I told her.

"Well, actually, it's not a real TED Talk," Julie said. "It's a TEDx Talk."

"What's the difference?" I asked.

"Well, a TED Talk, you know, that's a real TED Talk, whereas a TEDx Talk, that's like, a TED-*like* talk."

"Oh," I said, a little disappointed. "Well, what's the topic?"

"Liminality!" said Julie.

"Liminality?" I said.

"Yeah, because the Breuer's being rebuilt. It's halfway between what it was, and what it's going to become!"

"And you want me to do a TED Talk because—"

"A TEDx Talk."

"A TEDx Talk because—"

"Because Jenny. If you don't know about the in-between, then who does?"

I'm aware that the very liminality I'm lamenting here is, in fact, a state that others crave and celebrate, at least where gender is concerned. I know tons of nonbinary people who have found freedom and fun in a place beyond the constricting poles of male and/or female.

But there are plenty of others who object when something is neither one thing nor the other. It destabilizes the world, makes it seem as if everything we know can be called into question.

There have been nonbinary people throughout history, of course. Aristophanes recorded a myth that men were "born of the sun" and women "born of the earth." A third category, the *androgynous*, had been born from the moon.

Aristophanes suggested that this third group no longer existed. But I kind of want to tell him, Ari? Take a look around you, and then tell me if all the people you can see fall simply into one pile or the other. Maybe you should have dinner someplace other than the Agora once in a while?

Even now, among many good-hearted people, I hear resistance to the singular "they." *Oh, I want everyone to feel accepted,* they say. *But it's bad grammar! That's what I resent!*

Sometimes I suspect that what people really resent is not the change in grammar. What people resent is being told that the world that they have known has changed, and that even now they have to get used to something new.

Mrs. Sonny Bono, Jorge Mario Bergoglio, and Abraham Lincoln walk into a bar. Assuming you're the bartender, by what names will you address them?

Oh, wait, that's easy. Call them "Cher," "Your Holiness," and "Mr. President."

Because those are the names by which they are known.

The singular *they* once sounded funny to me, too. But lots of good things were unfamiliar at first, including (to name three) women's suffrage, Rhode Island–style hot-pepper calamari, and the opening chord of "A Hard Day's Night." I believe that most Americans really do yearn for a more just world, even if the changes that justice demands can take a long time to join the culture, or the language.

More simply, though, I'll call my students they, or "xir," or "xem" simply because calling people by the terms they prefer is a matter of respect.

(Even calling these terms "preferred" pronouns does a disservice, because people aren't choosing their identities out of fussiness or caprice; they are doing so, usually, as part of a hard-fought search for truth.) Using this language doesn't mean that I see the world through their eyes. But it does mean I greet them with an open heart.

To refer to people otherwise is to suggest to my students—or to Mr. Lincoln, or Señor Bergoglio, or Mx. Cherilyn Sarkisian La Piere Bono Allman—that I somehow know who they are better than they do. I call people by the names—and yes, pronouns—they have chosen, because to do so, in the end, is to simply treat my fellow human beings with love. And that strikes me as a good approach, both inside the classroom and out.

It will take a while before this language becomes commonplace, although probably not as long as the eighty-five years it took "Ms." to travel from *The Springfield Republican* to the pages of *The New York Times*. In the meantime, some people may need help understanding that some of the words we use to refer to one another are changing, and that these changes really do reflect a hope for a more just and compassionate world.

But that's OK, too. The Lord helps those that help xemselves.

The three writers who most influenced me pre-transition, as far as trans issues were concerned, were Jan Morris, Canary Conn, and Melanie Anne Phillips (the creator of the tape about developing a female voice). Morris was famous as a travel writer, before and after she published *Conundrum,* but the other two names are unlikely to ring a bell, unless you were a trans woman at a very particular moment in time. Canary published her book *(Canary: The Story of a Transsexual)* in 1974; as a male (sic) she'd been a minorly famous folk singer. Her memoir wasn't exactly *Infinite Jest,* but if you were trans and closeted in the 1970s, I promise it would have haunted you. I remember standing in the bookstore at the 30th Street train station, after my long days as a bank teller, looking at the cover. I could never quite bring myself to buy it, but as I waited for the train each scorching hot Philadelphia day, I'd leaf through its pages, staring at the photo spread in its heart with wonder and terror. She'd been a lumpy folk-singing boy, back in the day. Now she was this gorgeous woman.

Melanie Anne Phillips's tape inspired me, too. *Yes,* these works suggested. *It can be done.*

What's interesting to me now is not the role that these three women played, although I'm profoundly grateful that they were visible to me during a time when role models were few and far between. No, what haunts me now is the way that in later years, each of these women disappeared.

Correction: Jan Morris never disappeared, and after she published *Conundrum* she continued to write until her death, many years later, at the age of ninety-four. But she never took on the role of trans warrior. In 2018, she said that her transition was no longer the most important thing about her. She told the *Financial Times* she hadn't changed her writing "in the slightest. It changed me far less than I thought it had." Late in life she thought of herself as "both man and woman . . . or a mixture of both."

It makes me wonder how Jan Morris would have lived her life if the concept of a nonbinary identity had been more broadly understood, and accepted, during her day.

As for Melanie Anne Phillips and Canary Conn, they have vanished.

Three years ago I was asked by an editor at Godine if I would be willing to write a new introduction to *Canary,* were they to republish the memoir. He said that they had a team of people looking for her, but so far had turned up nothing. After 1978, more or less, she seems to have dropped off the face of the earth, although one online sleuth claims to have tracked her down to an apartment house in Texas.

Melanie Anne Phillips's story follows a similar arc. In 2023, the *Sounds Gay* podcast reported on the influence Phillips had back in the 1990s. But Melanie appears to have made a similar choice, to vanish off the radar. In one of her last public statements, she seemed to suggest she was, henceforward, going to deny that she had ever had a male past, and simply live her life as if who she had become was who she had always been.

It is a harrowing thing for me to consider—that these women, who had such a profound effect on me, would decide that having a public identity as trans was a burden so cumbersome that they chose instead to disappear, or (as in Morris's case) to downplay the importance of transition in the first place.

And they aren't the only ones. Renée Richards, who became a different kind of role model in the 1970s after playing professional tennis as a woman, has likewise kept a very low profile in her later years, although in 2007 she published a memoir, "No Way Renée." The *Times* titled a column on the book "The Lady Regrets."

Regrets, disappearance, insignificance . . . these aren't what I hope for in my later years. Although to be honest, the later years for me have already begun. Am I still here? Is it a good thing that I continue to shout into the megaphone, suggesting that trans people deserve kindness, and equality, and understanding?

It feels like a good thing. Most of the time. Although I will admit that being a whipping girl for the hard-hearted can surely wear a person down. I can understand all these women wishing to be seen for who they are, not *what* they are, or who they have *been*. There are lots of days when I look out the window and just wish everybody would leave me alone.

But it also breaks my heart that anyone would have to disavow their past. Surely if we are to find our peace, it will come from building a bridge between who we have been and who we have become. There is no shame in starting out one's life in one place, and then emigrating to another. Personally, I can say that finding my hard-won joy has been a source of strength and of courage. What else could it be, in the end, besides a strange and glorious gift? I am grateful for every tear I've ever shed. How else to know the real value of gladness, and of love?

Mine is not the joy of someone for whom everything was easy. I got here because I fought for it, and also because I inherited from my parents equal measures of cussedness and forgiveness. And because I wrote about it, too.

This is another difference between coming out then and coming out now. Once, a person who emerged as trans might look forward to an old age in which their past would have to be disavowed. In order to live in peace, a woman might have to lie, or regret, or disappear.

Now—with luck—a transgender person can look forward to a future in which our whole lives—both the Befores and the Afters—can be celebrated, and honored, and remembered.

A speaker at the 2023 Conservative Political Action Conference, Michael Knowles, told his audience that "transgenderism (sic) must be eradicated from public life entirely—the whole preposterous ideology, at every level."

But trans people aren't going to be eradicated, not unless we eradicate ourselves by disappearing in exhaustion and in shame.

Just because you cannot see someone, it does not mean she is invisible. Look at me, Michael. I'm standing right here.


In the spring of 2022 not one but two different institutions asked me to deliver speeches at their commencements. One of them, the College of the Atlantic in Bar Harbor, Maine, bestowed upon me the degree of Master of Philosophy, honoris causa. The other, Sarah Lawrence College in New York, gave me an honorary doctorate.

I gave pretty good speeches on both occasions, barn-burners, in fact. The graduating seniors had had the heart of their college educations stolen by the pandemic; this, plus the presidency of Donald Trump and the climactic insurrection by some of his idiot followers had left many of those young people more than a little cheesed off.

I attempted to give them a little hope, even as they looked out at a world in flames.

*At the heart of a lot of the trouble in our country*—I said—*is a simple inability to accept change, a refusal to accept that most things don't last forever, and in many cases, shouldn't last forever. It is hard to let go of the way things have been, but when we face injustice, we have to prevail. And make no mistake, to greet the world with love doesn't mean that you sit around with a dopey smile on your face while the world burns around you. For love to prevail it is necessary to greet the world with fierceness, to push back against injustice with both relentlessness and joy, wisdom and ferocity. Those who would turn back the clock to a time when women were denied the right to control their own bodies, to a time when LGBTQ people had to live in the shadows, to a time when people of color could be denied the right to vote— these people need to understand that they will have a fight on their hands—but that those of us engaged in this work are motivated not by fear but hope, not by intolerance but justice, not by hate, but love.*

As one of the members of the faculty later put it, "There wasn't a dry seat in the house."

I took my new degrees home and hung them up in my office. *Look,* I said to a professor friend who came to visit one day. *At long last! I'm a doctor! A Ph.D.!*

*Yeah,* she said. *Although these are degrees, you know, honoris causa.*

I said, *Right. Honoris causa! I'm a Doctor of Philosophy, honoris causa!*

She asked me, *You know what that means in Latin?*

I said, *No, what?*

She smiled. *It means, Not really.*

F ive years after I dreamed about writing a book with Jodi Picoult our novel, *Mad Honey,* debuted at number three on the bestseller list. (Me: "I'm so excited! We hit number three on the list!" Jodi Picoult: "Oh, no! Only number three?")

The publisher flew us around the world. One morning I stared out the window of the airplane at the clouds: cirrus, stratus, cumulonimbus. I had seen them from both sides now.

For the second time in my life, I was the author of a bestselling book. This time, I did not cry.

Later, Jodi and I flew from Seattle to Orlando, where Jodi was deter- mined that, before our evening performance, we would visit the Magic

Kingdom. Space Mountain. The Mad Hatter's Teacups. Thunder Mountain Railroad.

I remembered my child wailing and crying, as we'd entered the Haunted Mansion all those years ago. In the blink of an eye she had spread her wings, and taken to the sky. Ghouls and goblins sang their song from deep within the haunted house.

*Maddy!* she cried. *You promised me it was going to be funny.*

# HEARTS & BRAINS

There they are, in their Chevrolet Colorado, five dudes bouncing up and down as the truck grinds through the rugged American high country. Two guys up front, three in the back. Shania Twain is blasting on the stereo. The fellow in the middle is singing along. *"Oh, I want to be free to feel the way I feel. Man, I feel like a woman!"*

The other guys look deeply worried. But the person in the back just keeps happily singing away, even as the dude next to him moves his leg away. Just to be on the safe side.

This commercial aired back in 2004, and even now it's not clear to me if it's offensive or empowering, hilarious or infuriating. Shania Twain says she wrote "Man! I Feel Like a Woman!" after working at a resort where some drag queens were performing. "That song started with the title," she said. "Then it kind of wrote itself."

It's a fun tune, and I admit I kind of loved seeing that commercial. But at its heart is an issue central to our current political moment.

When someone says they *feel like a woman*, what exactly does that mean?

Across the country, conservatives are insisting that—and legislating as if—"feeling" like a woman, or a man, is irrelevant. What matters most, they say, is the immutable truth of biology. In spring of 2023, the Texas Department of Agriculture emplaced a new dress code, demanding that employees wear clothing "in a manner consistent with their biological gender." In Florida, a law signed by Gov. Ron DeSantis keeps "biological males" from playing on the women's sports teams in public schools.

This term, "biological males," is everywhere now. And it's not used only by right-wing politicians. People of good faith are also wrestling with the way trans people complicate a world they thought was binary. They're uncertain about when, and how, gender matters, and just how biological it is. Some want to draw a bright line in areas where maleness and femaleness might matter most—in sports, or locker rooms, or prisons. Others are trying to blur lines that used to be clearer. In 2022, a nonbinding student referendum at Wellesley, traditionally a women's college, called for the admission of trans men. The president of the college, Paula Johnson, pushed back.

So what, then, *is* a biological male, or female? What determines this supposedly simple truth? It's about chromosomes, right?

Well, maybe not. Because not every person with a Y chromosome is male, and not every person with a double X is female. The world is full of people with other combinations: XXY (or Klinefelter syndrome), XXX (or Trisomy X), XXXY, and so on. There's even something called Androgen insensitivity syndrome, a condition that keeps the brains of people with a Y from absorbing the information in that chromosome. Most of these people develop as female, and may not even know about their condition until puberty—or even later.

How can this be, if sex is only about a gene?

Some people respond by saying that sex is about something *else*, then—ovaries or testicles (two structures that begin their existence in the womb as the same thing).

What do we do then, with the millions of women who've had hysterectomies? Have they become men? What about women who've had mastectomies? Or men with gynecomastia?

Are these people not who they think they are?

It may be that what's in your pants is less important than what's between your ears.

In the last decade, there has been some fascinating research on the brains of transgender people. What is most remarkable about this work is not that trans women's brains have been found to resemble those of cisgender women, or that trans men's brains resemble those of cis men. What the research has found is that the brains of trans people are unique: neither female nor male, exactly, but something distinct.

But what does that mean, a male brain, or a female brain, or even a transgender one? It's a fraught topic, because brains are a collection of characteristics rather than a binary classification of either/or. There are researchers who would tell you that brains are not more gendered than, say, kidneys or lungs. Gina Rippon, in her 2019 book, *The Gendered Brain,* warns against bunk science that declares brains to be male or female—it's "neurosexism," a fancy way of justifying the belief that women's brains are inferior to men's.

And yet scientists continue to study the brain in hopes of understanding whether a sense of the gendered self can, at least in part, be the result of neurology. A study described by author Francine Russo in *Scientific American* examined the brains of 39 prepubertal and 41 adolescent boys and girls with gender dysphoria. The experiment examined how these children responded to androstadienone, a pungent substance similar to pheromones, that is known to cause a different response in the brains of men and women. The study found that adolescent boys and girls who described themselves as trans responded like the peers of their perceived gender. (The results were less clear with prepubescent children.)

This kind of testing is important, said one of the researchers Russo quoted, "because sex differences in responding to odors cannot be influenced by training or environment." A similar study was done in measuring the responses of trans boys and girls to echolike sounds produced in the inner ear. "Boys with gender dysphoria responded more like typical females, who have a stronger response to these sounds."

What does it mean, to respond to the world in this way? For me, it has meant having a sense of myself as a woman, a sense that no matter how comfortable I was with the fact of being *feminine,* I was never at ease with not being *female.* When I was young, I tried to talk myself out of it, telling myself, in short, to "get over it."

But I never got over it.

I compare it to a sense of homesickness for a place you've never been. The moment you stepped onto those supposedly unfamiliar shores, though, you'd have a sense of overwhelming gratitude, and solace, and joy. *Home,* you might think. *I'm finally home.*

The years to come will, perhaps, continue to shed light on the mysteries of the brain, and to what degree our sense of ourselves as gendered beings has its origins there. But there's a problem with using neurology as an argument for trans acceptance—it suggests that, on some level, there is something wrong with transgender people, that we are who we are as a result of a sickness or a biological hiccup.

Trans people are not broken. And, in fact, trying to open people's hearts by saying, *Check out my brain!* can do more harm than good, because this line of argument delegitimizes the experiences of many trans folks. It suggests that there's only one way to be trans—to feel trapped in the wrong body, to go through transition, and to wind up, when all is said and done, on the opposite gender pole. It suggests that the quest trans people go on can only be considered successful if it ends with fitting into the very society that rejected us in the first place.

All the science tells us, in the end, is that a biological male—or female—is not any one thing, but a collection of possibilities.

No one who embarks upon a life as a trans person in this country is doing so out of caprice, or a whim, or a delusion. We are living these wondrous and perilous lives for one reason only—because our hearts demand it. Given the tremendous courage it takes to come out, given the fact that even now trans people can still lose everything—family, friends, jobs, even our lives—what we need now is not new legislation to make things harder. We need understanding, not cruelty. What we need now is not hatred, but love.

When the person in that Chevy ad sings *Oh, I want to be free to feel the way I feel. Man, I feel like a woman!,* the important thing is not that they feel like a woman, or a man, or something else. What matters most is the plaintive desire *to be free to feel the way I feel.*

Surely this is not a desire unique to trans people. Tell me: Is there anyone who has never struggled to live up to the hard truths of their own heart?

Man! I feel like a human.

When I was fourteen, Leelah Alcorn wrote in her final note, *I learned what transgender meant, and cried of happiness. After ten years of confusion I finally understood who I was. I immediately told my mom, and she reacted extremely negatively, telling me that it was a phase, that I would never truly be a girl, that God doesn't make mistakes, that I am wrong. If you are reading this, parents, please don't tell this to your kids. Even if you are a Christian or are against transgender people, don't ever say that to someone, especially your kid. That won't do anything but make them hate themself. That's exactly what it did to me.*

In 2007, a sportswriter for the *Los Angeles Times*, Mike Penner, went on vacation. "Today I leave for a few weeks," Penner wrote in an April column. "When I come back, I will come back in yet another incarnation.

"As Christine.

"I am a transsexual sportswriter. It has taken more than forty years, a million tears, and hundreds of hours of soul-wrenching therapy for me to work up the courage to type those words. I realize many readers and friends will be shocked to read them."

I met Christine Daniels—as she renamed herself—at a convention of transgender people in Atlanta later that year. There used to be a lot of these conventions, places where trans people could safely gather for a weekend. There was one called the Gold Rush in Colorado; one called the First Event in Boston; and one called the Be-All in Chicago. In the years after *She's Not There*, I would attend many of these gatherings as a keynote speaker, or a member of a panel. There was a group of trans folks—mostly trans women—whom I'd see every few months back then: Mara Keisling, of the National Center for Transgender Equality; surgeons Marci Bowers and Christine McGinn; and Donna Rose, who'd briefly been a board member of the Human Rights Campaign, the political lobbying group for LGBTQ people in Washington.

It was quite a scene. I'd walk through the revolving door of a hotel and find myself, all at once, surrounded by up to one thousand other transgender people. There they were—strangely tall women, curiously short men—and for a few moments the world seemed as if some of its rules had been jubilantly rewritten. And then, a few moments after that, *ding!*, the world of the convention seemed normal, and everything outside those revolving doors seemed like the place that was weird. There were panels on everything from surgery to legal issues. There were gatherings for struggling loved ones. There were beauty contests and talent shows, political speeches and rock-and-roll bands.

One year, the then-president of the Human Rights Campaign, Joe Solmonese, stood before the convention and pledged his solid support for trans folks in all upcoming legislation, including in a bill called ENDA, the Employment Non-Discrimination Act. About a month after Solmonese's speech, the HRC announced that it now supported stripping trans protections out of the bill, and that ENDA would be for gay men, bisexuals, and lesbians only. Donna Rose resigned from HRC in the wake of that; it took years before many trans people would trust that organization again. Some of us have still not gotten over it.

There was also a remarkable bar scene at those conventions. I used to meet up with a banjo player that I knew named Molly, and the two of us would sit on stools, with me on Autoharp, and sing all the old folk songs we knew. One night, Molly and I stayed up until about 4 A.M. I remember looking up at one point and suddenly realizing that the whole place was now deserted, except for us two. We knew a lot of the same songs, Molly and me.

There was a plastic surgeon named Doug Ousterhout who used to buy everyone drinks in the bar, in hopes that his magnanimity would encourage people to consider Dr. O (as he was called) when time came for their tracheal shave, or their brow-ridge reduction, or their brand-new nose. I never had any surgery on my face, but I still remember sitting there between sets with Molly in the bar with Dr. O looking at me very, very carefully, until I said, "What?"

And he just said, kind of wistfully, "I could make you beautiful."

I said, "Wait. You're saying I'm not beautiful?"

He took me by the hand. "Oh, Professor," he said sadly.

That was the same year I met Christine Daniels. Her transition had caused a stir, as these things always used to do, pretty much up to and including the moment every trans person came out until Caitlyn Jenner. One year Chaz Bono came to Southern Comfort; another year it was Buck Angel, an adult film star. You never knew who you'd get.

Christine had read my book. The two of us sat in the bar talking about it. She wanted to know about Deedie—whom I'd called Grace in the book. "What can I do," she asked me, her eyes shimmering, "if my wife isn't Grace?"

I tried to explain that wives (and husbands, for that matter) get to decide whether they want to be married or not, and that trans folks who expect that their own transition will have no effect upon the people whom they love need to think a little harder. "But that's the thing," Christine said. "If I lose my marriage, I'm just not sure I can . . . do this."

At the time, when she said, "do this," I figured she meant go through transition. But Christine meant something else.

Leelah Alcorn was sent to Christian conversion therapists. There, she said, she was told that she was "selfish and wrong," and that she should look to God for help.

At age sixteen, she asked her parents if she could begin treatment for transition. They said no.

*I felt hopeless,* she wrote, *that I was just going to look like a man in drag for the rest of my life. On my 16th birthday, when I didn't receive permission from my parents to start transitioning, I cried myself to sleep.*

The day Christine Daniels came to work at the *Los Angeles Times* as Christine, her wife, Lisa Dillman, filed for divorce. Writer Steve Friess, in a story for *LA Weekly,* reported that Christine's transition was "marred by a series of blow-out arguments with Dillman and Dillman's parents." Dillman, who also worked at the *Times,* told her, "I don't even want to see you around the office unless I absolutely have to, and then I want to be as far away as possible. I don't want to be associated with it. I don't ever want to see you that way."

Then there was a fiasco involving *Vanity Fair,* which staged a whole photo shoot, intended to make Christine look like a glamour-puss, but which—in her view—made her look like a drag queen.

The same week as the divorce filing, Friess wrote, Christine suffered another blow. Paul Oberjuerge, a reporter for the *San Bernardino Sun*, attended a press conference for British soccer legend David Beckham, where he saw Christine. "She looks like a guy in a dress, pretty much," he wrote. "Except anyone paying any attention isn't going to be fooled—as some people are by veteran transvestites. Maybe this is cruel, but there were women in that room who were born women in body, as well as soul. And the difference between them and Christine was, in my mind, fairly stark. It seemed almost as [if] we're all going along with someone's dress-up role-playing. . . ."

On December 28, 2014, Leelah Alcorn wrote her suicide note. She scheduled it to be automatically posted on her Tumblr account later that day.

*I have decided I've had enough. I'm never going to transition successfully, even when I move out. I'm never going to be happy with the way I look or sound. I'm never going to have enough friends to satisfy me. I'm never going to have enough love to satisfy me. I'm never going to find a man who loves me. I'm never going to be happy. Either I live the rest of my life as a lonely man who wishes he were a woman or I live my life as a lonelier woman who hates herself. There's no winning. There's no way out. I'm sad enough already, I don't need my life to get any worse. People say "it gets better" but that isn't true in my case. It gets worse. Each day I get worse. That's the gist of it, that's why I feel like killing myself. Sorry if that's not a good enough reason for you, it's good enough for me.*

Christine Daniels went from a bubbly, enthusiastic woman to one who was increasingly depressed, isolated, and alone. "I don't feel like being Christine anymore," she told a friend. "I feel like pulling the plug."

In the end she returned to the *Times*—as Mike. But this version of Mike Penner wasn't anything like the pre-transition one. He was sad, exhausted. Mike and his now ex-wife occasionally had lunch together. But their marriage was done.

The day after Thanksgiving, Penner put on a blue shirt and jeans. He got into his Camry in the garage beneath his apartment with the motor running, and inhaled carbon monoxide until he was dead.

In the weeks that followed, there were two funerals—one managed for the family, for Mike Penner, and another, mounted by her friends in the trans community, for Christine Daniels.

Leelah Alcorn walked to a highway near her house, watched the passing traffic. Then she ran in front of an approaching truck, and was killed instantly.

*My death has to mean something*, she wrote in her final note. *Fix society. Please.*

Have we?

One by one, the gender conferences that had flourished in the '80s and '90s and '00s shut their doors. The Gold Rush died in 2012. The final Southern Comfort was in 2019, although it had been on its last legs since it left Atlanta in 2014 and tried for a second life in Florida. Two years before that, the Be-All came to an End-All.

A few of them, like the First Event, are still going; and a few new ones have started up. The Keystone Conference in Harrisburg meets each year, and a very big one happens in Philly each summer, although the Philadelphia Trans Wellness Conference is not so much about swimsuit competitions and makeup tips (although there's some of that) as it is about politics, and nonbinary identities, and intersectionality. This evolution is as good a metaphor as any for how trans politics—and trans lives—have changed since I came out twenty-five years ago.

On the whole, it reflects a positive movement for our people. I wouldn't go back to the old days, even if I had the chance.

But now and again I will think back to those nights of playing Autoharps and banjos as Dr. Ousterhout bought the drinks. There was one night when, during the evening's speeches from the podium, I duct-taped Mara Keisling to her chair. There was an afternoon when, after giving a reading from *She's Not There*, I walked outside onto a balcony and felt the warm rain of a sudden downpour soak me to the skin. I felt so young, standing there, so alive! I would love to feel that way again.

Most of all, I miss some of the friends I used to see at those conferences—Mara and Marci, Molly the banjo player, Donna Rose. We were good friends. Sometimes, friends are the difference between surviving this life, and not.

Now and again I remember Christine Daniels, and the time we overlapped at SoCo. I had stayed in touch with her during the final year of her life, and I had tried to offer her counsel, as best I could. Then, one morning, the blog she'd been writing ("Woman in Progress") at the *Times* came back, "page not found." I tried to tell her that the only person she needed to answer to was herself, and that there was no shame in being a less public person.

But it may be that I was not the right person to deliver that particular message.

The last note I got from her read, *The holidays and beyond have been a challenging time. I am recharging my battery on several fronts; I hope to blog again soon. But there has been a lot on my plate.*

I remembered that late-night conversation at Southern Comfort, and her plaint, *What can I do if my wife is not Grace?*

In the end, Christine's wife, in fact, was *not* Grace, and she had every right to make her own choices about what was going to be right for her own life. But I admit that the question Christine posed continued to haunt me, even after her life was over.

"Christine wasn't confused about what it meant to be a woman," one friend of hers said. "She died of a broken heart."

Even now, twenty-five years after my transition, sixteen years after her death, I sometimes hear Christine's voice in the middle of the night, when I wake from some unquiet dream. *What if my wife is not Grace?* she asks me. *What then?*

Grace, of course, was the pseudonym I'd given Deedie in *She's Not There*. It felt like a good choice when I wrote it, evocative of the way *grace* is sometimes described—as the gift that cannot be asked for, only received.

But it was not lost on me that, in fact, Grace was not Grace either.

# DAUGHTERS

**B**en and I pulled up at my haunted house, the snow still coming down. The front fender of the Vega was still crumpled. On his 8-track, the Beatles. *Remember,* I said. *Tell your parents it was me.*

I slipped up the back stairs. From the living room came the voices of my parents and some guests—the Thomases, from the sounds of it. I slid into my room, pulled the bolt, took off my clothes. My bra I stuffed with tube socks. I pulled on a black Danskin leotard and a paisley hippie skirt. I had a pair of Dr. Scholl's sandals, too. They were supposed to be good for your posture.

*Thank god,* I thought, with a tremendous sigh of relief. It was like a piece of glass had been in my shoe all day. Now it was gone.

I had no name then. I couldn't find anything that fit. I thought maybe—Elissa? Alice? Alyce? Elyce?

I sat down at my desk to do my homework. In German class we were translating Thomas Mann's *Tonio Kröger. Wer am meisten liebt, ist der Unterlegene und muß leiden,* I read. Whoever loves the more is at a disadvantage and must suffer.

My mother's voice called from downstairs. "Jim!"

"In the middle of something!" I said, irritated.

"The Thomases are telling us about a mystery!" she said, breathlessly. My friends secretly mocked my mother by calling her *Glinda the Good Witch,* which really wasn't much of an insult. Everyone loved Hildegarde. We imagined her, like Glinda, waving her wand, transforming into a floating lavender bubble.

"I'm doing my homework, Mom!"

"Come down!" she said. "I told them to wait for me to get you!" The stairs creaked as my mother ascended.

*We have a code red.* I yanked off the skirt and the leotard. My door-knob rattled. "Jim? Why is this door locked?"

"Just a second!" I unhooked my bra. The balled-up tube socks fell onto the floor.

"Are you all right?" asked Mom. "What's going on in there?"

"I'm fine!" I said, stuffing my gear beneath the mattress. Then I pulled my pants on. The belt buckle jingled. At the last second I pulled off my clip-on earrings, stuffed them in my pocket.

"Jim?"

I slid back the dead bolt, swung open the door.

"What?" I said. "*What?*"

Fifty years later, I lay on a beach in Cape Cod, feeling the summer sun upon my face. My wife and daughter were beside me, soaking up rays of their own. The Atlantic crashed before us.

Deedie and Zai and I had been on the Cape all week, drinking piña coladas, eating baskets of fried clams, watching seagulls hover and dive. (Seannie, working in Ann Arbor on the systems that guided driverless cars, couldn't take the time off.) One day, Deedie and Zai and I had gone on a whale watch and saw a big pod of humpbacks, plus a renegade minke. At one point, a half dozen humpbacks floated next to our ship with their giant mouths open, fish pouring in. A fantastic stench drifted past.

*Whoa,* I said to Deedie. What *is* that?

*Whale breath,* she said.

The day after Zai came out as trans, I had gazed out the window of the New York apartment as she drove off. Zai looked up me and waved, just before getting into the car.

*That's it,* I thought. *I'll never see my boy again.*

And yet.

In the weeks that followed, Zai was by almost any measure happier, more relaxed, more at peace, more herself. She had drifted around post-college, taking a temp job here, an acting job there—but for all that, had not quite found what felt like her mission. Now, out in the world as female, it occurred to Zai that she might be helpful to other people seeking counsel, seeking aid. She applied to graduate schools in counseling and therapy. She enrolled at a college in Cambridge, Mass.

Three years after that gruesome trip to New York—the one that had begun with the drive through the terrible snowstorm, and had concluded with one of her friends falling so heavily upon her that her catheter tube gushed with purple blood—three years later, our family had gathered again, this time to celebrate her graduation. We watched, tearfully, as she strode across the stage and accepted her degree.

By the fall Zai had taken a job as a counselor, with a specialty in drama therapy. Her experience as an actor, as well as a player of various role-playing games, had put her at the forefront of a new field. Using the devices found in theatre, and in RPGs like Dungeons & Dragons, Zai helped her clients to explore their own characters, to understand their own personal history and trauma, and to find their way to a better life. Soon enough she was authoring papers describing this new therapeutic method.

It was a process not so unlike the one I had found, in my own art, using the rituals of revision and reinvention through multiple drafts of story to find a better version of the self.

Zai had wound up, in her late twenties, not only as a successful transgender woman but also as a therapist, like Deedie. When asked about this by her friends, she laughed. "It's true," she said. "I've become *both* my parents."

I sat up on the beach, having dozed off in the hot sun, lulled by the sound of the ocean waves crashing again and again. Zai was lying on her towel beside me, but Deedie was gone.

"Where's your mother?" I asked.

"What?" asked Zai, pulling out an earbud.

"I asked where your mother got to."

"She's taking a walk, Maddy," said Zai. "And also getting away from the snoring."

I took this in. "I was snoring?" I said.

Zai shook her head. "Like a grizzly."

She sat up and looked toward the sea. Even in July, the Atlantic by Wellfleet is forbidding. It's bone-rattling cold, for one. For another, there's a layer of round stones rolling around about four feet from the shore, stones guaranteed to leave a few bruises if they knock against your shins. You had to be determined if you wanted to swim in an ocean such as this.

My daughter stood up. "I'm going in," she said.

She walked away from me. I thought of Ben. "Be careful," I said.

Zai rolled her eyes. "What could go wrong?" she asked and headed toward the sea.

Our neighbors, the Farnsworths, have an AFS student," explained Mrs. Thomas. "From China. They had her staying in their attic guest room."

"A beautiful room!" said Mr. Thomas. "Like a hotel!"

My parents and the Thomases and I were gathered around the fireplace. Above the mantelpiece, my grandfather—James Boylan—looked down on us from his painting. He'd been married, of course, to my colorful grandmother, Gammie, a woman who never quite got over being a flapper in the 1920s. I've written about her in the past, and why not: she was a character. When Deedie and I got married, in fact, she'd leaned against a piano at the reception, telling jokes, a martini in one hand, a cigarette in the other. At one point, I had looked over and seen her there, holding forth, a half dozen old men at her feet, enraptured.

She told the story about the night my father was conceived at that reception. It was one of her favorite stories. *Best screwin' I ever had!* she shouted.

But my *other* grandmother was a mystery to me, and not only because she had died when I was only six. Her name was Olga, but we called her Grandma Scheffler, a title as formal as *Your Excellency,* or *Reverend Mother.* I got the sense that Hildegarde had mixed feelings about her, too: proud of her mother's fierceness in the face of her drunken, abusive, abandoning husband, to be sure. But my mother was angry, too, for the life of poverty they all had lived through.

There weren't any paintings of Grandma Scheffler on our walls, anyway. Once, in a storeroom, I had found a single photograph of her with her many children, standing at the foot of the *Soldaten* monument in Berlin. My grandmother's face was ashen, like a woman who'd watched her house burn to the ground. Now they were on their way to America. On the back, in German, was my grandmother's shaky writing. *I do not love this country any more.*

Here were my parents, in wing chairs placed on either side of the fireplace. When we'd first moved into this house, the living room had been painted black. There was a yellow rug on the floor whose many brown stains made clear that the previous residents, the Hunts, had owned a pack of German shepherds. The day after we'd moved in, in fact, one of those dogs had found his way all the way from the Hunts' new apartment back to this house. He'd lain down on the front porch, waiting for his family to come home.

They didn't.

My sister and I loved the black living room, and had begged our parents not to repaint it. But my father was determined. *It's like a funeral parlor,* he said.

*We know! That's what we love about it!*

"So everything was fine with Jing," said Mrs. Thomas. She was a big woman with an updo and big glasses and swinging jowls. "Until last week."

I could feel the clip-on earrings in my pocket poking into my thigh. I hoped that they hadn't left a mark on my earlobes, like they sometimes did. How terrified I was, even as I sat there with my loving parents and their jowly friends, that the secret I bore would come out! Was it really so hard to imagine what was going on up on the third floor? Why did they think I locked my door, night after night?

"What happened last week?" I asked.

"Well," said Mrs. Thomas. "Mabel—that's Mrs. Farnsworth—called Jing down for dinner, only she didn't answer. They called her again and again, still no answer. They went up to her room, but the door was locked. They were afraid she was sick, or that she'd fainted? So Dirk broke the door down. They entered the room—and do you know what they found?"

"They found nothing!" said Mr. Thomas. He was drinking Virginia Gentleman, same as my father. Dad was his boss.

"What do you mean, nothing?" I said.

"I mean," said Mrs. Thomas. "The room was empty. There was no sign of Jing. The door was locked—even the windows were locked. Jing's homework was on the desk. A book was open on the bed. But she was gone."

"Vanished!" shouted Mr. Thomas. "Disappeared!"

I took this in. "But people don't just vanish."

My father took a long drag on his cigarette, then blew the smoke into the air. He looked at me, hard. "Or do they?" he said.

In 2019 the *Wall Street Journal* published a piece titled "When Your Daughter Defies Biology," an essay that decried the number of young women coming out as trans men. Of course transness has some of its roots in neurology, so in some ways it's actually *not* coming out that defies biology. But what really struck me in that essay was the way this emergence was described as a tragedy for *parents*.

In case there was any doubt about whose trauma is the one that matters, the subtitle to the piece was "The burden of mothers whose children suffer from 'rapid onset gender dysphoria.'" The final sentence is "As ROGD daughters rage against the biology they hope to defy, their mothers bear its burden, evincing its maternal instinct—the stubborn refusal to abandon their young."

ROGD, by the way—short for rapid-onset gender dysphoria—is not a clinical term. It's a political one, designed to undermine the validity of these young people's transitions.

The term originated a few years ago on three blogs with a history of promoting anti-trans propaganda. There has been only one study on it, in the journal *PLOS ONE*. But the study isn't about the children in question; it's about their parents, who were recruited for the study by ads placed in the conservative blogs that had invented the concept of ROGD in the first place.

There are other things worth observing here, one of which is the absence of fathers in this scenario of keening and regret. Don't these children have two parents? Is Dad so busy working at the Family Research Council that he doesn't have time to come home, and like, research his own family?

But above all, the most important thing to resist here is the idea that having a child come out as trans, or nonbinary, is the worst thing that could possibly befall that child. Transness, to some parents, is considered a fate worse than death. By which I mean, *actual death*. Given the high rates of suicide attempts among trans people—41 percent of us will give it a go at some point, according to one survey—you would think that having your child actually alive and happy is a state preferable to, you know: having a child that you have lost, forever. Because your child thought that they could never be happy in this world. Because your child thought that coming out as trans would mean being sundered from their parents. Because your child thought that, instead of being greeted with kindness and compassion at the most perilous juncture of their lives, they would meet with only cruelty, and anger, and someone who thought of your own quest for happiness as their own unbearable burden.

Because your child feared that their parent might express some of the grief that I myself had experienced, when my own child turned out to be someone like me.

If accepting Zai had been that hard for me, even given all that I know, what must parents who know *nothing* about these issues go through? How rare, I now understand, was someone like my own evangelical Christian mom, who at the moment of crisis quoted First Corinthians, and told me *love would prevail.*

Change is hard to accept, especially in things that we really just like goddamn fine the way they are, especially in things—in *people*, in fact— that we love more than any other. Who could possibly *want* a child whom we adore to suddenly change something as fundamental as their sex?

And yet our children constantly change before our eyes. One day they are little blobs you hold against your breast. The next day they are driving away, leaving you forever. That this is the nature of the world, and that we ourselves broke our own parents' hearts when it was our turn to drive away, is exactly zero consolation.

It has been remarkable, then, to watch the child for whom I had worried, and wept, now emerging as a settled and centered woman in the world. I was so grateful, and proud.

Of what had I been afraid? Was it really that my child's transition would fail to bring her happiness? Or was I really in mourning for myself—that if my child turned out to be someone other than whom I had thought, that I, too, was not quite the parent I had convinced myself I had been?

It makes me want to reach out to all the parents of all the transgender children in the world, to let them know that their child's coming out as trans is not some terrible fate, but—with a little luck—the thing that might well bring them joy, and success. And also to let them know *they are not bad parents for feeling an initial sense of loss.* That loss, I want to tell them, is not all that you will feel. In time you will find a new sense of pride, as your child, transformed, becomes a better version of themselves, a person whom you can admire not only for their accomplishments but for the way in which they have done the hardest thing imaginable—to have taken the risk of having their own parents turn their backs on them forever.

I sat up on the Wellfleet beach, a little sunburned. I'd been snoring again. There was no sign of Deedie, and now no sign of Zai. There were a dozen surfers in wet suits out by the sandbar.

I looked around. "Zai?" I called.

I t's a locked-room mystery," I told the Thomases. "Like 'Murders in the Rue Morgue,' by Edgar Allan Poe. Or 'The Speckled Band,' the Sherlock Holmes story. There are lots of them." I liked showing off in front of my parents and their friends. I had never been on a single sports team at Haverford. But I had read lots of books.

"The Father Brown stories," my mother added. She read lots of books, too.

"In those stories," I said, precociously, "it's like a puzzle you're trying to solve. But it's also a way of, like, thinking about people. *Because our hearts are locked rooms, too.*"

"Jim's going to major in *English* at college," my mother said.

"That's fascinating!" Mr. Thomas said. He was a big, sloppy man, given to shouting. "You know, Dick, what I always say. I say, 'People are funny!'"

"Yes," said Mrs. Thomas. "But what happened to Jing wasn't funny at all."

"It is if you think about it!" said Mr. Thomas.

"No, dear," said Mrs. Thomas, firmly. "It's not."

M y daughter had lived in a locked room. It still gave me a profound sense of shame, that I'd missed all the clues. We'd talked about this during the week in Cape Cod, as she and I dug into the Fisherman's Special one afternoon at a seafood shack. There had been a mountain of fried squid, fried clams, fried scallops, fried shrimp. Plus, *both* onion rings and French fries. Just to be on the safe side.

I was drinking an iced tea, instead of having a beer with all that fried food. Because I was trying to watch the calories.

"I feel so stupid," I'd told her. "For being so oblivious. Me, of all people!"

"You," she said. "Of all people."

I dipped the tentacles of a deep-fried squid into tartar sauce. "I'm so sorry," I told her. She picked up some deep-fried squid of her own, and popped it into her mouth.

"As the child of a storyteller," Zai said, "it sometimes felt to me like a—I'm not sure if *personal failing* is the right word, but I think I felt like, if I wasn't actually meeting the narrative that you had been writing about, then I—there was a way I was like, oh, jeez. This isn't a thing that I can do."

"Oh, Zai. That's heartbreaking to think about, because, like, in whose house could it possibly have been more okay to come out as trans? Given the work that I was doing?"

"You wanted people to look at your beautiful boys. 'Look how well-adjusted and normal and cisgender they are, despite the fact that I am trans.'"

"I know. Like you guys were proof that I was not a bad person. As if being trans was something that I should have been ashamed of!" I picked up a clam. "I was so intent on making you into the cis version of me that I wound up making you exactly into the trans version of me. The version that knew who she was but was afraid to talk about it. The version that—"

My throat closed up. I couldn't say another word. My eyes filled with tears. I put my clam down.

"Maddy," she said, putting her hand on my shoulder. "It's okay. Like I said, I've processed it."

I wiped my face with my napkin. "When you came out," I said, "there was a voice in me whispering bad things in my ear. Like, that you being trans was all my fault, that I'd done this to my child."

"And I was having the inverse reaction. You were worrying that you did this to me, and I was worrying, *I can't let her think that she did this to me.*"

I blew some air through my cheeks.

"What was that?"

"I was just—I don't know, Zai. This isn't easy."

"You sounded like a little whale."

"Like I just exhaled through my blowhole?"

Zai laughed. "You and your blowhole." She dipped some calamari into the cocktail sauce and popped it in her mouth. "Did I ever tell you the story of the saddest whale in the world?" she asked. This was the day after we'd stood on the boat as the world's murkiest stench had floated by. Whale breath.

"I'm not sure I want to hear the story of a sad whale right now."

"No, listen. There was a whale who couldn't talk to the other whales. Because, you know the song that they make, he couldn't make that song because his song was too high for the other whales to hear. All day long he sang his whale song but no one heard it. He was the loneliest whale in the world. Until—wait for it!—"

"I'm dying here," I said. Beyond the shack where we were eating, the ocean rose and fell.

"Until one day he met another whale, who had the same problem! Who also sang a song so high no other whales could hear—except this whale! Who became his friend! The two of them swam together the rest of their lives, and were never lonely again!"

I looked at my daughter. She was a beautiful young woman. "Is that supposed to be us? The two whales with the song that only we can hear?"

"I don't know, Maddy," Zai said, and it was at this moment that it was clear to me that she had, indeed, been trained as a therapist. "Is it?"

I had two memories of Grandma Scheffler, neither of them very clear. We were walking together through a small meadow in front of our house in Newtown Square. One of the trees had a band of white paint on its bark. A pipe from the house's perimeter drain emptied out there, too, making a little damp place. My grandmother reached for my hand. We walked together, my young hand in her old one.

Later, I was visiting her at the apartment of my aunt Erna and my uncle Jack, the railroad detective. They lived above a station in Glen Mills, Pennsylvania, where freight trains rumbled past day and night. We climbed a spiral staircase to get up there. In one room, my uncle was drinking beer while my aunt played the organ. In another, my grandmother lay in the dark. I crept into the dark room to say goodbye. She

didn't have any teeth. She said something to me, but I could not understand her.

During the fried seafood orgy, I had asked my child if she thought
her relationship with us had changed as she moved from son to
daughter.

"I feel like I've become more open with you," she said. "I mean, the
core of the relationship hasn't changed, I don't think. But I just feel like I
have gotten better at talking about what I'm dealing with, rather than just
putting on the older sibling smile. Telling you, *I'm fine, don't worry about
it. I've got it.* Because you were always more worried about Sean than me."

"I hate that you felt like you ever had to be like that. But I know what
that was like, having to put on the good face. When I was growing up, I
was always the good child, and my sister was the rebellious one."

"How long did that last?"

I laughed. "Until I came out."

We ate our squid. "So—when you think of growing up in Maine with
our family, what are some of the first memories that come to mind?" I
was hoping that her strongest memory was not of climbing stairs, and
locking a door.

"Pine trees," she said. "The lake. The smell of woodsmoke in the
house. Dog hair on everything." She looked away. "Some sort of music
was always playing."

A pair of lifeguards rushed past me, carrying first aid kits. There was
a small crowd gathering down by the water. Someone had fallen in
the sand. They weren't moving. I looked down the beach for Zai.

But she's not there.

A few days later," Mrs. Thomas continued, "Mabel was sitting in her
living room, reading the *Inquirer*. And then, as if from far away, she
heard a voice singing."

"Singing!" said Mr. Thomas. "Well, you know, Mabel's a little hard of hearing, and the song she heard seemed to come and go, and she wasn't even sure it was real at all."

"It could have been an illusion!" shouted Mr. Thomas.

"But it wasn't an illusion," said my father, quietly. "Was it?"

"Mabel walks around her house, trying to find out where this voice is coming from. It's hard because the song keeps stopping. As if someone were singing just to themselves."

"Which is what was happening!"

"Well, it was Jing, of course, but do you know where that girl was?"

The Thomases looked from face to face, hoping one of us might guess.

"The wall!" Mrs. Thomas said. "That girl was trapped inside the wall!"

I'd been aware, during our lunch, of how unafraid Zai seemed, how unconcerned she was with the occasional glances people shot at the two of us. "I have to ask you, Zai," I'd said. "Now that you're female in the world—do you feel safe?"

"Safe?" she said. "You mean from—"

"I mean that the world holds dangers for women that it doesn't hold for men. And as a very out queer person, there are additional dangers for you. I mean, passing—I hate that word, but you know what I mean— passing matters to me. But I don't know if it matters so much to you, and to people in your generation."

"Oh, I'm the spokeswoman for my generation now?"

"No, I just mean, does it matter to you? It can't be the same as it was—as it is—for me?"

"Sometimes," she said, "passing is about safety. And there are still a lot of places in this country where it is not safe to be visibly trans. I can feel myself like, clenching at saying this, but the ability to blend into society is sometimes necessary, in order to be safe."

I dipped a French fry into catsup.

"Do you feel safe?" I asked. I remembered the night in Hobart, Tasmania, when the footsteps of a stranger had drawn closer and closer to me on an abandoned street.

"When I was living in Boston," she said, "when I was living in Cambridge as a student, I felt a lot better about pushing the boundaries, and being visibly queer. I mean, I'm still incredibly visibly queer. I can't walk away from that."

"Do you *want* to walk away from it, Zai?"

"No. But since I started working in a much more rural, more conservative area, where queer identity is much less understood, I've been getting misgendered a lot more. It happens in stores, with clerks. Sometimes with my clients' parents. And that's—that has been weighing on me."

"It must feel really shitty," I said.

"It does. Anytime that someone sees something in you that you don't want them to see, when they see a part of yourself that you are not trying to project, it hurts."

In "Murders in the Rue Morgue," it turns out that the homicide has been committed by an escaped orangutan. In "The Speckled Band," the murder weapon is a poisonous snake.

As for Jing, she'd been hanging up her clothes in the attic closet when one of her dresses fell off a hanger and drifted onto the floor. The closet was partially unfinished, and instead of a wall at its back it just opened onto the attic. Above her were clouds of red fiberglass insulation; at her feet the rows of the house's beams ran parallel to one another, with more fluffy insulation packed between the beams. Jing bent down to pick up her dress, but it had fallen beyond the short, finished floorboards of the closet and onto the fiberglass beyond. She reached toward the dress, but it remained just beyond her grasp.

So she stretched out her hands a little farther.

Afterward she found it hard to explain what it had been like, falling through the insulation of the house, getting tangled up in the electrical wires, knocking her head against the beams. It was very dark, she said. Jing had cried out, hoping someone would hear.

"She'd be in there still if I hadn't been home!" Mr. Thomas shouted.

"He goes over there with a sledgehammer," Mrs. Thomas continued.

"And he starts whacking apart the wall. Plaster is flying everywhere! It's a sturdy old house, a hundred years old. Those walls are thick!"

"It took a lot of whacks, but eventually I busted through," said Mr. Thomas. "And there she was! Stuck back there, all wrapped up in fiberglass and dust! I didn't even know what I was looking at, at first!"

"You said it was like looking at something inside a cocoon," said Mrs. Thomas.

"That's right." Her husband nodded. "I did say that."

Let me ask you one more question, Zai," I said. We had eaten almost all of it: the scallops, the clams, the shrimp, the fries. "You know that I'm trying to write about the difference between manhood and womanhood, for this new book. Would you be willing to sum up that difference, what it means for you?"

Zai thought about it. "The wrapper," she said. "I mean, I think gender is fake, and that we have societal expectations that keep people in boxes and prevent them from experiencing the joy of things that are unnecessarily siloed off into man or woman."

"Okay. But humor me. If gender is fake, why is it necessary for people to change gender? Or to change sex?"

"Because," she said. "Just because gender is fake doesn't mean that one can't enjoy being whatever way we want to be. But I think we can decouple that from the idea of inherited gender roles."

"But if gender is fake, then why is it so important to be able to change our bodies? Is the thing we are changing sex, while gender remains fluid?"

"It's not about whether you hate who you are. It's more like, if you could change your gender, would you? If you could change the way that you look and the way that you present to the world, would you?"

She finished her squid, and looked at me.

"And if you could, and you want to, what's stopping you?"

Later, she told me that she'd first heard this line spoken by a video essayist on her YouTube channel, @PhilosophyTube. At the time, I'd just wanted to tell her about all the things that *did* stop me, in the days Before.

I'd been stopped because I didn't have a road map. I'd been stopped by Dr. Fernweh, the psychoanalyst, whose treatment had included everything except actually helping me. I'd been stopped because never once, in all the books I'd read, in all the TV shows and movies I'd ever watched, was there a character anything like me, or like any of the thousands of other trans women I would, one day, come to know.

"Zai, I think a lot of people will look at the two of us, and wonder if our family—and other families like ours, in which there is a parent and a child who are both trans—isn't this proof that transness is somehow genetic, that it's something that was passed down from me to you?"

She smiled at me. "Maddy, I think people looking at the two of us probably have a lot of opinions."

"But is there any truth to that, do you think? What makes people trans, anyway?"

Zai considered a tentacle. "Hell if I know," she said. "The real question is why it *matters* to people. Do we really need proof, like in our genes, or our brains, or anything else, to be who we are? Why do we need certification of it, or whatever? The only person who can tell you who you are is you."

I smiled. "You're reminding me, Zai, of this conversation I had with Edward Albee. He said—"

She rolled her eyes. "Jesus, Maddy. You know how that sounds, when you say, *One time when I was talking to Edward Albee*—I'm sorry to tell you this, but it just makes people hate you."

"Can I tell you this story or not?"

She sighed. "You're going to tell it to me whether I say yes or no, aren't you?"

"So Albee was, famously, adopted by a family in which he didn't fit in. And he used to always wonder who his real parents were. I mean, it obsessed him. One time, in talking to me about it, he mentioned this James Agee book, *A Death in the Family*, in which there's this scene where a child is being put to bed. *Sleep, soft smiling, draws me unto her: and those receive me, who quietly treat me, as one familiar and well-beloved in that home: but will not, oh will not, not now, not ever; but will not ever tell me who I am."*

The two of us sat there in our chairs at the seafood shack, looking at each other, mother and daughter, parent and child.

A waiter came over. "All finished?" he asked.

Jim," my father said, "play us something on the piano." He loved it when I played for him. Just a few years later, after he'd died, there were times when I could still feel him sitting there, listening.

"I have to get back to my homework," I said.

"Are you going to put that in one of your stories?" Mrs. Thomas asked. "Your mother said you love to write stories!"

"I don't know," I said. "I'm not sure what this story means." This was a lie. I knew exactly what that story meant.

"It's like I said," Mr. Thomas explained. *"People are funny!"*

"Jim's translating a story by Thomas Mann," said my mother. "For German class!"

"Now," Mrs. Thomas said, a light flickering on, *"your* mother was German. Wasn't she, Hildegarde?"

My mother's face went blank for a moment, as if she was sifting through many memories. "Why yes," Mom said. "But that was a long time ago."

Seltsam ist es. Beherrscht dich ein Gedanke, *thought Tonio Kröger,* so findest du ihn überall ausgedrückt, duriechst ihn sogar im Winde.

*It's strange. If you're obsessed with a thought, you see it everywhere, you even smell it in the wind.*

I climbed the long stairs back up to my room. I closed the door, and drew the dead bolt fast.

I got up from my beach towel and walked over to the place where the stranger had fallen.

"Maddy," said Zai, suddenly appearing by my side, as if arriving by parachute.

"Oh Zai," I said, so relieved, throwing my arms around her. "I was so worried."

"Worried about what?" she asked.

My voice caught. "I was afraid that it was you."

"Who?"

I nodded toward the man splayed out on the sand. I felt a little dizzy, and Zai grabbed me by the arm.

"You're okay," she said, and she clutched me harder. "I've got you."

She'd been doing that all week. The night before, as I ascended a long set of stairs from the seashore to the top of the bluff, she'd gently placed her hand on my back, to keep me from falling. Looking out for me.

Was it possible, I wondered, that Zai would be a better daughter to me, in the time to come, than I had been for my own mother? Was it possible, in fact, that she'd be a better daughter to me, than Hildegarde had been for Grandma Scheffler?

The stranger sat up. It was a man about my age, with glasses and a full head of gray hair, an intelligent face—almost professorial. It was not impossible that I'd have been a man much like this, if I'd never asked myself that question—*what's stopping you?*

I thought about my friend Ben, who had once been my twin, and the day Tim Ling had mistaken me for him. How strange it is that the world contains so many doppelgängers, or almost-doppelgängers: the people we might have become if, at a moment of crisis, we had made just one or two different choices.

A child stood next to the stranger—a grandchild, maybe? "I'm fine," the man said. He took his glasses off and wiped some of the sand off them with his thumb.

The lifeguards wanted to take him to the hospital, but he was having none of it. "I just fell down," he said, suddenly furious. "I don't need help!" He got back on his feet, but he still swayed from one leg to the other. He seemed to have lost his equilibrium.

The more he shouted about how he didn't need anyone's help, the clearer it was that help was exactly what he needed. But who could help him? To whom could he turn?

Deedie, returning from her walk along the sand, stood by my side. "What's going on?" she asked.

"That man fell down," I said, nodding toward the stranger.

"Is he all right?" Deedie asked.

"I don't know," I said. "Maybe."

The old man walked away, the young child's hand in his. Out in the ocean there were people laughing and shouting, playing in the waves. A young man chose to ride one in.

III

# EPILOGUE

## Cleavage

One of the stranger aspects of the word *cleavage* is that its definition contains its own opposite. Which is to say, that to *cleave* means to divide, to split something in half. Like the way gender divides humans, or the way politics divides a country.

But to *cleave* also means to stick to, or to adhere close to someone emotionally. Like the way the book of Mark suggests *a man shall leave his father and mother, and cleave to his wife; and the twain shall be one flesh. So then they are no more twain but one.*

And yet: cleavage also means the space that exists *between* two separated things. Like, you know: breasts. Or, as my mother used to call them, *boom-a-roos.*

When I told my friends that my book was going to be titled *Cleavage,* there was, in fact, a division in the categories of their reactions. At least one fellow laughed so hard he actually fell out of his chair. But another friend looked at me with tenderness and despair, like I'd hurt her feelings. All she could say was, *Really?* Which was a gentle way, I suppose of saying, *Oh, please please don't.* A third just seemed a little uncertain, at least until I told her the subtitle, *Men, Women, and the Space Between Us,* after which she smiled tightly and said, *Hm.*

I'm not sure, but how a person responds to this title might also depend on whether by *cleavage* one thinks I'm referring to the fundamental differences between men and women; or the overwhelming similarities

we all share as humans on this endangered planet; or even the third option, the whole question of *boom-a-roos* themselves.

I know there are some readers who probably wish there were more
breasts in this memoir and a lot less of everything else, and to these
readers all I can say is, I'm sorry there weren't more. I know I meant to fit
more of them into this when I started.

*Cleavage* is what linguists refer to as a *contronym*, a word with two
meanings that are opposite each other. Another name for this is a *Janus-
word.* Sometimes this is because a single word attains different meanings
over time. In other cases, words with different roots and histories come,
over time, to be spelled the same way. Cleavage is one of these; the word
meaning "to separate" comes from the Old English *clēofan* (to cut or
carve). But the word meaning "to adhere" comes from *clifian*, which
had a different pronunciation. The definition of cleavage to mean "the
space betwixt two bosoms" is relatively recent—the head of the American
Production Code Administration, one Joseph Breen, used it to describe
(disapprovingly) the space between the breasts of actress Jane Russell in
the film *The Outlaw.* This usage was amplified by an August 1946 issue
of *Time* magazine titled "Cleavage and the Code."

In the movie *The Aviator*, a producer says to Howard Hughes, "Howard, you really think they're going to let you put out a movie just about
tits?" And Hughes replies, "Sure. Who doesn't like tits?"

Actually I know plenty of gay men for whom tits are not at the top
of the to-do list. And I know many women, both those who like them and
those who are neutral on the subject, who would just as soon I not use the
word "tits," a word which feels a little argumentative. George Carlin, in his
famous monologue about the Seven Words You Can Never Say on Television, included it as one of the seven, although he also noted that *tits* doesn't
really belong on the list. "It sounds like a snack!" he said. "But I don't mean
your sexist snack. I mean new *Nabisco Tits!* And new Cheese Tits, Corn Tits,
Pizza Tits, Sesame Tits, Onion Tits and Tater Tits! Betcha can't eat just one!"

Oh, how funny I thought that was, back when I was a thirteen-year-
old boy. But back then, I thought a *lot* of things were funny.

I love that a single word can have all these meanings, because at various moments the journey I've been on has meant many different things to me, too. There are days when the fact that I began this life in one body and have ended it in another strikes me as miraculous. Other days, the fact that I'm trans feels like, possibly, the least important thing about me—or that, at the very least, it is something that was once important and has become less so over time. Other days, I'm right in the middle, spending most of my hours attending to my pizza oven and my dogs, only to find myself suddenly shoved in front of a television camera when the latest humiliating legislation has been unexpectedly unveiled in one of America's more mean-spirited statehouses.

I'm also well aware of the division between various parts of the transgender community—between the drag queens who would tell you that the most important aspect of our identities is *performativity*; and the transsexuals who might describe our condition as *medical*; between the cross-dressers whose identity is foregrounded in *fantasy*, to the young genderqueer or nonbinary souls who above all hope to either be *freed from the chains of gender*, or (on the other hand) to embrace all the ways in which *gender can be messed with and turned into a source of transgression and fun.*

These divisions—which of course are not separated into neat independent silos, but which also overlap in all sorts of ways—are sometimes echoed in the cleavages between various factions of the LGBTQIA+ community itself. There are some gay men and some lesbians who could not imagine two cohorts who have less in common with each other; other members of those same cohorts see our fates as inherently intertwined. There is yet more cleavage between those folks and trans people; some lesbians are irritated by the way some of their fellow-travelers have left a community of women and embraced lives as trans men, and others who have welcomed trans people of all stripes with open arms. In my own life I have known some gay men who have found me a whole lot less interesting, post-transition, and then there have been others who think I'm the cat's meow. Some of the gay men who think we share common ground base this insight on their own adoration of drag. When I point out that that most drag queens and I are up to two very different things, this can really piss some gay men off, especially those who hear my distancing myself from drag performers as criticism of the art itself.

The more I think about the word *cleavage,* the less it seems to mean to me, except of course for its ridiculous association with boom-a-roos, a word that never fails to make me smile, although this may be because I can only hear the word being spoken by my otherwise very elegant and dignified mother. (Although it was Hildegarde who unexpectedly suggested that instead of *She's Not There* I title my first memoir *Thanks for the Mammaries.*) It does feel, at times, as if the journey of transition has led me to my true self, as well as to what was once my own opposite—a journey that has resulted in at least one friend saying that I'd become unrecognizable to her and another saying, *You're exactly the same.* Early in transition I had another friend say that, while he loved the boy version of me, "the jury was still out" on who this Jenny person was, as if I might yet be revealed to be someone he had never known.

But who else would I be, besides a differently shaped and slightly happier version of myself?

As Groucho Marx once remarked, "Outside of the improvement you'll never notice the difference."

Deedie woke me up one fall morning. In one hand she held a steaming cup of coffee. "Good morning, Jenny Boylan," she said.

"This is nice," I said, but something in her voice made me think twice. "Isn't it?"

"Get dressed," she said. "There's something I need to talk to you about."

"Okay," I said, and took a sip. "Should I be worried?"

She gave me a look. "Get dressed," she said.

An hour later we were hiking up a trail a few miles north of our house, toward the summit of something called French's Mountain.

We'd hiked this trail a hundred times over the course of our marriage.

We'd taken our children as toddlers up this trail; I'd even walked it with my own mother when she was in her eighties.

A lot had happened since then.

Now our children were grown and flown. Zai was working in Boston; Sean was a mechanical engineer, living in Ann Arbor. They were adults, living their lives. How I missed them, every day! But they had done well for themselves. The kids were all right.

As we climbed together, Deedie took the lead, and I trailed behind. She's always been a better hiker than me. The mysterious ailment that I'd been suffering from for four years now—still undiagnosed—made hiking hard, at times almost impossible. I had to grab on to trees, sometimes, in order to keep from falling over.

Finally, we reached the summit and then stood there, looking at the lake below us, at the far line of mountains on the horizon, at the hills red and golden in the autumn light.

"So Jenny," she said, and swallowed. "Listen."

One day, not long after transition, I was driving around Devon, Pennsylvania, with my old friend Ben, in his hi-tech wheelchair van. We were going to Wawa for hoagies.

After his accident, he'd moved back into his mother's house, down by the train tracks in St. David's. We'd put pennies on the rails so the trains could smash them flat. Once, Julie—the girl from London for whom I'd hoped to buy that dragon robe—was there, too. She'd written to tell me how haunted she'd thought the whole situation was—me, my friend, those train tracks. *Those pennies,* she'd written me. *I don't know, there was something so sad.*

A few years later, the house next door to his mother's was sold, and a young woman moved in. Her name was Grace, an archaeologist. Now and again Grace came over, and she and Ben drank iced tea.

We pulled into the Wawa, and he turned off the engine. "Listen," he said. "I think I'm in love."

Grace, in this case, not being a pseudonym, but her actual name.

He rolled his wheelchair back from the steering wheel and looked at me. "She's building a ramp on the side of her house," he said. "Grace, I mean. From next door."

I nodded. That was very cool.

"Jenny," he said, for emphasis. "She's building a ramp! So I—" Tears shimmered in his eyes. *"So I can come over!"*

On the way back to his house, I told Ben that Deedie and I weren't sure what the future held for us. We loved each other, but we struggled. Things weren't made any easier by the well-meaning friends who suggested that what we needed to do was divorce.

One such swami had accused Deedie of being a martyr, as if the only reason she stayed with me was out of pity.

"Look at me, Jenny," Ben said, from behind the wheel of Red October. "Grace loves *me*! Not out of pity, but because I'm *me*."

His van was full of the smell of the hoagies: the sweet peppers and provolone and capicola. Our cheeks were shiny with oil.

"You'll find that, too," he said. "I promise. You'll find your way, back to each other."

It was a nice thought. But I did not know if it was true.

There are times when I think of my whole life as a *contronym*, a thing that all along is both itself as well as its own opposite.

How is it that I have made my way through this world, cleaving and cleaved? How have I lived my life as an older woman, the ghost of my boy self trailing close behind? Has the long journey of transition meant that my one self has been divided into two—one with a past, the other with a future? Or does it mean that I have found, at last, a sense of wholeness: one life, both the Before and the After?

Or does it mean that I exist between things?

In the end, the bodies we find ourselves in may matter less than the souls that inhabit them. And during our time on earth, it is surely no sin to do what you can to find your happiness within the body you're in.

It's a shame that finding your peace can cause such an uproar.

Russo once told me a joke about "an orphan with a heart of gold." In this story, someone sees a child in an alley laughing and smiling and cutting worms in half with a pair of scissors. A social worker is called in, to inspect what onlookers fear is the child's cruel streak.

Instead, as the social worker draws near, she sees the child holding the two halves of the worm up to one another.

"Look!" the child says. "Now you have a friend!"

We had reached the summit, my love and I. Deedie wasn't talking. I thought about the first time I'd ever seen her—standing on a stage, illuminated by a spotlight in David Mamet's *Sexual Perversity in Chicago*. One man asks the other, *Was she a pro?* The other, describing his date with Deedie's character, replied, *At this point, we don't know!*

"What is it," I said. My voice cracked. I could barely speak. "This thing you need to tell me."

"You," she said.

Me?

"Go on," I whispered. "Say it."

"Remember when we were at our wedding reception? And that friend of your sister's came over, and we were talking to her, and then a waiter asked you if you wanted a roll?"

I nodded.

"And you dropped to the floor, and rolled all around, and got dust all over your mourning coat? And then you stood back up and said, 'Don't mind if I do'?"

"Yes," I said quietly. Of course I remembered it. That's my problem. I remember everything.

"And Lauren said—?"

Deedie waited for me to finish. I whispered, "'You're going to have a funny life.'"

"Jenny," she said. "Lauren wasn't wrong."

Now I wasn't sure where she was going with this. "What do you mean?"

"I mean, I *have* had a funny life."

"But—?"

"But nothing," she said.

"But—*nothing?*"

"*Jenny.* Do you really think I could ever *not* love you? That I could ever not want to be with you, every day? Who on earth could ever want a life—that's *not funny?*"

"I bet a lot of people." I shrugged. "I bet a lot of people, they wouldn't want one."

"I know," she said. "But I'm not married to them."

She threw her arms around me, and we kissed, standing there on top of the mountain.

"Deedie—" I said, but my throat closed up. For once, I was completely speechless.

Years earlier, Rick Russo had stood in the doorway of my hospital room, in the hours after my surgery. He'd looked on as Deedie had sung me a song—"Two Little Boys," a tune she used to sing to our children when they were small.

*Do you think I could leave you dying,*
*When there's room on my horse for two?*
*Climb up here Jack quit your crying,*
*We'll mend up your horse with glue.*

I'd lain there in bed, gazing into her eyes.

*What I was witnessing,* Russo later wrote, *was a great love story. And it occurred to me, too, that if this was a great love story, I had no idea where we were on its timeline. For all I knew we might be nearer its beginning than its end.*

I had turned to Rick after Deedie finished her song, moments away from a deep sleep. "Russo?" I said. "Sing me a song?"

*It was a joke,* he wrote, *which was just as well. Sing? I could barely speak.*

The phone rang in my Colby office on a hot summer day. There was nobody in the department, August being the time when the campus usually cleared out, leaving no one except department chairs toiling away.

"Hello?"

"Hello, is this Professor Boylan?"

I allowed as how I was.

"This is Peter Houston. Do you know who he is?"

"Who?"

"He's on the Colby campus right now. He'd like to come and say hello to you."

"Who would?"

*"He* would."

Indeed: it was my eleventh-grade American History teacher, the one who believed it was a sin to use the first person. I hadn't given him much thought since the year of the Bicentennial, but considering it now, it was hard to imagine Mr. Houston as being overly enthusiastic about the whole switcheroo. You'd have to think anybody whose spiritual life was so unbending as to rule out the *actual use of the first person* was probably someone who took a dim view of stuff like, you know, *labiaplasty.*

Not to mention literary memoir.

But I invited him on up. Given my sanguinity when it came to pronouns like *xe* and *xem*, surely there was room in my world for a man who never used *I* or *me?*

A few minutes later he knocked on my door, and there he was. *Thumper.* It had been almost forty years since he'd taught me about the Kansas-Nebraska Act, and the Depression, and the civil rights movement, but there he was.

He looked me up and down. "You've changed," he said, and then added, pointing to himself, "but he's changed, too."

He sat down in my office chair. And then he told me his whole long story.

Later that same night, I returned home to find Deedie making chocolate chili in the slow cooker. Our very old dog Indigo, a black lab, was looking up at her with the eternal canine hope that some morsel might fall her way. Indigo was the same dog that, on one occasion, we had returned home to find covered from nose to tail with white flour. White pawprints had been tracked all over the house, including—incredibly—some on the dining room table. Indigo had just looked at us, like, *I don't know anything about this.*

Outside, on the lake, loons called, one to another. The Deedie light shone on the far-off shore.

"I love you," she said.

"She loves you too," I said.

Deedie looked at me, a little uncertain. Did I mean Indigo, the dog? "Wait," she said. "Who?"

I pointed to myself.

"*Her,*" I said.

# ACKNOWLEDGMENTS

I started writing this book under the title *Both Sides Now* half a dozen years ago and made so many false starts I can't remember them all, more proof, if any was needed, that the Heisenberg principle continues to have its way with me as a writer as well as a woman. I started rewriting this book in the summer of 2021 at the fabulous Civitella Ranieri in Umbertide, Italy, and continued that work during my year as a fellow at the Radcliffe Institute for Advanced Study at Harvard University in 2022–23. I'm profoundly grateful to the folks at Civitella as well as at Radcliffe for their support. And then there are the presidents, provost, and faculty of Barnard College of Columbia University, who have supported my work at every turn, and to whom I am profoundly grateful. This crew includes Deb Spar, Sian Beilock, Laura Rosenbury, Linda Bell, Peter Platt, Lisa Gordis, Ross Hamilton, Mary Gordon, Ken Chen, and above all, the saintly Chris Baswell. I love them all like crazy.

Writers and editors who provided counsel are too numerous to name, but I'm especially indebted to Richard Russo, Andrew Greer, Jodi Picoult, Maggie Nelson, Gary Fisketjon, Clay Risen, James Bennet, Jim Dao, Chris Suellentrop, Mary Karr, and Timothy Kreider.

I want to thank my agent, Kris Dahl at CAA, who has stood by me for thirty-three years now. I think this is probably the last book we will work on together, and that breaks my heart. But how grateful I am for the role she has played in my life! We have traveled a long, long road together, Kris. I would never have been able to take a single step without you.

Above all my love goes out to my editor, Deb Futter, who first edited *She's Not There* in 2003, and to whose fond embrace at Celadon I returned with the memoir *Good Boy* in 2020.

Some of this material has been published previously, although in such radically different form most of it is unrecognizable, at least I hope so. From 2007 to 2022, I was contributing opinion writer for the *New York Times*, and some of the ideas in this book first saw the light of day as columns for the op-ed page; others surfaced in a similar manner in columns written for the *Washington Post*. Parts of the chapter "The Unit" were originally included in an essay for the anthology *On the Couch: Writers Analyze Sigmund Freud*. The title of that essay was "Penis Envy." About half of the chapter "Rogues & Pixies" originally sprouted as an essay in *Now Comes Good Sailing*, an anthology of work about Henry David Thoreau. And some of the passing references to Charlie Brown as a modern-day Boy of Constant Sorrow were first published in the book *The Peanuts Papers* and excerpted in the *New Yorker* under the title "What 'Peanuts' Taught Me About Queer Identity" (although my original title was "You're Weird, Sir"). All three of those anthologies were edited by Andrew Blauner, a good editor, agent, and friend.

The chapter "The Heisenberg Variations" was originally conceived as the Julia S. Phelps Annual Lecture in the Arts and Humanities at Harvard, and later reedited yet again as a talk for the Bread Loaf Writers' Conference of Middlebury College. The original title for those talks was *The Heisenberg Variations: Invention, Imagination, and Uncertainty*, a title I shamelessly cribbed from my dear mentor at Hopkins, John Irwin, who saw something in me as a grad student in 1986 that I did not yet see in myself. (John Irwin gave this same title to his lovely collection of poems, published under the name of his alter ego, John Bricuth.) Professor Irwin, please know now and forever that *as long as I got a biscuit, you got half.* Parts of the section of that Harvard talk, focusing on my mentor John Barth, were themselves originally part of an essay for the *New York Times Book Review*, and published under the title "A Twist in Her Plot."

All of this inventing and reinventing, taking a paragraph from one story and grafting it onto another, reminds me of Richard Russo's comments about my surgeon. *I don't know if Dr. Schrang was the one who actually came up with the idea of using a penis to create a vagina, of turning one highly sensate organ in upon itself to produce another, but if so, he gets points for imagination in my book. Either that or he just lived through the Depression and, like my maternal grandmother, hated to waste anything.*

I, too, hate to waste anything. That said, I have diligently tried to avoid an exact retelling of any story I have told before, lest I start channeling my own grandmother and her irrepressible desire to tell the story of my father's conception again and again. Still, some of the facts of my life previously published in earlier memoirs and essays were necessary to revisit once more, in order for readers to catch up with me. I hope this wasn't too annoying. Those previously published books include *She's Not There* (2003); *I'm Looking Through You* (2008); *Stuck in the Middle with You* (2013); and *Good Boy* (2020).

It is necessary to state clearly that many names in this work were changed in order to protect people's privacy, and that some of the distinguishing aspects of their appearance or characters were altered as well, for the same reason. Some beautiful people were made ugly; a few schlubs were cleaned up nicely, in order to veil them, too. Does this turn my work from truth to fiction? I don't believe so, but I know very well how sticky this business can be. I've done my best. As a writer I confess that I am of the school of Frank McCourt, who once said that *memoir is a painting of a life, not a photograph.* To this I can only add that there are some photographs that don't tell the truth, either, and that there are many paintings, some of them abstract, that seem to me to tell the truth far more piercingly than a photo, just as there are some works of fiction that do a better job of capturing the truth than an autobiography.

Still, if anything here deviates from the truth, it is surely less likely to be a deliberate intention to bamboozle anybody, and more because my memory has failed.

Readers seeking counsel for themselves or loved ones are encouraged to reach out to GLAAD, at glaad.org; or the National Center for Transgender Equality, at transequality.org; or the Human Rights Campaign, at hrc.org; or their local PFLAG or GLSEN chapter.

These passages can be joyful, or they can strip the bark right off a person, depending. I am hoping that all my readers can find what they need to make their way in the world. Even now, I believe in the thing that Hildegarde promised, that love will prevail.

And I hope all of us can somehow answer the summons given to the narrator of *Night-Sea Journey*, as he makes his way into the unknown:

*Love! Love! Love!*

# ABOUT THE AUTHOR

**JENNIFER FINNEY BOYLAN** is the author of nineteen books, including *Mad Honey*, coauthored with Jodi Picoult. Her memoir *She's Not There* was the first bestselling work by a transgender American. Since 2014 she has been the inaugural Anna Quindlen Writer in Residence at Barnard College of Columbia University; she is also on the faculty of the Bread Loaf Writers' Conference of Middlebury College and the Sirenland Writers Conference in Positano, Italy.

She is the president of PEN America, the nonprofit protecting free speech and free expression in this country and worldwide and, from 2011 to 2018, she was a member of the board of directors of GLAAD, including four years as national cochair.

From 2022 to 2023, she was a fellow at the Radcliffe Institute for Advanced Study at Harvard University. She graduated from Wesleyan University and Johns Hopkins University, and she holds doctorates honoris causa from the College of the Atlantic, Sarah Lawrence College, the New School, and Wesleyan.

For many years she was contributing opinion writer for the opinion section of the *New York Times*. Her work has also appeared in the *New Yorker*, the *Washington Post*, the *Boston Globe*, *LitHub*, *Down East*, and many other publications.

She lives in Maine and New York with her wife, Deirdre. They have two children, a daughter, Zai, and a son, Sean.